1001
Garden Plants

1001
Garden Plants

TIPS AND IDEAS FOR GARDEN LOVERS

Text by Antje Rugullis
Photographs by Modeste Herwig

Bath · New York · Singapore · Hong Kong · Cologne · Delhi · Melbourne

This edition published by Parragon 2010

Copyright © 2008 Parragon Books Ltd

Queen Street House, 4 Queen Street, Bath BA1 1HE, UK

ISBN 978-1-4454-0874-3

Printed in Indonesia

Text: Antje Rugullis

Photographs: Modeste Herwig

Layout, editing, typesetting, picture editing, lithography:
Makro Chroma Werbeagentur, Hilden, for the German edition

English-language edition produced by Cambridge Publishing Management Ltd

Translation: Susan James, Michele McMeekin, Theresa Pike,
David Darrah-Morgan, Catherine Landenberger

Project Editor: Diane Teillol; Copyediting: Diane Teillol & Alison Coupe

Proofreading: Joanne Osborne; Indexing: Marie Lorimer

CONTENTS

BULBS AND TUBERS

Stores of Splendid Colour, not Just for Spring

If you want to enjoy spring in all its intense colours, you simply can't ignore these flowers: once winter is over, tulips, daffodils, and crocuses adorn the garden with an incredible wealth of different species. In the summer and autumn, lilies and dahlias expertly go on with the show. And the truly practical thing about these miniature power plants is that they are quite uncomplicated and truly undemanding. They are true survivors. There are very few things that bulbs and tubers cannot forgive, and essentially these include waterlogging and rodents. But they can be protected from both by planting in well-drained soil and placing the bulbs, if necessary, in little wire baskets.

They look their most impressive in groups. So plant them in groups, even a little close together. If you delay cutting back the leaves until they have yellowed – the flower should, however, be cut off straight after it has wilted – you can look forward to more magnificent flowers next spring. This is because the plant's strength is withdrawn to the bulbs, its storage organs, through the leaves. Bulbs and tubers also reproduce themselves, so simply separate them now and again, and you will see that they quickly accept new locations.

20–60 cm   Summer

Allium caeruleum syn. A. azureum
Blue ornamental onion, blue-of-the-heavens

About 30 to 50 star-shaped, cool sky-blue flowers arrange themselves skilfully to make an unusual, spherical, dense umbel. The narrow, upright leaves adorn the lower third of the single-shoot stems. Ornamental onions prefer moderately nutrient-rich soil in full sunlight, but are in other respects fairly undemanding. Plant the bulbs in the autumn. Propagation takes place by means of bulblets or self-seeding. This fine species of *Allium*, which is the only one with such marvellous blue flowers, deserves a good visible spot; it is also particularly attractive in herb or rose gardens.

Allium cernuum
Nodding onion, lady's leek

The little bell-shaped flowers, pink to amethyst in colour, nod playfully as they dangle from the stiff upright stem. This unusual, enchanting garden plant with a definite 'wild' look about it is most attractive in a group, among shorter bedding plants or together with other *Allium* species. It prefers a sunny spot in well-drained soil rich in nutrients. *Allium cernuum* is fairly undemanding and grows well. It is perennial, with green leaves in the winter.

| | 30–60 cm | | Summer | | | | |

Allium christophii Persian onion, star of Persia

Its airy, star-shaped flowers look just like a purple firework. Up to 20 centimetres in diameter, the proud flowerheads sit on their upright stems and, whether in a rock garden or a bed of plants, form an eye-catching feature that is impossible to ignore. Its long, ribbon-like, lanceolate leaves are early arrivals. Star of Persia loves sunny flowerbeds and well-drained soils. Plant the bulbs in the autumn. It is easy to care for; put fertiliser on the soil about every two years. To propagate, take bulblets; also self-seeding. **Tip:** this plant looks particularly good in a flowerbed with long-stemmed, late tulips in the same colour range. The dried flowerheads also make very attractive dried flowers and keep for a long time.

| | 30–60 cm | | End of spring | | | | |

| ↕ 15–20 cm | ✿✿ | Late spring to early summer | ❄❄❄ | ✹ | 🌱 | 🪣 | ✿ |

Allium karataviense 'Ivory Queen' Turkestan onion

The low-stemmed, spherical flowerhead, formed of delicate, pinkish-white stars, peers out from a pair of broad, almost tongue-shaped, bluish-tinged leaves. It displays itself to the astonished gaze of the observer for up to three weeks. A true attraction. Together with colourful perennials, it works well as a team in sunny flowerbeds and rockeries, as well as – more rarely for *Allium* species – in semi-shade. It likes well-drained soil. Dig in the bulbs in the autumn. *Allium karataviense* is as easy to care for as its fellow species. You can propagate it using bulblets or seed. **Tip:** in their first year, the young plants of all *Allium* species require winter protection. The optimum substratum for *Allium* is, by the way, a sandy loam.

| ↕ 10–35 cm | ✿✿ | Early to late summer | ❄❄❄ | ✹ | 🪣 |

Allium flavum Yellow onion

Brilliant yellow distinguishes *Allium flavum* from the purple colours of the rest of the family. The bell-shaped, partly pendant, small flowers are arranged in a loose umbel. The restrained grey-blue of the foliage forms a discreet contrast. The plant prefers a dry, stony site in full sun. It is particularly effective set among reddish-flowering small perennials or ground cover. Plant in the autumn. Easy to care for. Propagate by bulblets or self-seeding.

| ↕ 20–40 cm | ✿✿ | Late spring to early summer | ❄❄❄ | 🌱 | 🪣 | ✿ |

Allium moly Lily leek, golden garlic

This is a really versatile little show-stealer. The bright golden-yellow flowers of *Allium moly* bloom in dense, small umbels. When the plant finds a spot it likes – in well-drained soils, including fresh soils, in semi-shady locations – it quickly spreads by dividing its bulbs and seeding. **Tip:** makes a scented cut flower. Ideal for planting under shrubs. Will harmonise with blue and violet plants. If it becomes a nuisance, cut the flowerheads as soon as flowering is over to avoid self-seeding.

10–50 cm | Late spring to early summer

Allium roseum Rosy garlic

This pink-flowered ornamental garlic species has a delicate and filigree appearance. The flowerheads are relatively large and the plant can reach widely differing heights. Planted in the full sun in well-drained soils, it will not need much care and will quickly spread to form a dense carpet through bulblets and dividing bulbs. *Allium roseum* makes a good cut flower for vases.

Allium sphaerocephalon
Drumstick, round-headed garlic

The pretty carmine-red flowers of globe garlic are arranged in particularly dense flowerheads, slightly elongated and ovoid in shape. Their thin, yellowish-green leaves wilt even while the plant is flowering. It loves the full sun and well-drained soils, dry in summer. Otherwise, it is an undemanding plant. Plant in the autumn. The plant propagates by means of bulblets and self-seeding. **Tip:** it looks really good among grasses and ground-cover plants. Also suitable for extensive root growth. It makes a fine cut flower.

50–80 cm | Early to high summer

Allium triquetrum Three-cornered leek

The loose, bell-shaped flowers of this triple-edged ornamental leek, all hanging down to one side, are of an almost translucent white, decorated with fine, green central stripes on the inside. Low-growing and definitely dainty, *Allium triquetrum* requires a moist, well-drained, nutrient-rich site in the shade or semi-shade. In good conditions, it will spread quite widely. It will thrive in sunny locations if given enough water. Plant in the autumn.

20–40 cm | Late spring

| 🌱 60–100 cm | ✿✿ | Early to high summer | ❋ ✳ | ✶ | 🥬 | ⚱ | ❗ |

lstroemeria aurea syn. *A. aurantiaca* '*Orange King*' Peruvian lily, lily of the Incas

his plant will put up with frost for short eriods, but requires light winter mulch for rotection. Plant it in beds of perennials r at the edges of shrubberies; it will need upporting canes. It also needs sufficient noisture and occasional fertiliser. It can ake sun or semi-shade.

| 🌱 50–70 cm | ✿✿ | Early to high summer | ❋ ✳ | ✶ | 🥬 | 🍵 | ⚱ | ⚱ | ❗ |

Alstroemeria ligtu hybrids Peruvian lily, lily of the Nile

This plant, a classic of floral bouquets and arrangements, also makes a fine impression in the garden and provides magnificent colour with a touch of the exotic. These hybrids bloom in splendid shades of pink, salmon pink, and yellow, with marked contrasting stripes. They especially thrive in semi-shade with loose soils rich in nutrients. In sunny locations, they need to be well watered in their first few weeks. **Tip:** do not cut off the stalks once flowering is over, but pull them off the plant with a strong twisting motion; this will stimulate the tuber to form shoots. Provide light winter mulch with leaves or straw. The plant may cause skin irritation.

Amaryllis belladonna 'Durban'
Belladonna lily

'Beautiful lady' is a name rightly given to *A. belladonna*, for its scented, funnel-shaped flowers are truly noble and gorgeously beautiful. The sturdy flower stalk bears six or more flowers. 'Durban' is a strong pink colour; other varieties range from white to rose pink to red. The leaves of *A. belladonna* appear before the flower, but die back quickly before the actual flower stalk appears. Plant in spring in moderately nutrient-rich, well-drained soil. The plant loves sunny, sheltered locations such as, for instance, south-facing walls and good winter cover. Tends to naturalise. **Tip:** support the flowers with a cane if necessary.

30–80 cm   Late summer to autumn

Anemone blanda 'White Splendour'
Grecian windflower

In the very early spring, when the first rays of the sun are melting the covering of snow, the innumerable white starry flowers of 'White Splendour' are to be seen. They look most effective under shrubs and in rockeries. Planted en masse, the effect is simply enchanting.

10–20 cm   Early to mid-spring

Anemone blanda 'Blue Shades'
Grecian windflower

With bright mid-blue on their short stalks, the star-shaped, flat flowers announce: 'Spring is here'. In undisturbed locations on loose, humus soil with good drainage, the plant forms dense carpets of flowers. It is an ideal flower to allow to naturalise in meadows, rockeries, and borders. Plant in the autumn or spring. Propagate by dividing the tubers. **Tip:** in the autumn, mulch with a thin layer of compost. Goes well with primroses and crocuses.

10–20 cm   Early to mid-spring

Anemone coronaria 'De Caen'
Lilies-of-the-field, poppy anemone

A host of brilliant red, blue, violet, white, or pink calyces consisting of remarkably broad petals, with a black wreath decorating the centre: *A. coronaria* cannot be overlooked in flowerbeds or rockeries. It looks its best in groups or planted together with wild tulips, alpine squill, and low grasses. Its favourite spots are sunny to semi-shady, on light, sandy soils. The plant does not like to be too moist. Plant in the spring or the autumn. In the winter, in temperate latitudes, it requires a mulch of leaves or compost for protection, as it is not frost-hardy. The plant likes to remain undisturbed, so only dig out the tubers after flowering if necessary, then dry and store them in a frost-free place. **Tip:** before planting, soak the tuber in water for one or two days; this stimulates rooting. A popular cut flower.

25–40 cm | Late spring

10–20 cm | Mid-spring to early summer

Anemone nemorosa
Wood anemone, European thimbleweed

A. nemorosa is a true child of the forest. It enjoys the spring sun and in summer tends to prefer the shade. This makes the borders of deciduous woodland an ideal habitat – fresh, humus soils that are dry in summer. There they will display their delicate white, pink-tinged flower calyces, with the intensely yellow wreath of stamens in the middle. Tripinnate, deeply-notched, grass-green foliage. The flower is undemanding and forms carpets. Propagates by division of the rhizome. Plant in the autumn. Looks particularly good in 'wild' gardens. **Take care:** contact with the plant sap may cause skin irritations. If you are sensitive, wear gloves.

Up to 25 cm. | Early spring

Anemone pavonina Peacock anemone

This pretty flower hungrily raises its fiery red, cup-shaped flowers towards the sun. The peacock anemone's delicate individual flowers also appear in pink and purple, usually with a white centre. Because of its Mediterranean origin, it loves sunny locations on light, sandy soils. Ideally, the plant should be mulched in winter or spend the winter months free of frost in sand. Its wild plant character means that it is very well suited to 'natural'-look flowerbeds and rockeries.

30–50 cm | Late spring to early summer

Anemone sylvestris Snowdrop anemone

The creamy-white flowers with their yellow-gold stamens are attached to long stems and are simply breathtaking in their effect. The plant will tolerate sunny and semi-shady locations and well-drained, humus soil. *A. sylvestris* spreads quickly through runners. **Tip:** anemones, of whatever species, should preferably be planted in groups of at least five plants.

Arisaema candidissimum Cobra lily

Proud and magnificent are the words that spring to mind when you see the flower of *A. candidissimum*. The fresh pink and white of the spathe – the term for the bract that surrounds the club-shaped flowerhead – is a real eye-catcher in any garden. The tripinnate leaves grow to quite a size and provide an exotic touch. The small flowers are delicately scented. Typical woodland plants, they prefer a cool, moist, shady or semi-shady location in moist, humus, slightly acidic soil. They are well suited to woodland borders. The best time to plant is the autumn. Propagate by seed or by taking bulblets. In dry weather, give sufficient water. In habitats where the climate is harsh, protect the plant with a winter mulch of leaves and twigs. You can also provide winter protection by digging the tuber in deep up to 30 centimetres. If necessary, dig out the tuber and allow it to overwinter in the fridge.

 40–60 cm | Early to late summer

| 20–40 cm | Early summer | Late summer to late autumn | | | |

Bulbocodium vernum Spring meadow saffron

The delicate, pink to violet star-shaped flowers seem to shoot straight out of the ground without stalks. Toward the end of the flowering period, the leaves follow and continue to grow until they fade back in the summer. These pretty spring flowers are ideal for rockeries and woodland or shrubbery borders; together with fritillaries, wild daffodils, and crocuses they will form a carpet of spring flowers. They like a sunny to semi-shady position. Even and sufficient moisture in the ground is important, so water plentifully in the growing period. The bulbs cannot be stored; plant immediately after purchase. Plant in late summer/autumn. When the leaves have died back, you can remove the bulbs from the ground and take off bulblets. **Take care:** all parts, especially the seeds, contain colchicine. Extremely poisonous and therefore not suitable for gardens where there are children.

| 60–80 cm | Late spring | | | | | |

Arum italicum Italian lords and ladies

This plant is a real attraction, with an unusual flowerhead and bright red berries. Its sagittate, glossy green leaves come out in spring, and in early summer the plant displays its yellowish flowerhead, surrounded by the large, yellow-green spathe. In summer it bears decorative red berries, ideal for flower arrangements. It will tolerate sunny to semi-shady, sheltered locations on fresh, nutrient-rich soils. Easy to care for. In habitats where the climate is harsh, protect in winter. Propagate by bulblets or seed. **Take care:** all parts of the plants of the arum species are poisonous.

| 10–20 cm | Early spring | | | |

Camassia cusickii Cusick's camass

Its tall candle-shaped flowerheads are the high point of a spring garden. The racemes bear pale blue flowers with a touch of purple. As a whole, it is easy to care for. It is winter-hardy, but a winter mulch is nonetheless recommended. Cut the flowerheads off after blooming, unless you want to harvest the seeds. Good neighbours in the flowerbeds might be tulips, or members of the *Geranium, Iris,* or *Polemonium* species. The soil needs to be sufficiently moist, and the site should be sunny or semi-shady. Propagate by bulblets or seed. The camass makes a beautiful cut flower.

100–200 cm | High summer to mid-autumn

Canna indica hybrids Indian shot

This exotic beauty offers a broad range of colours – from scarlet to golden yellow – and is esteemed for its splendid flowers and lush, ornamental foliage. Glowing colours and an impressive growth height make it a confident attraction. The foliage, too, with its shades ranging from green to crimson and bronze, is conspicuous. *Canna* looks good planted among summer flowers in harmonising colour ranges. During the growth period it needs plenty of water and nourishment; apply fertiliser about every two weeks. Cut off blooms when they have finished flowering. After flowering, cut back to a hand's width. In regions subject to frost, dig out the rhizome, dry it and store it in a cool place. In spring, cut the rhizome into sections making sure each section has a bud of new growth and plant in late spring. The site should be sunny and sheltered from wind, in nutrient-rich, well-drained soil.

10–15 cm | Late summer to autumn

10–15 cm | Early spring

Chionodoxa luciliae Glory of the snow

The graceful, brilliant blue star-shaped flowers thrust their way impatiently through the last of the snow toward the spring sun. Their pretty shades of blue make them well suited to planting among yellow heralds of the spring in shrubbery borders or in rockeries. Easy to care for, they prefer a sunny position in loose soils. Plant in the autumn. Take off the bulblets in the autumn; propagation by seed is also possible.

Colchicum autumnale Autumn crocus

The elegant pink to purple calyces of *Colchicum autumnale* resemble those of the spring crocus, but do not appear until the late summer, stretching upward toward the sun's last warming rays. The plant is leafless, for the leaves do not appear until the following spring. The autumn crocus prefers sun and fertile, well-drained, fresh soils. *Colchicum autumnale* is fairly undemanding. It looks best under shrubs or in flowerbeds where, at this late season, it can still make a few splashes of colour. Propagate by dividing old clumps in the summer or through bulblets. **Take care:** in all *Colchicum* species, the parts above ground are highly poisonous.

15–20 cm | Late summer to autumn

Colchicum speciosum Showy colchicum

C. speciosum, a somewhat larger species, has large, broad flowers in blue-violet or white. The flowers look a little like small tulips. Their soil and location requirements are similar to those of *C. autumnale. Colchicum* usually has several flowers growing from one bulb. Plant the bulbs in groups. **Take care:** this plant is very poisonous.

Crinum × powellii Cape lily, Powell's crinum lily

The elegant air of this plant is strongly reminiscent of lilies. Up to 15 radiant, scented, funnel-shaped flowers — white or pink — on the tall, sturdy stem make it an effective single plant. However, by planting it in small groups, you can achieve a truly magnificent explosion of flowers. The plant develops best in sunny, warm, sheltered locations, for instance, in front of a south-facing wall. It prefers moist soils, rich in nutrients and well drained. Water freely during the growing phase. In winter, cover with a thick mulch of leaves or brushwood. If allowed to develop undisturbed, it will become more magnificent year by year. If you take bulblets off for propagation, these will only flower after three or four years.

100–150 cm | Late summer to autumn

Crocosmia × crocosmiiflora 'Lucifer'
Montbretia

'Lucifer' sets a blazing, scarlet exclamation mark, preferring to be planted in sunny beds among other bulbs and perennials. It is less prolific in its flowering in semi-shade. It is relatively easy to care for, as long as it is watered regularly in the growing phase. Cut off dead flowerheads just below the last blossom. Leaves and twigs make a good protective winter mulch. In the right position, *C. crocosmiiflora* will form dense groups, spreading through runners. The soil should be light and well drained. Plant in spring. Also makes a good cut flower.

50–80 cm | High summer

5–10 cm | Early spring

Crocus chrysanthus 'Cream Beauty' Snow crocus

C. chrysanthus flowers very early indeed. The variety 'Cream Beauty' delights us with its restrained cream-coloured flowers with their golden-yellow insides. Its dainty appearance would not lead you to believe that it is an extremely robust, modest, and enduring representative of the species. It spreads slowly but constantly in sunny locations with well-drained, reasonably fertile soils and if allowed will form lavishly flowering clumps. Plant the little bulbs in the autumn. Crocuses look their best in dense clumps and, if the colours are skilfully blended, can become a real attraction. 'Cream Beauty', for example, would look well in a cushion of purple flowers. It is ideal for rockeries, light shrubbery borders, or in the lawn. Leave the foliage until it yellows. Take care when mowing the lawn. No further care is needed.

10–15 cm | Autumn

5–10 cm | Early spring

Crocus speciosus Autumn crocus

This plant flowers in the autumn. Colours vary according to species: pale blue to dark violet with darker stripes or white with orange stripes. It has an orange stigma. This plant prefers a sunny location on well-drained soil. Plant in the summer. An undemanding garden companion.

Crocus tommasinianus 'Ruby Giant' Woodland crocus

A strong colour, a delicate form: this spring-flowering crocus, dark purple in colour, is excellently suited to naturalising and soon forms magnificent carpets of intense colour. *Crocus tommasinianus* not only is very resistant to wind and rain, but also has a long flowering period. Absolutely easy to care for. **Tip:** makes an ideal source of food for bees.

5–15 cm | Early spring

Cyclamen coum Persian violet

Hearing the name 'cyclamen', you might be reminded of Grandma's potted plants. However, if so, you would be doing the delicate *C. coum* an injustice. It is a very sturdy and hardy garden plant, and can flower reliably year after year in semi-shady, wind-sheltered sites on humus, well-drained soils. This little spring bloom with its distinctive, long-stemmed flowers in white, pink, or crimson and its kidney-shaped leaves does, however, like to be left undisturbed and in peace. It is easy to care for. Sprinkle humus over it every two years in spring or autumn. Mulch in the winter with twigs and pine needles. Plant the corms horizontally in the late summer or autumn. Propagate by seeds.

Cyclamen hederifolium Hardy cyclamen, ivy-leafed cyclamen, sowbread

C. hederifolium is especially hardy. The different species of cyclamen are distinguished not so much by the flower as by the shape of their leaves. This one, for example, has ivy-like leaves, green throughout the winter, with conspicuous silvery-green markings. The flowers appear either before or together with the young leaves. This autumn-flowering cyclamen is tolerant of semi-shady but also sunny locations and is considered frost-hardy. However, in regions with a harsh climate, prepare a winter mulch. **Tip:** pre-grown potted plants are easier to plant in position than the corms.

10–15 cm | Autumn to June

Cypripedium calceolus Yellow lady's slipper

A pretty rarity. This winter-hardy orchid species has crimson flowers with a bright yellow lip. It feels most at home in a sheltered spot at the edge of a shrubbery or in a semi-shady rockery. The plant prefers moist, fertile, alkaline soils. Mulch in the winter.

30–40 cm | Late spring to high summer

Dahlia Dahlia

They bring the sun back into your autumn garden. Next to tulips, dahlias, with their rich variety of colours, shapes, and species, are the most popular of bulb plants. These asterids appear in all colours except blue. They are divided into different groups according to the shape of the flower:

Single-flowered dahlias

These are mostly low-growing members of the species, with open centre flowers that consist of a simple ring of broad ligulate florets around a flat yellow centre (mignon dahlias). They have a disk-like appearance.

Anemone-flowered dahlias

These have one or more rings of generally flat petals surrounding a dense group of tubular florets. The latter are longer than those of single-flowered dahlias and therefore the form is not disk-like. The flowers have a semi-closed centre.

Collerette dahlias

A simple ring of generally flat ligulate florets. In each floret of this outer ring there are additional smaller florets, which give the visual effect of a second, usually smaller, inner ring. It looks like a collar or ruff. The centre is flat, as with the single-flowered dahlias. Semi-closed centre.

Waterlily dahlias

Large, but generally few petals, flat to curved in a bowl shape, not rolled. The overall impression of the flower is therefore flat. Closed centre.

Decorative dahlias

Densely filled with many small, flat petals, the edges lightly curled inward, bending back slightly toward the stem. The effect is lush and plump.

Ball dahlias

These have round but also flattened shapes. Densely-placed ligulate florets, rolled inward for more than half their length. Closed centre.

Pompon dahlias

A miniature version of the ball dahlia. The petals are, however, rolled for more than half their length, so that you can look down them as if down a tube. Closed centre.

Cactus dahlias

Narrow, pointed petals, rolled backward for more than half their length. The petals are positioned straight or very slightly curving upward toward the centre. Closed centre.

Semi-cactus dahlias

These are similar to cactus dahlias but generally have broader petals. The petals are only rolled backward at the tips. Closed centre.

Miscellaneous dahlias

These include dahlias that do not belong to one of the above groups: peony dahlias, giraffe dahlias, orchid dahlias, laciniated dahlias.

▶ Dahlia 'Garden Show'
Anemone-flowered dahlia

This flower has a superb colour combination of delicate pink and red. With its warm bronze shade in the centre, 'Garden Show' is about to steal the show from all its rivals. Flowerhead 12 centimetres across.

80–100 cm | High summer to late autumn

Dahlia Dahlia

80–120 cm | High summer to late autumn

80–100 cm | High summer to late autumn

◀ *Dahlia* 'Lambada' Anemone-flowered dahlia
The name sounds like a Latin American dance. And the delicate pink and beige shades will make your garden dance. This flower is also excellently suited to containers. Flowerhead 16 centimetres across.

70–80 cm | High summer to late autumn

▲ *Dahlia* 'Bridesbouquet'
Collerette dahlia, yellow bird

Innocence in pale creamy off-white, with a 'collar' in the same shade. Flowerhead 7 centimetres across.

◀ *Dahlia* 'Night Butterfly' Collerette dahlia
'Night Butterfly' conquers all hearts in its mysterious dark purple, almost black costume with the fine, white ruff in the centre. 6 centimetres across.

Dahlias deserve their position among the most popular garden plants because they guarantee colourful and dense flowers from high summer to the frosts of the autumn. These wonderful, spectacular flowers love locations that are sunny but not too hot and in the open, where they can develop undisturbed. Even if they do not demand uninterrupted sun, dahlias are barely tolerant of shade. The soil should be fertile, humus, slightly acid, and well drained, as the tubers may begin to rot when waterlogged. Dahlias also have the reputation of not liking contact, so they should always be planted with sufficient gaps. Planted in containers, dahlias in the autumn are a treasure for patios and balconies. The taller varieties make wonderful cut flowers, which keep well if the water is changed daily.

▶ *Dahlia* 'Twiggy' Waterlily dahlia

Bright pink 'Twiggy' makes a good cut flower. The touch of delicate yellow in the centre is particularly pretty. Flowerhead 12 centimetres across.

100–120 cm · High summer to late autumn

◀ *Dahlia* 'Arabian Night' Decorative dahlia

Dark crimson, almost black, and mysterious, this flower is among the most select treasures in the dahlia kingdom. Flowerhead 12 centimetres across.

80–100 cm · High summer to late autumn

▶ *Dahlia* 'Café au Lait' Decorative dahlia

This large-flowered decorative dahlia is one of the most elegant varieties available; it has a subtle mocha shade with a tinge of delicate pink. A prolific bloomer, it will also look eye-catching in a vase. Flowerhead 25 centimetres across.

80–100 cm · High summer to late autumn

D. 'Mystery Day' Decorative dahlia

This variety is very dominant in its effect. The luxuriant flowers of 'Mystery Day' have a strong colour, a fuchsia red with dainty white tips. Flowerhead 14 centimetres across.

90–120 cm · High summer to late autumn

◀ *Dahlia* 'Boy Scout' Ball dahlia

This is quite a feminine shade for a 'Boy Scout', but nonetheless a very ornamental dahlia. Flowerhead 7 centimetres across.

70–90 cm　High summer to late autumn

Dahlia Dahlia

◀ *Dahlia* 'Bantling' Pompon dahlia

'Bantling's' orange flower ball looks so perfect, almost like something from another planet. Even if the flower is small, 'Bantling' can nevertheless reach the impressive height of over 1 metre.

▼ *Dahlia* 'Nescio' Pompon dahlia

Not all reds are equal. The colour has never been as glowing, as exhilarating, as powerful as it is in 'Nescio'. It is so intense, it takes your breath away.

90–120 cm　High summer to late autumn

75–100 cm　High summer to late autumn

However, it is not so very easy to enjoy the splendour of dahlias. They do require care and attention. But a little care is well rewarded, many times over. After the first frost, you will need to dig out your dahlia tubers and gently knock the soil off them. Then place them in peat or dry sand and keep them over the winter in a frost-free, cool, well-ventilated room. In frost-free regions, you may leave the dahlias in the ground over the winter. In areas where there is a slight risk of frost, cover with a deep layer of mulch. In late spring, you can plant the tubers back in the garden again, but divide tubers that have been with you for several years first. During the growth period, regularly add fertiliser rich in nitrogen, as this stimulates leaf growth. From high summer onward, add fertiliser rich in potassium to promote flower formation. The taller varieties need supports, to which the new shoots should be tied at regular intervals. In order not to damage the tubers, knock in the support first and then plant the tuber. Regularly cut off dead flowers. In dry periods, give plenty of water, close to the ground.

▶ *Dahlia* 'Apricot Star'
Cactus dahlia

Here is 'Apricot Star', in its light, free, and easy outfit. The salmon-pink flower with its creamy heart displays a particularly attractive colour combination. Flowerhead 15 centimetres across.

| 100–120 cm | High summer to late autumn | | |

| 70–90 cm | High summer to late autumn | | | | |

▲ *Dahlia* 'Mondeo' Cactus dahlia

The colouring – golden-yellow, changing to orange in the tips – is reminiscent of a cool, refreshing summer drink. Flowerhead 10 centimetres across.

Dahlia 'Burning Love' Semi-cactus dahlia
Was it named after the famous song by Elvis? At any rate, the effect is wild and smouldering. Flowerhead 10 centimetres across.

| 100–120 cm | High summer to late autumn | | | |

Dahlia 'Cha Cha' Semi-cactus dahlia

A truly attractive play of colours for your garden or your vase. Flowerhead 12 centimetres across.

| 90–100 cm | High summer to late autumn | | |

Dahlia Dahlia

◀ **Dahlia 'Melody Gypsy'** Semi-cactus dahlia

The small-flowered, medium-height 'Melody Gypsy' looks radiant in pale rose pink with a little yellow centre. It makes a good cut flower. Flowerhead 12 centimetres across.

▼ **Dahlia 'Nuit d'Été'** Semi-cactus dahlia

In the darkest wine red, almost black at the centre, 'Nuit d'Été' brings a hint of shade to the most brilliant sunlight. Flowerhead 12 centimetres across.

| 50–70 cm | High summer to late autumn | | |

| 100–120 cm | High summer to late autumn | | |

▼ **Dahlia 'Bishop of Llandaff'** Peony dahlia

Peony dahlias are like single-flowered varieties, but have more than one ring of florets. 'Bishop of Llandaff' is a true classic: a brilliant red flower with contrasting dark leaves. Flowerhead 10 centimetres across.

| 90–120 cm | High summer to late autumn | | |

▶ *Dahlia* 'Classic Masquerade'
Peony dahlia

It has no need to hide. The red flame-like streaks on the terracotta to orange background are truly eye-catching. It looks particularly attractive with its purple to black leaves. Flowerhead 10 centimetres across.

◀ *Dahlia* 'Classic Rosamunde' Peony dahlia

The warm pink to purple petals make for a friendly atmosphere. The dark leaves form a decorative contrast. Flowerhead 10 centimetres across.

| 🌱 25–50 cm | ✿✿ | High summer to late autumn | | ✳ | ✴ |

| 🌱 80–100 cm | ✿✿ | High summer to late autumn | ✳ | ✴ |

Dahlia 'Promise' Laciniated dahlia

Laciniated dahlias are cactus dahlias with petals that are split or serrated at the ends. 'Promise' is a sulphur-yellow variety with such split-tipped petals.

| 🌱 120–140 cm | ✿✿ | High summer to late autumn | ✳ | ✴ | 🫖 | 🪴 | 🏺 |

5–15 cm Winter to very early spring

Eremurus × isabellinus 'Pinokkio' Foxtail lily

Stiffly upright, pointing skyward like a rocket before blast-off, 'Pinokkio' is an ornament to the summer garden. The densely-packed individual flowers on the truly impressive flower stalk glow in coppery yellow to orange shades in front of dark trees and shrubs or in flowerbeds. Their essential requirement is for a sunny, warm, and wind-sheltered spot on well-drained soil rich in nutrients, with no risk of waterlogging. After flowering, cut the flower stalks back to half-way down the stem. Mulch in winter with leaves and brushwood. If necessary, also protect the leaf shoots in the spring from cold weather damage. As the root stocks are friable, care is advisable when planting. Plant in late summer. Do not divide the rhizome until three or four years have passed. Makes an attractive cut flower.

20–35 cm Spring

Eranthis hyemalis Winter aconite

This sturdy little marvel will cheer up a melancholy spring garden with a scented carpet of flowers in almost blinding yellow. It is an undemanding little plant and has few requirements where soil and care are concerned. In semi-shade or light spring shade, it will spread – through bulblets or seed – along the borders of shrubbery or woodland, under bushes or on scanty lawns. Plant in the autumn. The bulbs are very sensitive to dehydration, so do not store. **Take care:** all parts of the plant, particularly the bulb, are poisonous. **Tip:** *E. hyemalis* is an excellent source of food for bees.

80–120 cm Early to high summer

Erythronium 'Citronella' Dogtooth violet

The rather unflattering common name was given to this airy crown-shaped beauty because of its egg-shaped, whitish bulb, which does indeed resemble a dog's canine tooth. The delicate yellow pendent flowers with their dark yellow anthers will reward a site in semi-shade and fertile, humus soil by plentiful flowering. Keep the plants moist during the growth period, but avoid waterlogging, and keep them rather drier after flowering. In areas with a harsh climate, a winter mulch of leaves and brushwood is required. Propagate in late summer by means of bulblets and seeds. This plant has decorative foliage.

Freesia lactea Freesia

In temperate zones, this plant is more familiar as a scented cut flower. Planted in the spring, the flowers will appear in summer. Plant in the autumn in frost-free regions to obtain flowers in the spring. It requires fertile, moist, well-drained soil.

20–40 cm | Summer

Eucomis bicolour Pineapple lily

This plant can't disguise its African origin. The unusual exotic flowering cylinders of *E. bicolour* are a gorgeous attraction for the eye when set in front of dark trees or shrubs, large stones, or in summery flowerbeds. The pale green star-shaped flowers with their pink edges hang from a tall stem crowned with a tuft of leaves. The plant owes its name 'pineapple lily' to this visual arrangement. It will display its conspicuous magnificence in fertile, well-drained soils in sunny to lightly-shaded, sheltered locations. Keep the soil evenly moist during the growing period; add fertiliser if required. In mild climate zones, winter mulch is enough protection. In areas with a harsher climate, lift the bulbs out of the soil and put them in winter storage in a cool, dry place from the autumn onwards. Plant in mid-spring. Once the leaves are yellowing, bulblets can be removed for propagation.

30–60 cm | Late summer

Fritillaria imperialis 'Blom's Orange Perfection'
Crown imperial fritillary

Its graceful and impressive pose and its lavish elegant flowers make this a star of the typical cottage garden. The brightly-coloured, orange to red bell-shaped flowers are particularly effective in small groups and planted close to other spring-flowering plants, such as *Tulipa*, *Narcissus*, *Myosotis*, in harmonising shades. The plant loves sunny, warm sites with well-drained soils rich in nutrients. Cut back the dead flowerheads down to the first leaves on the stem. Once the leaves have yellowed, cut the imperial fritillary back to just above ground level. Add fertiliser regularly. In all other matters, the plant, in keeping with its imperial status, likes to remain undisturbed. Plant in high summer. Do not store the bulbs for long. Propagate by bulblets. There are also red and yellow varieties. **Tip:** the sharp scent of its bulbs is supposed to keep off voles and other rodents. **Take care:** all parts of the plant contain toxins.

| 80–150 cm | Early summer | | | |

Fritillaria meleagris Chequered lily, snakehead fritillary

Year after year, the chequered lily in its charming little checked costume displays grace and elegance. The broad, attractive, nodding flowers are in fact marked with the graphic precision of a chessboard. While *F. imperialis* grabs all the attention, this variety unfolds quite modestly in semi-shady, cool locations in fertile, moist soil. Planted among low-growing spring flowers, our little friend can achieve skilful effects. It will grow undisturbed, too, in moist meadows or in ponds or shrubberies and woodland borders. It will show its gratitude for the right position by problem-free and profuse growth. Do not store the bulbs for long periods, but plant in the ground in the late summer. Replant bulblets immediately after removing them.

| 15–30 cm | Late spring | | | |

| 10–20 cm | Late spring to early summer | | | |

Fritillaria michailovskyi Maroon fritillary

A dark beauty, *F. michailovskyi* has bell-shaped, violet-brown flowers with a yellow rim and the same colours on the inside, all on a delicate, slender stem. It is a perennial species and thrives in flowerbeds in cottage gardens and rockeries in sunny locations with rather dry, well-drained soil. It tolerates very little moisture.

Fritillaria pallidiflora Pale-flowered fritillary

This low-growing, pale yellow flower with broad, blue-green leaves has up to four fairly large pendent flowers per plant. It needs humus, well-drained, and fertile soil in a sunny location. The flowers have a slightly unpleasant scent.

30–40 cm | Late spring to early summer

100–150 cm | Late spring

Fritillaria persica 'Adiyaman' Persian fritillary

F. persica is definitely one of the most unusual varieties of this species and the spring garden is the richer for this highlight. Up to 30 enchanting, scented, brownish-purple bell-shaped flowers hang from a single stalk. This ornamental beauty is best admired among plainer neighbours, surrounded by grasses or ferns. As it is a mountain plant, it also manages well in drier soils. It loves sheltered, very warm sites. If the location is right, it needs very little care. However, a protective mulch of brushwood is recommended for the winter. Propagate by bulblets.

Fritillaria raddeana Fritillary

In appearance, this plant resembles a smaller version of F. imperialis but it is less colourful. F. raddeana has a rather more restrained, pale yellow-green flowerhead, but its demands regarding care, site, and soils reveal their relationship. Sunny spots with well-drained, fertile soil are desired. See also F. imperialis.

60–70 cm | Early spring

10–30 cm · Early to mid-spring

Gagea lutea Yellow star of Bethlehem

A very uncomplicated and undemanding guest in your garden is yellow *G. lutea*, which does, however, not look its best unless in company. As a solitary plant, it is somewhat lacking in expression, but in a group it becomes a very visible sea of flowers. It works particularly well when planted under trees and shrubs or leafy hedges. It requires light spring sun and moist, humus-rich soils. Plant in the autumn. Propagate by seed or by removing bulblets once the leaves have died back.

Galanthus nivalis Snowdrop

This tiny, radiant white flower is one of the first to raise its head bravely in the unfriendly winter garden. Tough and hardy, it defies snow and frost. Because the weather is usually harsh, *G. nivalis* prefers to flower in the sun, but after flowering it will tolerate shade and semi-shade. It will thrive, therefore, under deciduous trees and shrubs or bordering hedges. In moist, humus-rich soil it will soon naturalise, propagating itself through bulblets and self-seeding to form luxuriant carpets. It is in no way a solitary plant. Its innocent white will look positively radiant in the company of *Eranthis hyemalis*, crocuses, anemones, or *Cyclamen*. The filbert-sized bulbs are planted in early autumn. Larger snowdrops are suitable vase flowers and give out a delicate scent. **Take care:** *G. nivalis* is not as innocent as it looks. All parts of the plant are poisonous.

10–15 cm · Winter to early spring

Galtonia candicans Summer hyacinth

G. candicans is surely the most impressive of the summer-flowering bulbs. Slender, tall, all in white, it is decorative not only in flowerbeds, but also in vases. It displays its somewhat exotic splendour in sunny, sheltered locations, supported by plenty of water and fertiliser. The soil should be fertile and loose. In the autumn, cut off dead flowers and in areas where the winters are harsh dig out the bulbs and store them in a dry and cool place. This plant is sensitive to frost. Plant in spring. Propagates by seed, more rarely by bulblets. The flower is delicately scented.

100–150 cm Late summer

▶ *Gladiolus* 'Flevo Cosmic'

This short-stemmed, exotic-looking beauty is a member of the *Primulinus* group. The delicate, greenish-yellow flowers have bright pink tips and a dark brown eye in the centre. A magnificent sight.

| | 40–60 cm | | Early to late summer | | | | |

Gladiolus Gladiolus

| | 40–60 cm | | Early to late summer | | |

| | 90–110 cm | | Early to late summer | | |

◀ *Gladiolus* 'Flevo Smile'

Creamy off-white flowers, their effect further strengthened by two pale yellow petals each. A whisper of red in the centre completes the ensemble.

| | 60–120 cm | | Early to late summer | | | |

▲ *Gladiolus* 'May Bride'

Take a look: tall and slender, with radiant white flowers, lightly tinged with yellow on the inside. A splendid large-flowered plant.

◀ *Gladiolus* 'Oberbayern'

Large-flowered, violet to dark blue variety with creamy-white centre. This variety is not winter-hardy – store the bulbs in a protected place for the winter. A member of the Butterfly group.

Time for a comeback. Thanks to the fashion for all things retro, the stern and upright but elegant gladiolus is returning victorious to gardens and vases. With its great variety of colours and the long, profusely-studded flowerheads, it brings plenty of atmosphere to the summer garden, where it prefers to be in full sun, in warm and wind-sheltered flowerbeds with deep, sufficiently moist but well-drained soils rich in nutrients. The plant does not like to be waterlogged, and a little coarse sand in the hole when planting can help prevent this. Plant the bulbs in spring; the taller varieties will need support. Gladioli look good in groups among medium-height summer flowers and perennials. In regions where there is a risk of frost, the bulbs must be taken out of the soil in late autumn, when the leaves turn yellowish-brown. To store over the winter, brush off the soil, allow the bulbs to dry and remove remaining foliage. Keep them in a dark, cool, and frost-free place. Remove bulblets from the old bulbs in the autumn for propagation. The old, dried-up bulbs can be thrown away.

▶ *Gladiolus* 'Priscilla'

Big, white flowers, looking decorative with their yellow throats and pink-edged petals. A sturdy bloomer.

◀ *Gladiolus* 'Traderhorn'

The brilliant red flower spike of 'Traderhorn', up to just over 1 metre tall, stands stern and upright. Inside, the flower is ribbed with white. Large flowers.

| 100–150 cm | Early to late summer |
| 100–150 cm | Early to late summer |

▶ *Gladiolus byzantinus* subsp. *communis* Cornflag

A winter-hardy variety with sturdy growth, which spreads well through its rhizomes. It is very undemanding, requiring only sun and ordinary soil. It is a favourite for cottage gardens and wild perennial plantings.

| 80–100 cm | Mid-spring to early summer |

Gladiolus tubergenii 'Charm'

This flower really does have a lot of wildflower-style charm. It flowers in early summer; the flowers are crimson red with a great variety of shades. Ivory throat. This flower also looks good in a vase.

| 30–60 cm | Early summer |

Hyacinthoides hispanica 'Danube'

Spanish bluebell, Hispanic hyacinthoides

The delicate bluebell adds a fresh note of blue to spring gardens. It is an excellent plant for wild-look gardens, where it can, if allowed to naturalise, soon create lush, blue carpets of flowers. *H. hispanica*'s distinctive features are a broader, more erect flowerhead and broader leaves than *H. non-scripta*. In the right location, both species need little care. Add a little compost every few years and water in longer spells of dry weather.

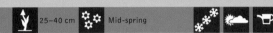

25–40 cm   Mid-spring

Hyacinthoides non-scripta 'Bluebell'

English bluebell

In Britain in the spring, thousands of bluebells cover forest borders and meadows with their blue flowers. *H. non-scripta* will also flower in gardens, very profusely and year after year, in cool, semi-shady spots such as the edges of shrubberies and woodlands or as a border for shady areas. The soil should be well-drained, moderately rich in nutrients, humus and fresh, even moist in spring. Plant in the autumn. Propagate by separating plants from the flower patches or by taking bulblets. There are also white and pink varieties.

20–40 cm   Early summer

▶ *Hyacinthus orientalis* 'Amethyst'

Seductive and radiant, the opulent tubular flowers of 'Amethyst', set in dense spikes, glow in a mysterious violet pink. They are a true ornament for a spring flowerbed.

15–25 cm   Mid-spring

Hyacinthus Hyacinth

The hyacinth is definitely one of the classics among spring flowers, with its magnificent flowerheads with their slightly Baroque appearance, its bright, lovely colours, and its unmistakable scent. Despite its intensely colourful and rather plump appearance, the flower looks best in groups. Planted with *Myosotis*, *Viola*, or *Bellis*, it will liven up the spring flowerbed or decorate sunny shrubbery borders. It prefers a warm, sheltered spot in the sun. The soil should be well drained and rich in nutrients; a light sandy soil is best. In the growth phase the plant requires sufficient moisture and nutrients, but waterlogging must be avoided. In harsh climates, a light winter mulch of brushwood is recommended. Particularly with double-flowered hyacinths, the flower spikes tend to autumn over, and a small stick can give helpful support. Cut the dead flowers off straight away but leave the leaves until they turn yellow. Over the years, the splendour of the hyacinth's flowers will be reduced. Either plant new bulbs or carefully remove bulblets after the leaves have died back or plant in the autumn in a different location. The flower provides plenty of food for bees and bumblebees. Also suitable for vases. Hyacinths are poisonous, and there is a danger of skin inflammation.

20–25 cm   Late spring

20–25 cm   Mid-spring

▲ *Hyacinthus orientalis* 'City of Haarlem'

'City of Haarlem', in pale yellow to ivory, shows restraint in its appearance. It is quite an old variety, and reliable. Single flowers.

◀ *Hyacinthus orientalis* 'Delft Blue'

'Delft Blue' – right away, the name tells you the colouring of this beautiful and densely packed flower spike. Single flowers.

▶ *Hyacinthus orientalis* 'Festival'

Multiflora hyacinth

'Festival', with several flower spikes, has a looser and more informal effect than the single-stemmed varieties. Each bulb has five to seven shoots, guaranteeing a lavish bouquet of scented flowers. The plant is hardy in bad weather.

15–20 cm Mid-spring

Hyacinthus 'Paul Hermann'

This variety of hyacinth is a pleasure for the senses, with its large, pink to violet flower spike and intense scent. It is a special attraction for flowerbeds or rockeries or as a potted plant.

20–25 cm Mid-spring

10–20 cm · Mid- to late spring

Ipheion uniflorum Springstar, spring starflower

The delicate six-pointed star of *I. uniflorum* has radiant white, blue-tinged, or violet petals, prettily marked with a dark stripe down the middle. These spring flowers have a sweet scent, while the leaves smell rather of garlic. This easy-to-care-for, sturdy little plant will quickly spread to form a carpet of flowers in sunny, sheltered locations on loose, moist but well-drained soils. It looks very good in the company of *Crocus*, *Narcissus*, and *Scilla*. Winter protection is needed. Plant in the autumn.

Ixia 'Uranus'

The dark lemon-yellow flowers have a dark red, almost black centre. They love sunny, warm, sheltered spots and well-drained, sandy soils. Water well in the growing phase, but leave fairly dry after flowering. Take the bulbs out of the ground in the autumn and allow to overwinter in a pot at 50 to 59°F (10 to 15°C).

40–60 cm · Early summer

Leucojum aestivum 'Gravetye Giant'
Summer snowflake, giant snowflake

'Gravetye Giant' likes to aim higher than its smaller relations. It has up to eight bell-shaped white flowers on each stem. It looks pretty near water, in light shade on wet, humus soils. Plant the bulbs in the autumn and then allow them to develop undisturbed; this lets *L. aestivum* spread without too much effort. **Take care:** *L. aestivum* is poisonous.

60–90 cm · Late spring to early summer

| Up to 10 cm | | Late spring | | | | |

eucojum nicaeense Nice snowflake

he smallest and most delicate of the snowflakes
as white bell-shaped flowers that appear in late
pring. In flowerbeds, rockeries, or containers, they
dd a bright touch. However, in contrast to the rest
f the family, *L. nicaeense* prefers the warm rays of
e sun, which it is used to in its French homeland,
nd a moist, well-drained soil. It can survive the
inter in a protected, sunny place, but give it a light
rotective mulch of leaves and brushwood. Plant
nicaeense in the autumn. **Tip:** all the snowflakes
re suited to growing in small containers and make
ood cut flowers.

| 20–30 cm | | Early spring | | | | | |

Leucojum vernum Spring snowflake

They might be small, but the round-bellied, nodding flowers of
L. vernum, with a yellow-green spot at the tip of each of the white
petals, simply catch the eye. In semi-shady spots with fresh, even
moist, humus-rich soil – the edges of shrubberies, for example, or a
bed of heath plants – they will soon spread to form luxuriant ground
cover. It is undemanding, and has two further advantages: it has a
lovely scent and is very popular with bees and other insects because
of its nectar. Once the leaves have died back, bulblets can be removed
or the bulb groups divided. Seed propagation is also possible. Plant in
late summer. **Take care:** *L. vernum* is poisonous.

Lilium 'Apeldoorn' Asiatic hybrid

The sturdy 'Apeldoorn' makes a lively splash of unmissable
orange. It has lush, cup-shaped flowers.

| 70–90 cm | | Early to high summer | | | | | |

Lilium Lily

The lily's flowering period is one of the high points
the summer garden has to offer. Its elegant and noble
stature and the scent of its flowers give it an irresistible
charm. The multitude of colours and shapes of this versatile
cosmopolitan is also overwhelming. There are lilies in
almost every colour except blue. The flowers have spotted
or striped patterns or are plain and single coloured. They
come in cup, bowl, trumpet, funnel, bell, or turban shapes.
Bearing long-lasting flowers, the lilies are divided into

eight classes of hybrids and a further class comprising
the botanical species. The Asiatic hybrids are the most
important class for cultivating in gardens. The lilies in the
trumpet class have splendid large flowers and are easy
to cultivate, with a beguiling scent. The oriental hybrids
are sometimes a little sensitive, but the very large flowers
are appealing.

◀ *Lilium* 'Bright Star' Trumpet lily

It lives up to its name: there is a bright yellow star on the backward-curving, ivory-coloured petals. A scented variety, which tolerates lime soils.

100–150 cm	High to late summer

Lilium Lily

60–80 cm	Early to late summer

This most impressive bulb plant looks good almost anywhere: in shrubberies, woodland, or cottage gardens, or planted among bushes or roses. It's also very ornamental in big pots or as a cut flower in a vase.

Most species like a place in full sun for the flowers and shade for the bulbs. Some, however, will tolerate semi-shady sites with a good deal of light. Well-drained, neutral, or acid soils, enriched with rotted organic material, are accepted by most species. Heavy soils should be lightened with coarse gravel before planting, in order to avoid waterlogging. The bulbs are planted in the autumn or in spring. Tall species should be given support. Water regularly in the summer and add fertiliser rich in potassium. Regularly remove dead flowers. Mulch with peat in the autumn. As this noble plant is also very popular with snails, slugs, and lily-leaf beetles, these should be collected and removed before there is nothing left of your lilies. **Tip:** if you are inexperienced in growing lilies, try one of the more robust hybrids first.

100–120 cm	Early to high summer

▲ *Lilium* 'Côte d'Azur' Asiatic hybrid

In rockeries, summer flowerbeds, or containers; little 'Côte d'Azur' looks pretty anywhere.

◀ *Lilium* 'First Crown' Oriental hybrid

Gorgeous, beautiful flowers in a warm orange-bronze shade with fine pink markings. A scented early-flowering variety.

▶ *Lilium* Golden Splendour Group
Trumpet lily

Umbels with large yellow flowers at right angles to the stem. Scented.

120–200 cm | High summer

◀ *Lilium* 'Mona Lisa' Oriental hybrid

The most common of the pink hybrids. It is fairly easy to care for and has a beguiling scent.

90–120 cm | Late summer

▶ *Lilium* 'Monte Negro' Asiatic hybrid

The large flowers on their sturdy stems, curving right back, are delightful in their elegant shade of dark red. An exclamation mark in any garden.

90–120 cm | Early to high summer

Lilium 'Star Gazer'
Oriental hybrid

A true star, with no prima donna habits. This popular red to pink lily variety is not only incredibly beautiful and marvellously scented, but also very robust and easy to cultivate, making it ideal for 'beginners'.

100–150 cm | High to late summer

◀ *Lilium auratum* var. *platyphyllum*
Gold-banded lily

The conspicuous golden-yellow stripes on every petal are the trademark of the gold-banded lily. The flowers of this species, which comes from Japan, are up to 30 centimetres in diameter.

100–150 cm | Late summer

Lilium Lily

80–150 cm | High summer

60–150 cm | Late summer to early autumn

◀ *Lilium candidum* Madonna lily

Christian symbol for purity. An evergreen variety, protect with a mulch of brushwood from the autumn onward. Rather demanding.

100–150 cm | Early summer

▲ *Lilium hansonii* Hanson's lily

The curled-back petals give the impression of a small turban. Brilliant orange-yellow flowers.

◀ *Lilium lancifolium* Tiger lily

An exotic touch for the late summer garden. This robust species prefers moist, acid soils.

▶ *Lilium martagon* var. *album*
White Turk's cap lily

Up to 50 small, pure white nodding little flowers come out in high summer. All of them have the back-curving petals.

| | 120–140 cm | | High summer | | |

◀ *Lilium pyrenaicum* subsp. *pyrenaicum*
Pyrenean lily

Though the little lemon-yellow flowers are pleasing to the eye, they are not famed for their scent.

| | 30–100 cm | | Early summer | | |

▶ *Lilium regale* Regal lily

This splendid plant is not selfish with its charms. The broad, trumpet-shaped, white blooms with their crimson stripes on the outside have a seductive scent. This is a wonderful plant for containers and cut flowers.

| | 90–130 cm | | High summer | | |

Lilium speciosum
Japanese lily

It forms bunches of up to 12 large flowers. It grows best in moist, acid soils. An undemanding plant with long-lasting flowers, it has a delicate scent, and is ideally suited to growing close to a patio or garden seat area.

| | 100–170 cm | | Late summer to early autumn | | |

Mirabilis jalapa Marvel of Peru, four o'clock flower, beauty-of-the-night

You really can't accuse this plant of being miserly with its charms, and yet the flower of *M. jalapa* is very shy, showing its full splendour for only a single night. It is a good thing that this perennial, scented, repeat bloomer has flowers in plenty, a profuse mass of them, and in a great variety of colours. For this is its speciality: glowing flowers in many colours – red, yellow, red and yellow together – on the one and same plant. If planted in a sunny, sheltered place in fertile, loose soil, it will start to open its delicate buds in the afternoon and begin its flirtation with the dark. If there is a risk of frost, remove the tuberous roots from the ground in the autumn and store them for the winter in earth in a cool and dry place. Plant in late spring.

50–70 cm | Early to late summer

Muscari armeniacum Armenian grape hyacinth

Here is a sight that ought not to be missing from any garden – when the cone-shaped flower spikes of *M. armeniacum* crowd together in great numbers to make a cobalt-blue carpet, impossible to overlook, every year, spring after spring. There is always the right place for *Muscari* to make a show, whether in spring flowerbeds, rockeries, or the borders of shrubberies. The plant loves a sunny to semi-shady spot with well-drained, moist, fairly fertile soil. Plant in the autumn. **Take care:** poisonous and a skin irritant.

10–20 cm | Late spring

Muscari comosum 'Plumosum' syn. 'Monstrosum'
Tassel grape hyacinth

Definitely a late bloomer, *M. comosum* takes the stage only when the last tulips have almost finished. An unusual feature in this undemanding species is that the flowers surround the stem like loose spikes. The 'tassel' consists of sterile, blue to violet flower stems that bunch together to form a feathery, bushy crown. This presumably serves to attract the attention of passing insects.

20–40 cm | Late spring to early summer

Muscari latifolium
Bicolour grape hyacinth, wide-leaf grape hyacinth

M. latifolium has a surprise for us: harmonising shades. The upper flowers are pale blue; the small, spherical lower flowers are a mysterious dark blue, almost blue-black. This species also thrives in rockeries or lawns.

10–20 cm | Late spring to early summer

Narcissus Narcissus

Narcissi are divided into twelve classes according to the shape and length of the wreath of outer petals (perianth), the number of flowers per stem, and the time of flowering.

Trumpet narcissus
Usually a single flower. The trumpet (corona) is at least as long as the petals of the perianth. Early to mid-spring.

Large-cupped narcissus
Single flower. Corona is at maximum the length of the petals, at least one-third as long. A great variety of shapes and colours. Spring.

Small-cupped narcissus
Single flower. Corona is shorter, at maximum one-third as long as the petals. Spring.

Double narcissus
Perianth and corona, or corona only, filled with petals. Single flower. Early to mid-spring.

Triandrus narcissus
Nodding flowers with short corona and turned-back petals in the perianth. Two to three flowers per stem. Strongly scented. Mid- to late spring.

Cyclamineus narcissus
Nodding flowers. Turned-back petals in the perianth, long, narrow corona. Early to mid-spring.

Jonquilla narcissus
Usually several flowers. Short, broad corona with flat, broad, rounded petals. Mid- to late spring.

Tazetta narcissus
These form scented tufts of flowers. Flat, broad-petaled perianth with small, cup-shaped corona. Usually in two colours. Moderately frost-hardy. Mid- to late spring.

Poeticus narcissus
Single flower. Large white perianth and red-edged, relatively small, coloured corona. Late spring to early summer.

Split-cupped narcissus
Usually single flowered. The corona is split and partly turned back. Spring.

Wild narcissus
Wild forms of the classes described. These flower between the autumn and spring.

Miscellaneous narcissus
Hybrids not assigned to any other class.

N. 'Slim Whitman' Large-cupped narcissus

'Slim Whitman' is an ideal variety to allow to naturalise, even in shady locations. With a creamy perianth and a light orange-to-yellow corona, this flower is truly eye-catching.

35–50 cm   Spring

Narcissus Narcissus

Plant and wait. The instructions for this genus, rich in many varied species, really are that short and simple. Beauty and strength have eased their upward path and made them the most popular of spring flowers.

Once in the ground, their annual comeback delights us year after year, with a splendid and extravagant show. They don't even make any great demands of us. The soil should be moderately fertile and well drained – neither dryness nor waterlogging will be tolerated. In a dry spring, therefore, it will be necessary to water. Narcissi are hungry for the spring sun, but will accept semi-shady places. This makes them the ideal planting for leafless shrubbery borders. But they also bring a brilliant spot of colour to rockeries, flowerbeds, or lawns. They should never be planted singly; the more numerous they are, the more they will be admired. But they can also develop wonderfully in the company of *Muscari* or tulips. The bulbs should be planted in the soil in September, to allow them to root well before the winter.

15–30 cm   Spring

25–50 cm   Early to mid-spring

▲ **N. 'Segovia'** Small-cupped narcissus

This delicate beauty will not only draw all eyes to itself but also attract bees and butterflies. A little jewel for every garden.

◀ **N. 'Petit Four'** Double narcissus

The lush apricot to pink crown contrasts prettily with the white perianth.

▶ *N.* 'Rip van Winkle' Double narcissus

It looks a bit shaggy, but the small-flowered, low-growing 'Rip van Winkle' is a tried and tested classic among the narcissi.

◀ *Narcissus* 'Tahiti' Double narcissus

The red and yellow, large-flowered 'Tahiti' does indeed add a brief touch of the South Seas to spring gardens.

15–20 cm   Early to mid-spring

25–50 cm   Early to mid-spring

▶ *Narcissus* 'Hawera' Triandrus narcissus

Lemon yellow, elegant, and delicately scented. There are five to six little nodding flowers on each stem. 'Hawera' is ideal for rockeries.

15–20 cm   Mid- to late spring

Narcissus 'Thalia'
Triandrus narcissus

The tall-growing 'Thalia' proudly bears one to three virginal white flowers on each stem. This Narcissus is a reliable and long-lived spring companion. It will also naturalise in suitable locations.

25–40 cm   Mid- to late spring

◀ *Narcissus* 'Jack Snipe'

Cyclamineus daffodil

Behind the sulphur-yellow corona lies the perianth with its back-curving, creamy petals. 'Jack Snipe' is almost unsurpassed when it comes to longevity and profusion of flowers. Shapely growth and elegance.

20–35 cm | Early to mid-spring

Narcissus Narcissus

◀ *Narcissus* 'Jetfire' Cyclamineus narcissus

'Jetfire' is an extravagant and impressive member of the cyclamineus narcissus class. The orange to red corona stands out against the lemon-yellow, back-curving petals.

20–30 cm | Early to mid-spring

20–30 cm | Mid- to late spring

30–40 cm | Mid- to late spring

▲ *Narcissus* 'Bell Song' Jonquilla narcissus

This charming variety also appears in two colours. The pale pink, cup-shaped corona sits on creamy-white petals.

◀ *Narcissus* 'Pipit' Jonquilla narcissus

'Pipit', in brilliant yellow, may be small but is not easy to overlook.

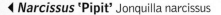

Once the leaves have died back, bulblets can be removed. These should be stored in a cool and dry place until it is time to plant in the autumn. The foliage should always be left until the plant has died back completely, and only removed when the leaves can be easily pulled off. This is the only way of guaranteeing a profusion of flowers for the next year. If the withered leaves get in the way when mowing the lawn, simply tie them up in bunches and mow around them.

Narcissi also make outstanding cut flowers. However, they do not do well in a vase with other cut flowers, as they produce a poisonous sap. Put them in water on their own for a day before placing them in arrangements with other flowers. A piece of charcoal in the water will neutralise the poison. **Take care:** all parts of the plant, and especially the bulbs, are poisonous.

Most species of narcissus are winter-hardy. The jonquilla and tazetta hybrids, and the wild narcissi, require the frost protection of a leaf and brushwood mulch.

▶ *Narcissus* **'Geranium'** Tazetta narcissus

'Geranium' offers three to six scented, orange and white blooms per stem. It is pretty as a picture and ideal for naturalising.

30–45 cm Mid- to late spring

◀ **'Actea'** Poeticus narcissus, poet's daffodil

Scented, and with a festive look, 'Actea' brings a long-lasting show of flowers into the spring garden. It is almost matchless in its simple elegance.

35–50 cm Late spring

▶ *Narcissus poeticus* **var.** *recurvus* Pheasant's-eye narcissus

This variety of the poeticus narcissus makes itself known both with its conspicuous flower and with its intense, spicy scent. It is one of the last narcissi to flower.

35–40 cm Late spring

Narcissus bulbocodium
Hooped-petticoat narcissus

This low-growing wild narcissus species has an unobtrusive but enchanting charm. Its flowers look a little like a wide, swaying lacy skirt, hence its name. Ideal for rockeries.

10–20 cm Early to mid-spring

Ornithogalum umbellatum
Star of Bethlehem, sleepydick

The milk-white star-shaped flowers of *O. umbellatum* cover the sunny and semi-shady borders of shrubberies and rockeries with foaming profusion. As the plant spreads easily, it is well suited to natural-look plantings on humus, loose soils. However, it only shows its flat, small stars around midday, and for the rest of the day its flowers remain closed. It is quite undemanding, though. Plant it in the autumn in small groups. It is easy to propagate by seeding or bulblets.

| | 10–30 cm | | Late spring to early summer | | | |

Oxalis acetosella Wood sorrel

The little plant with the cheerful, nodding white flower cups and the dainty, pale green foliage looks so graceful and harmless. And yet its tendency to expansion leads it to make veritable campaigns of conquest and drive out anything that gets in its way. As a forest and ground cover plant, *O. acetosella* is particularly suited for planting under shrubs and trees. It feels most at home in such shady locations with humus, moist, acid soils. On the one hand, it is by no means delicate, but on the other it is very sensitive to stimuli. If the weather is bad, it closes its flowers. If you touch the horizontally positioned leaves, they will after a short while droop downwards. It needs a lot of moisture all the year round, but is otherwise easy to care for. Can be propagated by dividing the clumps, by bulblets or seed.

| | 5–10 cm | | Late spring | | | |

25–40 cm | Mid-spring to early summer

Ranunculus asiaticus **hybrids** Buttercup, Persian buttercup

It's a lovely little plant. The intense brilliance of its ball-shaped flowers, with their fresh, clear colours ranging from red to pink to orange, yellow, and white, can be seen from quite a distance. There are single and double forms. In brief, this bulb has something for everyone. Depending on the weather, you can start planting early in the spring. Before planting, place the tubers in water for three or four hours. The site should be sunny and sheltered, with a well-drained, humus soil rich in nutrients. Rockeries or the borders of flowerbeds are ideal. Keep moist during flowering and if required add fertiliser once a week. After the leaves have died back take the tubers out of the ground. Allow to dry for a few days, then store in a cool and dry place. Divide the tubers or take off bulblets. **Tip:** if you plant the tubers in batches over a period of time, you can enjoy the blooming plants for weeks.

40–60 cm | Early summer

Roscoea auriculata

This slender, extraordinary flower should only make its appearance in the company of plain neighbours such as grasses and fern. It loves cool, light shade and reasonably fertile, moist, well-drained soil. Plant the root stock deep in the winter. Before the frost, mulch the planting site with a thick layer of leaves. If required, store the rhizomes in sand for the winter, keeping them slightly moist and cool.

10–20 cm | Spring

Puschkinia scilloides Striped squill

Small, cute, easy to care for. These attributes give a brief, precise portrait of this spring flower. Plant it in the autumn in little groups under trees and shrubs, in the lawn or in the rockery, and enjoy it for a long time.

10–20 cm ❀❀ Spring

Scilla siberica Siberian squill

This little blue jack-of-all-trades is very versatile. In light shade, under deciduous shrubs and trees, it will quickly naturalise; in lawns and rockeries it will accompany tulip, yellow *Narcissus*, or other *Scilla* species. It needs a reasonably fertile, well-drained soil rich in nutrients. Apart from that, its demands are few. The bulbs should be planted soon after purchasing. Plant in the autumn. A light mulch of compost in the winter will protect the Siberian squill.

Sternbergia lutea Winter daffodil

Surprisingly, the autumn garden often doesn't get the care that it deserves. And yet there are such cheerful flowers for the autumn, such as *S. lutea*. Thanks to its radiant yellow-gold flowers, it is able to bring a touch of life and vigour to weary rockeries and in front of leafless shrubberies. True to its Mediterranean origin, it loves sunny spots with stony soil, dry in summer. Plant in the summer in groups. During this rest period, you can also divide the clumps of bulbs. However, we would like to point out here that the same applies to *S. lutea* as applies to many other plants: it will best develop its full splendour if it is left undisturbed. In areas with a harsh climate a good winter mulch of leaves or brushwood is needed. After flowering, however, the bulbs may be kept in boxes over the winter.

10–20 cm ❀❀ Autumn

100–150 cm ❀❀ Summer to early autumn

Tigridia pavonia Peacock flower, tiger flower

T. pavonia, with its extravagant scarlet pattern of spots on a yellow background, has a touch of the unique. Economical, it opens its red, yellow, orange, or white petals for a single day only. However, as it has plenty of flowers, the spectacle continues for some weeks. For its spectacular appearance – which is, by the way, best if planted in groups – it needs sun, warmth, and a fertile soil. Keep the plant evenly moist during flowering, but tending toward dry after the flowers have died. In the autumn, take the rhizomes out of the ground and store them for the winter at 41 to 50°F (5 to 10°C).

| 20–40 cm | Early spring to early summer |

Trillium grandiflorum White trillium, large-flowered trillium, snow trillium

The lovely geometric form and the rich green of the foliage radiate an incomparable calm all by themselves. However, this relaxing effect is further enhanced by the wide open, brilliant white flower of *T. grandiflorum*. As a woodland plant, it is particularly well suited to shady parts of the garden. This makes it the ideal flower to plant under rhododendrons or trees. It is demanding when it comes to soil: it requires a loose, moist but well-drained, acid humus. It should be given sufficient water especially in spring. To protect from dehydration in the summer, spread a mulch of bark or pine needles on the ground. Plant *T. grandiflorum* in the autumn. To ensure good drainage, place some expanded clay into the planting hole. **Tip:** plant in groups covering a large area. The rhizomes can be divided. However, once they have begun to sprout, they are best left alone.

| 50–60 cm | Early summer |

Triteleia laxa 'Queen Fabiola' Ithuriel's spear, grassnut

In deep purple-blue, 'Queen Fabiola' stands with great dignity, a dense umbel of flowers on its long stem. The grass-like leaves, on the other hand, are quite inconspicuous. This summer bloomer is ideal for wild gardens and rockeries. It looks good together with *Geranium*, *Sedum*, or low-growing grasses, and also makes a pretty cut flower. As the plant will not tolerate wet conditions, sandy, nutrient-rich soils are ideal. Keep moist during the growth period, and stop watering during the rest period, after flowering. If the soil is too wet or frosty in the winter, remove the bulbs from the ground after flowering and store in a dry place. If they are to stay in the ground for the winter, mulch with a layer of brushwood. Plant in the autumn, and propagate by bulblets.

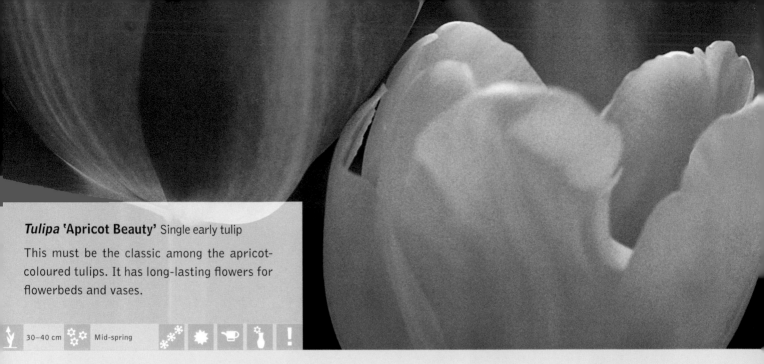

Tulipa 'Apricot Beauty' Single early tulip

This must be the classic among the apricot-coloured tulips. It has long-lasting flowers for flowerbeds and vases.

| 30–40 cm | ✿✿ Mid-spring | ❄ ✸ ☕ 🏺 ! |

Tulipa Tulip

| 35–45 cm | ✿✿ Mid- to late spring | ❄❄❄ ✸ |

| 30–40 cm | ✿✿ Mid-spring | ❄❄ ✸ |

◀ *Tulipa* 'Christmas Dream'
Single early tulip

The large-flowered 'Christmas Dream' comes in all-over fuchsia pink.

| 25–35 cm | ✿✿ Mid-spring | ❄❄❄ ☕ |

▲*Tulipa* 'Monte Carlo' Double early tulip

The large, luxuriant double flower of 'Monte Carlo' is betting on yellow. A truly beautiful, eye-catching flower.

◀ *Tulipa* 'Prinses Irene' Single early tulip

The lovely orange flower with pink, flame-like streaks brings in an atmosphere of spring, as well as a delicate, sweet scent. The flower will tolerate full sun.

It is almost impossible to imagine a spring garden without tulips. The extraordinary range and the most varied forms of flower shapes, colours, sizes, and blooming times have, quite simply, made this flower the darling of the garden. A classification that divides the numerous species and varieties into 15 classes does justice to the plant's versatility:

Single early tulips

Cup-shaped tulips with sturdy stems, these flowers open very wide. They withstand wet weather well. Some are scented. Mid- to late spring. They last well, and are easy to cultivate. This is a popular garden tulip. 15 to 45 centimetres.

Double early tulips

The double cup-shaped flowers on their sturdy stems are long-lasting. Mid-spring. Outstanding cut flowers. 30 to 45 centimetres.

Triumph tulips

The cone-shaped, single flowers withstand wet weather well. They have taller stems than

▶ *T.* 'Orange Princess' Double early tulip

This double variety of 'Prinses Irene' also has a delicate, sweet scent.

◀ *T.* 'Peach Blossom' Double early tulip

A tender pink and a gentle scent of honey: the popular 'Peach Blossom', with its cheery, long-lasting flowers, makes for a spring atmosphere.

| | 35–45 cm | ✿✿ Mid-spring | ✳✳✳ | ✺ |

| | 20–30 cm | ✿✿ Mid-spring | ✳✳✳ | ✺ |

▶ *Tulipa* 'Abu Hassan' Triumph tulip

The contrasting colours of 'Abu Hassan' provide a touch of Eastern flair. The red-brown petals have a fine vanilla-yellow edging. Long-lasting blooms, even as a cut flower.

| | 40–50 cm | ✿✿ Mid- to late spring | ✳✳✳ | ✺ |

Tulipa 'Ice Follies'
Large-cupped tulip

An extravagant flowering variety with large, heavy flower calyces. The petals are streaked in more than one strong colour and the calyx opens wide. The plant prefers a sheltered site.

| | 30–50 cm | ✿✿ Mid- to late spring | ✳✳✳ | ✺ |

▶ *Tulipa* **'Negrita'** Triumph tulip

Distinctive 'Negrita' comes in a very dark shade of violet. This tried-and-tested bloom is noted primarily for its hardiness. It is well-suited to naturalising.

40–50 cm Mid-spring

Tulipa Tulip

50–60 cm Mid-spring

50–60 cm Mid-to late spring

◀ *Tulipa* **'Daydream'** Darwin hybrid

The large flowers of 'Daydream' put splashes of glowing orange red into the spring garden. At the end of the flowering period, its flowers open wide.

50–60 cm Mid-spring

▲ *Tulipa* **'Golden Parade'** Darwin hybrid

The slender golden-yellow flowers of 'Golden Parade' stand sternly upright. At the start of the flowering period, the flowers are still elegantly closed.

◀ *Tulipa* **'Pink Impression'** Darwin hybrid

This splendid reliable bloomer is quite 'pretty in pink', and yet still somehow restrained.

early tulips. Outstanding cut flowers. Mid- to late spring. 35 to 60 centimetres.

Darwin hybrids

These have the largest flowers of all garden tulips and their thick stems make them extraordinarily resistant to bad weather. The flowers open into wide bowl shapes toward the end of the flowering period. Mid- to late spring. 50 to 70 centimetres.

Single late tulips

These tend to be slender, egg-shaped flowers with a satin-like shimmer, perched on sturdy stems. They are well suited to warmer climates. Late spring. 45 to 75 centimetres.

Lily-flowered tulips

Elegantly shaped tulip in magnificent colours. Slender, long flowers with pointed, often back-curving petals. Late spring. 45 to 65 centimetres.

Fringed tulips

Finely incised petal margins give their name to the 'fringed tulip'. The flowers are

▶ *Tulipa* **'Recreado'** Single late tulip

Balanced on the end of its tall stem almost like a violet-coloured egg, 'Recreado' makes an extraordinarily elegant garden and cut flower.

◀ *Tulipa* **'Mariette'** Lily-flowered tulip

The ladylike 'Mariette' keeps its petals tightly done up. Beautiful as a poem.

50–60 cm Late spring

50–60 cm Late spring

▶ *Tulipa* **'Mona Lisa'** Lily-flowered tulip

The flower lives up to its name. The yellow and red streaked 'Mona Lisa' is surely one of the most beautiful and mysterious of the lily-flowering tulips.

50–60 cm Late spring

Tulipa crispa **'Aleppo'**
Fringed tulip

The fringed tulips (which derive from *Tulipa crispa*) are unusual and definitely something special. They are known for their profuse flowering. The 'Aleppo' variety is pretty as a picture with its red and yellow petals and also looks good in a vase.

50–70 cm Late spring

◀ *Tulipa* **'Blue Heron'** Fringed tulip

With soft violet petals and a white, fringed edge, 'Blue Heron' brings a romantic mood to your garden.

50–60 cm | Late spring

Tulipa Tulip

◀ *Tulipa* **'Laverock'** Fringed tulip

A glowing yellow colour and with a long fringe, dainty 'Laverock' is guaranteed to set new trends in your garden. Indulge yourself...

50–60 cm | Late spring

50–60 cm | Late spring

▲ *Tulipa* **'Green River'** Viridiflora tulip

Only a few flowers have green among their basic colours. 'Green River', truly delightful, comes in green and orange.

◀ *Tulipa* **'Groenland'** Viridiflora tulip

This is quite a beauty: pale pink, marked with green stripes and a touch of cream. It looks especially beautiful in front of a green and white background.

50–60 cm | Late spring

elegant and long-lasting. Late spring. 35 to 65 centimetres.

Viridiflora tulips

Especially attractive tulips, these are mostly distinguished by green markings that run vertically down the petals. Late spring. 40 to 60 centimetres.

Rembrandt tulips

Slender single flowers with stripes or streaks. Late spring. 45 to 65 centimetres.

Parrot tulips

Large flowers with bizarre split and curled margins, these usually have several intense colours. The flowers open wide toward the end of the flowering period, making the stalks bend. This flower makes a lovely single item for a vase. Late spring. 30 to 60 centimetres.

Double late tulips (Peony-flowered tulips)

Lush, double, bushy, often very large flowers, these are simply gorgeous. They are unfortunately sensitive to wind and rain.

▶ *Tulipa* **'Hollywood Star'** Viridiflora tulip

With a name like that, no wonder it likes to put on a bit of a show: a blazing red with delicate green to surround it.

◀ *Tulipa* **'Flaming Parrot'** Parrot tulip

The unusual shape and the conspicuous red-streaked markings make 'Flaming Parrot' a particularly splendid highlight. It makes an ideal cut flower.

50–60 cm | Late spring

▶ *Tulipa* **'Libretto Parrot'** Parrot tulip

In restrained cream and white with a touch of pink, 'Libretto Parrot' is all innocence. Pure romance.

30–35 cm | Late spring

50–60 cm | Late spring

55–60 cm | Late spring

◀ *Tulipa* **'Salmon Parrot'** Parrot tulip

This impressive salmon-pink variety is particularly effective in its colouring because of the creamy-yellow edging. It looks beautiful in groups or flowerbeds or as a solitary flower in a vase. Always plant parrot tulips in a spot sheltered from the wind, because the large flowers make them tip over easily.

Bulbs and Tubers 63

T. 'Weber's Parrot' Parrot tulip

The fascinating variety 'Weber's Parrot' is almost too gorgeous to be true. The lush, frilled petals in delicate ivory white with crimson to pink edging have something of a Baroque look about them. This variety will tolerate full sunlight.

| 35–40 cm | | Late spring | | | |

Tulipa Tulip

| 40–45 cm | | Late spring | | |

| 10–20 cm | | Mid-spring | | |

◀ *Tulipa* 'Angelique' Double late tulip

The pretty pink flower of 'Angelique' enchants us, not just because of its dainty pink colour, but also with its pleasant, delicate scent. This is a true classic for a romantic garden.

| 45–55 cm | | Late spring | | | |

▲ T. 'Lilac Perfection' Double late tulip

'Lilac Perfection', in a group, will form a purple sea of flowers. This sweet-scented variety has the conspicuous large flowers typical of its class.

◀ *Tulipa* 'Ancilla' Kaufmanniana hybrid

This little beauty looks good in flowerbeds and rockeries. The flowers are pink and red on the outside, pure white in the inside with the red ring in the centre.

These doubles flower in late spring. 35 to 60 centimetres.

Kaufmanniana hybrids

Also known as waterlily tulips because they open like waterlilies in the sun and close again in the evenings. The inside is often a different colour from the outside. These are usually two-coloured single flowers. Botanical tulip. Very robust. Early to mid-spring. 15 to 30 centimetres.

Fosteriana hybrids

Large, single flowers that open wide. Botanical tulip. Also suitable for less sheltered sites. Mid-spring. 20 to 60 centimetres.

Greigii hybrids

Very decorative foliage with brown-striped or spotted patterns and lightly wavy edges. Flowers open wide in the sunlight. Colours are usually shades of red, white, and yellow. Early to mid-spring. Botanical tulip. 15 to 30 centimetres.

▶ **T. 'California Sun'** Kaufmanniana hybrid

In brilliant yellow and red, the spirited 'California Sun' radiates *joie de vivre*.

◀ **T. 'Early Harvest'** Kaufmanniana hybrid

A narrow yellow edging surrounds the orange-red petals of the early-flowering, pretty 'Early Harvest'.

10–25 cm   Early to mid-spring

10–25 cm   Early spring

▶ **Tulipa 'Jeantine'** Kaufmanniana hybrid

Graceful, with pointed, slender flowers, 'Jeantine' is apricot and pink on the inside with a yellow centre. On the outside, the petals are scarlet. An early-flowering variety with long-lasting blooms.

10–20 cm   Early to mid-spring

Tulipa 'Scarlet Baby'
Kaufmanniana hybrid

The attractive dark-red 'Scarlet Baby' is one of the smallest varieties in the Kaufmanniana class. In a mass, its brilliant red has an almost intoxicating and passionate effect.

10–20 cm   Early to mid-spring

◀ *Tulipa* **'Concerto'** Fosteriana hybrid

Conspicuous in its beauty, the almost magnolia-like 'Concerto' spreads out its modest white petals and proudly displays its golden-yellow centre.

15–20 cm Mid-spring !

Tulipa Tulip

30–40 cm Mid-spring

50–60 cm Mid-spring

◀ *Tulipa* **'Orange Emperor'** Fosteriana hybrid

In the brightest shade of orange, 'Orange Emperor' will definitely see that you get variety in your flowerbed. If you are bold enough, mix it with red and salmon-pink shades.

35–45 cm Mid-spring

▲ *Tulipa* **'Purissima'** Fosteriana hybrid

Also known as 'White Emperor'. In the purest white, 'Purissima' looks good in rockeries, flowerbeds, and bridal bouquets.

◀ *Tulipa* **'Sweetheart'** Fosteriana hybrid

Creamy-white edges adorn the delicate yellow 'Sweetheart'. Planted en masse, the sight is incomparable.

Multiflowered tulips

Not an official class but often classified separately because of their popularity. Single late tulips have multiflowered varieties, as do triumph, greigii, and botanical tulips.

Other species

This final class comprises, in particular, the wild tulip species. These are excellently suited to naturalisation, low in growth, and include some scented species. Tulips are surprisingly modest plants which give a lot of pleasure over a long period of time. There are only two conditions which they insist upon as relatively essential: protection from waterlogging, to prevent the bulbs from rotting, and a place in the sun. Most tulips will manage in semi-shade, but their flowering suffers visibly. The optimum conditions are a well-drained soil rich in nutrients, full sunlight, and if possible shelter from the wind.

Tulips look best in groups, and you can plant 50 to 60 flowers together. In flowerbeds, borders, and rockeries (low-growing wild species are particularly suitable here), they

▶ *Tulipa* **'Easter Surprise'** Greigii hybrid

The fascinating 'Easter Surprise' displays a sophisticated shift in colour from lemon yellow to a warm shade of orange in the tips.

◀ *Tulipa* **'Lady Diana'** Greigii hybrid

Almost unsurpassable in elegance, this flower may be unique but still looks best planted en masse.

| | 25–35 cm | | Mid-spring | | |

| | 25–30 cm | | Mid-spring | | |

▶ *Tulipa* **'Mary Ann'** Greigii hybrid

The flowers of Greigii hybrids open fully in sunlight and display their decorative insides, which as here with 'Mary Ann' resemble a skilful mosaic.

| | 20–25 cm | | Mid-spring | | |

| | 40–50 cm | | Late spring | | |

◀ *Tulipa* **'Colour Spectacle'**
Multiflowered tulip

With bright red streaks and three to seven flowers per stem, 'Colour Spectacle' is a pleasure to see in flower. And it is not only a fine sight in the garden, it also makes an excellent cut flower.

Bulbs and Tubers 67

Tulipa 'Orange Bouquet' Multiflowered tulip

This single, late-flowering variety has deep orange blooms. The flower on the main stem is usually larger than those on the side stems.

| 40–50 cm | Late spring | | | | | |

| 10–15 cm | Very early spring | | |

| 10–15 cm | Very early spring | | |

◀ **Tulipa clusiana var. chrysantha** Wild tulip

The noble wild tulip *T. clusiana* looks as if it has been painted. The elegant, pointed flowers are sulphur yellow with shiny red outer petals. This flower will tolerate full sun.

| 20–25 cm | Mid-spring | | |

▲ **Tulipa humilis** Wild tulip

In the sunshine, *T. humilis* will open its pink to purple flowers and display its yellow insides. When closed, it looks a little like a crocus.

◀ **Tulipa linifolia 'Batalinii'** Wild tulip

This magical, low-growing beauty has lovely lemon-yellow flowers. It is known as a profuse bloomer, able to form whole colonies in a few years.

make eye-catching islands of colour. The range of colours is practically legendary, from white to purple-black, from delicate edges to flame-like streaks. But tulips also make a good show in containers, pots, window-boxes, and of course in vases.

Tulips tolerate rather dry soil, but need moisture in the ground when flowering. Dead flowers and seedheads should be cut back as soon as possible to half the height of the stem, to prevent formation of seeds robbing the bulb of its strength, but leaves can be left until they turn yellow. This allows the bulb to ripen fully. A change of site helps after profuse flowering, otherwise the bulb can remain in place for years. Once leaves have died, remove bulbs and bulblets to dry out; store them in a cool, dry place until planting season in the autumn.

All parts of the plant are slightly poisonous. Prolonged contact can lead to so-called 'tulip bulb dermatitis', with skin irritation.

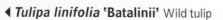

▶ **Tulipa saxatilis** Candia tulip

Lilac-pink flowers with a yellow heart. This is a most rewarding and dainty flower.

◀ **Tulipa sylvestris** Wild tulip

T. sylvestris, sturdy and spreading freely, enriches any rockery. The yellow, bell-shaped flowers also have an enchanting scent. The plant will tolerate semi-shade.

15–20 cm · Very early spring

20–30 cm · Mid-spring

▶ **Tulipa tarda** Wild tulip

This multiflowered miniature tulip, with star-shaped, scented flowers, bears up to eight scented blooms on one stem. In the sunshine, it will open its creamy-white flowers and display its eggyolk-yellow centre. Excellent for naturalising, this plant makes good ground cover.

10–15 cm · Mid-spring

Tulipa turkestanica
Wild tulip

The cream-white, almost parchment-coloured, star-shaped flowers with their yellow central eye dangle in great numbers on their slender stems. *T. turkestanica* is one of the earliest-flowering of the wild tulips.

15–20 cm · Very early spring

Zantedeschia aethiopica Calla lily, arum lily

Elegant and secretive, exotic and expressive: this many-faceted beauty from southern Africa can hardly be praised too much. The chalice-shaped, curved 'petal' – botanically speaking, it is actually a bract – will not really settle for any one individual colour, but generally shows variations on white, ivory, or green, or blends into rose pink, orange, or even black. The dark green of its long arrow-shaped leaves provides the perfect contrast. *Z. aethiopica* loves light, warm locations, but it will tolerate semi-shade, as long as the site is warm enough. In summer, it needs a good deal of water – it is, after all, a swamp plant – and therefore a sufficiently moist soil. After flowering, stop adding fertiliser. Varieties range from winter-hardy to frost-sensitive. In cold regions, winter protection will be needed; or you can store the tuberous rhizome over the winter in dry sand in a frost-free place. **Take care:** all parts of the plant are poisonous.

40–75 cm Early to mid-spring

Zantedeschia aethiopica 'Green Goddess' Calla lily, arum lily

The unusual green and white 'Green Goddess' is one of the most important varieties of *Z. aethiopica*. A few more general items of information: *Z. aethiopica* also makes a very good container plant, and this method of planting is particularly recommended for colder climates. Propagate by taking off side shoots from the rhizome or by dividing. A very decorative and long-lived cut flower.

60–100 cm Late spring to high summer

ANNUAL PLANTS

A Summer Blaze of Colour

The annuals have their grand performance in the warm months between spring and autumn. However, they flower and thrive for a single summer only, and then die back. This early end is part of their survival strategy, allowing the plants to put all their strength into the production of resistant seeds. The annuals need to be sown every year, from early to late spring, either in seed trays or pots or directly in the flowerbed. Much less effort is required if you purchase young plants. When the fruit are ripe, however, many of the annuals tend toward self-seeding, which is not always desired. Should the seeds from the previous year still be in the ground, they will germinate when the soil reaches the right temperature and become fine plants that bloom splendidly in the summer. Many of the plants we class as annuals are perennials living several years in their homelands, but having problems with frost in more northerly latitudes.

Most annuals love the sun and many will extend their flowering period if dead flowers are removed.

Ageratum houstonianum Bluemink

Bluemink creates magnificent cushions of flowers, covered with long-lasting, bunched little blooms in purple, pink, blue, or white, and according to variety the plants can reach up to 80 centimetres. The shorter varieties look very decorative in low plantings, rockeries, and window-boxes, while the taller ones make good background plants and cut flowers. In its tropical and sub-tropical home, bluemink will turn woody, becoming a shrub. In cooler regions, it will not survive a winter in the open air and is therefore cultivated as an annual. It prefers a fertile and moist, but well-drained soil. As it cannot tolerate drought, it needs to be watered in dry weather. Cut off dead flowers. Sow in early spring in a temperature of 61 to 64°F (16 to 18°C), and plant out in the open in late spring. Sowing directly in the open is not recommended. *A. houstonianum* has an almost magnetic effect on butterflies.

Amaranthus caudatus Love-lies-bleeding

The splendid crimson flower spikes of *A. caudatus*, casually dropping almost to the ground from the end of the tall stem with its pale green leaves, look attractive and exotic. The very long-lasting flowers look their best in borders of showy tall plants or in cottage gardens as a solitary or container plant. It loves the sun and a moist but well-drained soil moderately rich in nutrients. Special care is not required. The plant self-seeds profusely. **Tip:** also makes a good cut flower and dried flower, as it keeps its colour for a long time. It attracts butterflies.

60–100 cm | Summer to early autumn

Amaranthus hypochondriacus
'Green Thumb' Prince of Wales' feather

Like fingers pointing, the bright yellow-green spikes of 'Green Thumb' stretch upward. This green rarity has something of the air of coming from another planet into our gardens. The plant looks particularly impressive combined with large-leafed plants or plants with flowers in contrasting colours such as strong reds and yellows. It prefers warm, sunny, and sheltered sites in moist, well-drained, and humus soil.

Up to 60 cm | Summer to early autumn

Antirrhinum majus 'Peaches and Cream'
Snapdragon, garden snapdragon

The erect plant *A. majus*, with its long-lasting flowers, is a classic in cottage gardens and summer flowerbeds and comes in a whole palette of colours ranging from white, yellow, orange, red, violet to near black, and also in various heights. The striking two-toned flowers of the low-growing variety 'Peaches and Cream' form thick racemes at the ends of the stem. These short-lived flowers, mainly cultivated as annuals, should be cut from time to time, including the stalk, to keep the plant flowering. It prefers a sunny spot in a well-drained soil, rich in nutrients. **Tip:** *A. majus* is an excellent and popular cut flower.

Up to 25 cm | Late spring to late autumn

Up to 120 cm | High summer

triplex hortensis 'Red Plume'
arden orache

Red Plume' stands stern and upright, omehow grass-like. Its many purple-tinged eaves and red stem make it an attractive, ontrasting complement for a summer bed f tall plants or flowers. As it is not wind-ensitive, it will make good wind protection or lower plants. The yellow-green flowers re rather inconspicuous. The plant equires moist but well-drained soil. In ry weather, give plenty of water to avoid vilting. Cut dead flowers off before the eeds are formed, otherwise garden orache vill spread profusely. **Tip:** *A. hortensis* is an ld-fashioned vegetable. The leaves can be used in salads or cooked like spinach.

Up to 45 cm | Early summer to late autumn

Brachyscome iberidifolia Swan River daisy

This cheerful profuse bloomer has marguerite-like flowers, in violet, blue, pink, or white. You can choose either those with a yellow centre or the Splendid series, where the centre is black. Suitable for planting in flowerbeds, rockeries, or window gardens. It likes nutrient-rich, dry soils.

30–70 cm | Early summer to autumn

Calendula officinalis Pot marigold

This very hardy plant, popular in gardens and as a cut flower, comes with yellow, cream, or orange flowers, single or double, in tall-growing or dwarf varieties. *C. officinalis*, also used as a medicinal plant, likes medium heavy, moist soil. It looks gorgeous in cottage gardens or summer flowerbeds. Cut off dead flowers to encourage flowering. As it is a strong self-seeder, you can enjoy this flower's presence year after year. **Tip:** you can eat the petals. The base of the flower, however, has a bitter taste.

20–120 cm   Early summer to autumn

Callistephus chinensis China aster

The wide range of the magnificent China aster can be seen in its many variations in height, in shape, and colour of flowers. There are dwarf varieties and tall ones growing over 1 metre – the latter also make good cut flowers. The flowerheads are single, semi-double, or double. The many lively colours, usually in crimson or violet-blue, but also in white, yellow, red, or pink, ensure a brilliant display in the flowerbed or in a pot. The plant will tolerate any cared-for soil in full sun.

Centaurea cyanus Cornflower

We are all familiar with the picture of these simple, pale blue flowers in summer fields of grain. But there are also white and pink varieties, single and double flowers. At any rate, the cornflower provides the ideal splash of fresh colour among perennials, roses, phlox, or in summer flowerbeds. The plant prefers a wind-sheltered site with a well-drained soil rich in nutrients. It needs no special treatment, being rather undemanding. It will even tolerate a certain amount of drought. The taller varieties should be supported so that they do not break in the wind. If you do not want to take the trouble with replanting seedlings, sow *C. cyanus* directly in the open from mid-spring onward. **Tip:** bees and butterflies are most interested in cornflowers.

20–80 cm   Late spring to high summer

Up to 75 cm   Summer

Clarkia amoena

Farewell to spring, satin flower, godetia

Charming *C. amoena* displays its papery, silky flowers for weeks on end in the summer. It struggles in moist, hot conditions, but in well-drained, fairly fertile soil it will send out shoots again the next spring, with no problems. Whether you plant it in a cottage garden or in a summer flowerbed, it looks its best planted en masse.

Up to 30 cm | **Summer**

Coreopsis tinctoria **'Mahogany Midget'** Golden tickseed

The brilliant scarlet flowers with their yellow centre make this miniature plant rise to the occasion in summer. This flower will enjoy any well-drained soil in the sun or semi-shade. Remove dead flowers to encourage repeat flowering.

90–120 cm | **High summer to autumn**

Cleome hassleriana syn. *C. spinosa* **'White Queen'** Spiderflower

The exotic and rather bizarre-looking *C. hassleriana* owes its less than charming name to the long, protruding stamens of its flowers, which look like spiders' legs, and the prickles on its leaf stems. The scented 'White Queen' is a good variety to complement summer flowerbeds. As the plant has an upright, almost unbranched habit of growth, it should be planted in groups so that it can be seen from a distance. A light, nutrient-rich soil (it can also be sandy) in full sun is ideal. In order to encourage profuse repeat flowering, regularly pinch out the seedpods. Grow in pots or seed trays from the early spring onward and plant out in the open in late spring. There are also varieties with pink, red, and violet flowers.

Up to 90 cm | **High to late summer**

Cosmos bipinnatus **Sensation range** Garden cosmos

The delicate pink flowers really do look their best in profusion. The dainty, feathery leaves of the Sensation varieties are just as attractive as the large, luxuriant flowers. This pretty flower loves warm, moist, well-drained, moderately fertile locations. You will extend the flowering period if you remove the dead flowers. However, do leave some seeds to ripen, so that it can self-seed. Sow directly in the flowerbed in late spring.

Dorotheanthus bellidiformis Livingstone daisy

The Livingstone daisy is distinguished by a creeping growth habit, small, daisy-like flowers, and brilliant colours: purple, red, orange, yellow, or white. It flowers busily all summer long, making magnificent cushions of colour. Plenty of sun – because it only opens its finely rayed flowers in sunshine – and dry ground will ensure that it becomes lovelier every day. This annual looks particularly good as ground cover in flowerbeds, in rockeries, or borders, but also does well in containers. It likes fairly poor, dry soils. Flowering is prolonged if dead flowers are regularly removed.

| | 10–15 cm | | Early to late summer | | | |

Eschscholzia californica
California poppy

The bowl-shaped flowers have a silky gleam and look as if they have been painted. They rise up on their tall stems as if craning their necks for the best view. Whether the flowers are pink, yellow, orange, red or white, double or crimped, *E. californica* brings colour and lightness to flowerbeds and rockeries. A little peculiar in its habits, the bushy plant with the finely pinnate, bluish-green foliage only shows itself completely open in sunshine. A poor, well-drained soil in full sunlight is therefore recommended. *E. californica* self-seeds easily and will appear next spring if the ground is left undisturbed over the winter.

| | Up to 30 cm | | Summer | | | | |

15–30 cm Late spring to early autumn

Gazania hybrids Gazania, treasure flower

This sun-worshipper presents its individual flowers in a selection of bright, conspicuous colours, in shades of yellow, pink, orange, red, and white, usually with a darker pattern on the petals. On rainy days, however, or in shady places, the flowers will remain closed. If sparingly watered, the plant will flower fairly profusely, so a site in full sun with a slightly sandy, well-drained soil is recommended. Not much care is needed. Pinching off the dead flowerheads and occasionally adding fertiliser will extend the flowering period. In areas where there is a risk of frost, gazanias are cultivated as annuals. In a sheltered, well-lit spot this summer bloomer can overwinter, as long as the temperature is between 46 and 50°F (8 and 10°C).

Gypsophila elegans Showy baby's breath

Flowering in white or pink, *G. elegans* is especially suited to bring a light and airy touch to summer flowerbeds. This markedly branched, bushy plant bears a wealth of delicate star-shaped flowers, which also look good as a decorative addition to summer bouquets. *G. elegans* needs little in the way of water or nutrients, but it does prefer soils with lime content, in full sun if possible. The tall varieties should be tied to prevent them being bent or broken.

30–60 cm Summer to autumn

elicia amelloides
ue daisy, blue marguerite, kingfisher daisy

mass of lavender-blue, daisy-like flowers
ses from a voluminous dark green cushion
foliage. All it needs is sun and a poor
t well-drained soil. Rain, however, will
nsiderably restrict its flowering. The
ant can overwinter. Propagate by cuttings
late summer or seed in spring.

Up to 60 cm High summer to early autumn

| ↑ | 1.5–2 m | ✿✿ | Summer | ⁂ | ✸ | 🫖 | ⚱ |

Helianthus annuus 'Autumn Beauty'
Common sunflower

Van Gogh couldn't have painted this sunflower to look any more beautiful. 'Autumn Beauty' displays warm, autumnal shades with mahogany red, yellow-gold, or bronze-red ligulates (the 'petals' are actually separate small flowers called ligulates). The flowers are up to 15 centimetres across and daisy-like in form. The flower is shown to best advantage planted in front of house walls or fences or as a background planting.

Helianthus annuus 'Teddy Bear' Common sunflower

If you don't have space for the large varieties, you can still have these glowing summer flowers in your garden if you plant dwarf sunflowers. 'Teddy Bear' is one of the low-growing varieties and has enchantingly soft, filled, yellow flowerheads, which, dwarf or not, nevertheless can reach a diameter of up to 13 centimetres. Impressively, this sturdy little plant can manage to turn whole flowerbeds into a sea of yellow, and it is well suited for growing in containers too. However, it does need plenty of nourishment. In all cases you should guarantee it a good supply of nutrients and water, and a loose, well-drained soil with no danger of waterlogging. You can sow the seeds directly into the growing position in late spring. **Tip:** in a vase, *H. annuus* will keep for longer if most of the foliage is removed and the freshly-cut stalk end is held in boiling water for about half a minute. This will prevent the spread of bacteria.

| ↑ | Up to 60 cm | ✿✿ | Summer | ⁂ | ✸ | 🫖 | ⚱ |

Helichrysum bracteatum
Bracted strawflower

Because it reacts badly to frost, *H. bracteatum* is cultivated as an annual in cold climates, though in its Australian homeland it is often perennial. The parchment-like flowers, yellow, white, red, or rose-pink, only open fully in sunlight and provide bright spots of colour in flowerbeds or borders. The plant is, however, very sensitive to waterlogging. It makes an ideal dried flower.

| ↑ | 10–100 cm | ✿✿ | Early summer to early autumn | ✳ | ✸ | 🫖 |

| 15–20 cm | | Late spring to autumn | | | | |

patiens walleriana 'Peach Swirl'
sy Lizzie, patience plant

is wonderful bushy repeat bloomer's
undance of dainty flowers brings a wealth
colour to dark areas of the garden. Busy
zie lives up to its name and flowers with
xhaustible energy, even if assigned to a
t very sunny spot. Apart from the glowing
each Swirl' variety, which has bright pink
tals that catch the eye even under dark
shes, there is a wide range of colours
m white through orange and salmon
k to deepest violet. Some are even two-
loured. This plant, generally cultivated
an annual, is an indispensable plant for
werbeds or containers. It likes a wind-
eltered, humus, moist but well-drained
e. It thrives best with a regular supply of
ter and occasional fertiliser.

| 60–80 cm | | Summer | | | | |

Lavatera trimestris 'White Beauty' Annual mallow

The splendid white funnel-shaped flowers and the bushy growth of
'White Beauty' will certainly attract the eye. This typical cottage garden
plant is very effective, not just in beds of tall and perennial plants, but
also in front of wooden fences. It likes well-drained, moderately fertile
soils. Avoid waterlogging. Bind up tall plants in exposed places.

15–20 cm | Late spring to early autumn

Lobelia erinus Edging lobelia, annual lobelia

It forms a long-lasting, blooming carpet of innumerable dainty little flowers, with glowing colours from blue and purple to pink or white. The numerous varieties of *L. erinus* include outstanding cushion-forming ground cover for borders and flowerbeds, and trailing varieties for containers and hanging baskets. It likes humus, moist soils in sun or semi-shade and should be watered regularly to keep it moist. The seed germinates in sunlight and can be sown in pots or seed trays in early spring, but should not be covered with soil. Transplant into the open in late spring. Shorten by about one third after initial flowering, and it will bloom again.

Lobularia maritima Sweet alyssum

An enticing scent of honey drifts above the lavish, flat cushions of sweet alyssum flowers, very popular as filler for empty spaces in the flowerbed, planted under tall-stemmed plants or as ground cover between roses. It also finds a spot in cracks in walls or paving. The little cup-shaped flowers, which attract plenty of insects, bloom in white, pink, or a delicate violet, and their sheer numbers almost completely cover the grey-green foliage. It is a good idea to cut back the plant after the first flowering to encourage it to sprout again. Sweet alyssum prefers a sunny location and nutrient-poor soil. It will also tolerate a maritime climate and is self-seeding.

5–30 cm | Late spring to early autumn

Matthiola incana 'Cinderella Lavender'
Tenweeks stock

M. incana, originally a semi-shrub, is cultivated as an annual in cooler climates. This low-growing member of the 'Cinderella' series is a genuine early and long-lasting bloomer, ideally suited for borders in cottage gardens or containers. In the garden, it characteristically branches out and bears more than a single flowerhead, but in a pot it remains very compact and usually bears only one. Any moist, well-drained soil in a sheltered spot will be accepted.

20–25 cm | Early summer to early autumn

Up to 25 cm | High to late summer

Nemesia strumosa 'KLM'

Named after the Netherlands airline whose company colours it bears, 'KLM' appears in a rich blue and elegant creamy white. It also has a little yellow throat. This undemanding flower forms pretty, profusely-blooming cushions in summer beds and containers.

60–90 cm | Late summer

Ioluccella laevis Shellflower, bells of Ireland

he effect of upright *M. laevis* is of omething rather out of the ordinary, ut very attractive. The shellflower is stinguished by pale green funnels. These re not petals, but bracts, set thickly on e tall, unbranching stems. The tiny white owers, although they are even scented, o not really show up in this arrangement. hese out-of-the-ordinary flowers are very opular with florists and flower arrangers nd make the plant an unusual enrichment or summer flowerbeds, but it looks best lanted in groups. It looks especially izarre when the bracts become white-eined and papery during seed production. or its habitat, the shellflower will tolerate ny moist, well-drained soil. Occasional ertiliser will encourage growth.

Up to 40 cm | Early summer to autumn

Nicotiana × sanderae 'White Bedder'

Nicotiana × sanderae is a relative of the tobacco plant. A short-lived perennial, it is often cultivated as an annual. The large flowers of 'White Bedder' are borne by a plant with bushy growth and show their pure white colour all day long. In a sheltered, moist, well-drained location it will flower repeatedly for a long period and needs no special care except for cutting off the dead flowers and watering during drought. **Take care:** contact with the leaves can lead to skin irritation.

Annual Plants 83

Nigella damascena
Love-in-a-mist, devil-in-the-bush

This plant, with its mysterious names, is worth a little attention, for it is one of the most interesting sights the garden has to offer. *N. damascena* produces delicate flowers, in blue, white, yellow, or pink, surrounded by a wreath of very finely pinnate leaves. This gives the impression that the flowers are surrounded by a mist. Equally worth seeing are the round fruit, which are often used in dried flower arrangements. In a sunny position and on well-drained soil this marvellous flower can be enjoyed without extra work. **Tip:** the plant is self-seeding if you leave a few seedpods standing.

Up to 50 cm | Early summer to early autumn

Papaver rhoeas Corn poppy

There is something missing in the summer garden without the very fine-petaled flowers of *P. rhoeas*, in delicate pastel or bright red, which shimmer as if they were made of fine, crinkled silk. In natural-look gardens they are simply indispensable. This undemanding plant thrives in every kind of soil and only needs watering in long dry periods. If you leave the seedpods to ripen, corn poppies will self-seed.

Up to 90 cm | Summer

20–30 cm | Late spring to late autumn

Petunia 'Prism Sunshine' Petunia

The popular petunia hybrids are available in almost all shades of colour, in different habits of growth and with various shapes of flower. The velvety flowers are star-shaped, veined or have crinkled edges; sometimes they are double flowers. 'Prism Sunshine', which belongs to the Grandiflora group, radiates both elegance and freshness with its large flowers: finely greenish-yellow veined, pale yellow to cream-coloured, funnel-shaped. This repeat flowerer likes light, well-drained soils in flowerbeds or containers. Both dry and over-wet conditions are undesirable. Remove dead flowers regularly.

10–20 cm · Summer

Portulaca grandiflora 'Everbloom' Rose moss

The slightly creeping *P. grandiflora* with its fleshy leaves and charming, satiny flowers that look so much like musk roses is an ideal plant for hot, dry, sandy places in your garden. The only things it cannot stand are waterlogging and low temperatures. For rockeries, as ground cover or as a container plant.

2–3 m · High summer to late autumn

Up to 45 cm · High summer to early autumn

Phlox drummondii Annual phlox

P. drummondii, the annual variety of the classic cottage garden plant, offers a short but intense pleasure. Its wealth of intensely-coloured, flat flowers in white, yellow, salmon pink, rose pink, red, or violet make the single or multicoloured phlox an indispensable attraction in any summer flowerbed. The plant, with its erect, bushy growth, which comes in low-growing and taller varieties, likes well-drained, humus soil in full sunlight. If you cut the flowers back hard after the first flowering, down to 10 to 15 centimetres, you encourage a second bloom. **Tip:** the flowers are edible and can be used in salads.

Ricinus communis 'Carmencita' Castorbean

The surprising thing about *R. communis* is its powerful growth, which allows it to achieve its full stature in three months. In warmer regions, this branching shrub is perennial, but in cooler latitudes it is usually cultivated as an annual, because it is not frost-hardy. 'Carmencita' is distinguished by unusual, bronze-red foliage, reminiscent of chestnut leaves. Spikes on the ends of the stems bear the flowers, with the yellow male flowers below and the reddish female ones above. The conspicuous spherical, reddish-brown seedpods are thorny. This decorative foliage plant looks impressive in larger, sunny flowerbeds, in front of walls, or in large containers. It needs a well-drained soil very rich in nutrients, and plenty of water. **Take care:** the seeds are extremely poisonous.

Rudbeckia hirta 'Irish Eyes' Blackeyed Susan

The daisy-like, bright yellow flowerhead with the green button in the centre rises high on its rough-haired, erect stem. The long flowering period, right into the late autumn, means that 'Irish Eyes' can bring a last warm touch of colour into a summer flowerbed. 'Irish Eyes' makes a charming colour combination with fat hens, blueminks, and asters. The plant is fairly undemanding but prefers a sunny spot with moist, semi-heavy soils rich in nutrients.

60–75 cm | High summer to late autumn

Salvia farinacea 'Strata' Mealycup sage

The bushy *S. farinacea* with its mealy grey bloom looks particularly good in rockeries or raised beds among tall perennials. Two-coloured 'Strata', an especially attractive example of this species, has lavender and blue flowers on its spikes, giving it a lovely silver-blue shimmer. The mealycup sage is quite an undemanding plant, which thrives on very well-drained, slightly dry soil in full sun. *S. farinacea* is a perennial, cultivated as an annual in regions at risk from frost. It can, however, survive the winter if kept frost-free indoors.

Up to 60 cm | Late spring to autumn

Sanvitalia procumbens
Mexican creeping zinnia

The small, closely-crowded, golden-yellow, button-shaped flowers are simply delightful. They look like a miniature version of the sunflower and carry on flowering tirelessly right up until the first frost. This creeping, branching ground cover with the elongated ovate leaves makes pretty borders, or covers less attractive surfaces of the flowerbed. Any loose, well-drained soil in full sun will be accepted. This tiny plant needs little care, though the dead flowers should be cut back regularly to allow flowering to continue into the autumn.

Up to 20 cm | Early summer to late autumn

| 20–70 cm | Early summer to early autumn |

Solenostemon scutellarioides syn. *Coleus blumei*
Painted nettle, dwarf coleus

If you can't resist the attraction of these colourful foliage plants, you run the risk of succumbing to painted nettle fever. Bizarrely patterned in red, yellow, pink, or green, with wavy, serrate or smooth leaf edges, the painted nettle will provide variety in your summer flowerbed. It likes well-drained, humus soil.

| Up to 50 cm | Summer to early autumn |

hizanthus × wisetonensis
or man's orchid

summer, the cheerful, orchid-like flowers ver the whole plant and for weeks they ovide a brilliant sea of colour in white, low, rose pink, or violet. This delicate wer is a little on the sensitive side, for it l only reveal its full splendour in sheltered aces under ideal conditions. If the weather too hot or there are heavy showers of rain, will refuse to put on its lavish summer play, and you will have to be satisfied th the fine, fern-like leaves. You will then ed to try again next year. Among the other nditions are fertile, moist, well-drained l and full sunlight. **Tip:** the flowers will ep for up to four weeks in a vase.

| 30–120 cm | Early summer to early autumn |

Tagetes erecta hybrids
African marigold, Aztec marigold, American marigold

The large, filled, spherical pompons in shades of fresh yellow or bright orange rise nobly above the dark green, feathery leaves. These tall-growing plants make an excellent background planting for summer flowerbeds and borders. And apart from their eye-catching ball-shaped flowers, they are also wonderfully sturdy and easy to care for, making them one of the essential classics of formal flowerbed design.

Annual Plants 87

20–60 cm | Summer to late autumn

Tagetes patula hybrids French marigold

Over and over again, these plants bloom in shades of yellow, red, or brown, or in lively combinations of these shades, with double or single flowers. The dwarf varieties form dense little bushes. They are often planted in summer flowerbeds as colourful filling-in plants or to make borders. These tireless bloomers prefer sunny sites with nutrient-rich soil. There is only one disadvantage: they are, without a doubt, high on the list of slugs' and snails' favourites.

Tagetes tenuifolia 'Ornament'
Dwarf marigold, signet marigold

'Ornament' is a real long-lasting bloomer. On its stems it bears numerous single, red-brown flowers, which are particularly hardy when exposed to rain. When compared to the hybrids, *T. tenuifolia* can be distinguished by its more delicate, finely divided foliage. A place in the full sun in any normal soil will suffice for this prettily patterned plant, allowing it to develop to its full capacity. Can be used for flowerbed edging, for beds of tall plants and perennials, and rockeries. Snails and slugs avoid *T. tenuifolia*.

Up to 25 cm | Early summer to late autumn

Tanacetum parthenium Feverfew

Perhaps *T. parthenium* isn't suited to playing the lead, but the attractive, daisy-like, often double, white and yellow flowers and the aromatic, daintily pinnate, fresh green foliage make it into an attractive co-star in flowerbeds and borders, or in the herb garden. This is a short-lived perennial, usually cultivated as an annual, but it can certainly survive mild winters. Any well-drained soil is welcome.

20–60 cm | Early summer to early autumn

| 20–30 cm | Summer to autumn | | | |

Tropaeolum majus 'Whirlybird Orange' Nasturtium

Touchingly bright splashes of colour; in contrast to the vigorously growing annual climbers of the *T. majus* species, the Whirlybird series comprises dwarf bushy annuals with single or semi-double flowers. 'Whirlybird Orange' forms compact little mounds covered with a wealth of fresh, orange-coloured blooms. The semi-filled flowers raise their heads to peer out of the foliage as if curious, and make a fine eye-catching feature. They thrive in most soils, but prefer nutrient-poor, moderately dry to moist soils and a sunny location. This plant is ideal ground cover for designing flowerbeds, borders, containers, or window-boxes.

| Up to 150 cm | Late summer to autumn | | | | | |

Tithonia rotundifolia
Mexican sunflower, clavel de muerto

The annual Mexican sunflower is considered a real magnet for butterflies. Planted singly or in groups, it will form a lovely background planting for flowerbeds and looks particularly pretty in natural, 'wild' gardens. However, it also makes an impressive container plant. It develops proper little branching bushes with rough, almost triangular leaves. The range of colours of the zinnia-like flowers comprises a fiery orange, a glowing yellow, and a strong red. The plant needs full sunlight and fertile, well-drained soils. In dry weather, give sufficient water. **Tip:** It makes a good cut flower. To ensure the flower lasts a long time, hold the ends of the stems briefly over a flame shortly after cutting, then place them in warm water.

| Up to 45 cm | Summer | | | |

Ursinia anethoides Dill-leaf ursinia

The bushy, branching ursinia with its finely pinnate leaves reveals itself to be a marvellous repeat bloomer, producing ever more new golden-yellow flowers with their crimson markings all through the summer. Even in bad weather, its pretty flowers are radiant. An evergreen perennial, mostly cultivated as an annual, this plant loves sites in full sun with a sandy, fertile soil.

Xeranthemum annuum Immortelle

Set on erect, branching, slender stems, with leaves covered with felted hair, the delicate flowers have papery-white, pink, or violet bracts. The plant needs moderately fertile, well-drained soil. It is well suited to drying.

25–75 cm | Late summer to early autumn

Zinnia elegans 'Envy' Elegant zinnia

Z. elegans, erect, popular, and not in the least old-fashioned, comes in a wide range of heights, flower shapes, and sizes. Yet all varieties are enchanting because of their velvety, marguerite-like flowers, which come in almost every imaginable colour. The conspicuous double-flowered 'Envy' displays a cool, bright greeny-yellow, making semi-shady places simply glow. A wonderful cut flower, this plant prefers fertile, well-drained soil.

Up to 75 cm | Early summer to early autumn

Zinnia elegans 'Orange King' Elegant zinnia

Planted in groups, 'Orange King' is a striking attraction in a bed of perennials or summer flowers. This annual cottage garden plant is, however, also an ideal complement for vegetable gardens, where it brings plenty of fresh colour if planted between cabbages and lettuce. The more often it is cut, the more it will flower, and dead flowers must be regularly removed. It prefers a site in full sunlight. As zinnias are very sensitive to cold, it is best not to plant them until the late spring.

60–80 cm   Early summer to early autumn

BIENNIAL PLANTS

Wonderful Flowers Every Other Year

In contrast to annual summer flowers, which need only a few months to develop from simple seeds to splendid flowers, biennials need a longer period of preparation. To develop flowers and seeds, they need two growth periods and one winter. Only if sown very early in a site with favourable conditions will they flower in the same year.

In the first year, most biennials form a sturdy leaf rosette. The magnificent flowers then arrive the next spring. Before the plant completely dies back, numerous seeds will ripen, which most perennials distribute generously over the entire garden. But biennial summer flowers can of course also be sown as part of garden design or for the most part bought as pre-cultivated young plants.

Seeds can be sown in the summer in little seedling pots before being planted out in autumn in the desired open-air spots.

 1.2– 2.5 m Summer to early autumn

Alcea rosea Hollyhock

Proud and upright, the impressive, magnificent flower spikes with their rough, generally heart-shaped leaves stand tall. Peering from the axils where leaf joins stem, the numerous single or double individual flowers seem to be keeping an eye on what happens in the garden. *A. rosea* has flowers in white, yellow, and various shades of pink and red, including a mysterious red black. The bowl-shaped flowers, especially the single ones, are popular stopping places for bees and butterflies. They are at their loveliest in natural-look gardens, together with other cottage garden flowers, perhaps planted in front of a garden or house wall, a fence, or a pergola. Planted in a group, they make a romantic feature that is sure to catch the eye. This tall plant is usually cultivated as a biennial, but will self-seed. It is recommended that you allow the young plants to grow and remove the mother plant. **Tip:** without their stamens, the young flowers of *A. rosea* can be enjoyed in salads.

Alcea rosea 'Nigra' Black hollyhock

The flowers of *A. rosea*, with their deep, dark red, almost black shimmer, have a distinctly magical effect. This marvel of dark colour will look its fascinating best in large cottage or herb gardens. Hollyhocks are happiest in full sunlight and in moderately fertile, very well-drained soil. In exposed places, they need the support of a stick to prevent the flower spikes bending or snapping. In dry locations, ensure the plant receives plenty of water.

Up to 2 m · Summer to early autumn

Bellis perennis Lawndaisy

The cheeky little double flowerheads, pink, white, or red, peer out of flowerbeds or containers in the spring. This sturdy cultivated variety looks nothing like the wild European daisy. A charming, somehow old-fashioned plant, it is cultivated as a biennial and loves sunny to semi-shady spots in well-drained, moderately fertile soil. You can extend the flowering period by removing the dead blooms. Little *Bellis* also looks very pretty in small bouquets or posies.

5–20 cm · Early spring to early summer

Campanula medium Canterbury bells

With loose racemes of large, bell-shaped flowers, double or single, in blue, white, or pink, Canterbury bells appear to be ringing in the summer. The lavish profusion of flowers of this popular cottage garden plant makes it a worthwhile addition to flowerbeds and borders in natural-look gardens. But it also makes an especially decorative cut flower. It demands nothing more than a nutrient-rich, moist but well-drained soil and watering on dry days.

 60–90 cm · Late spring to high summer

🌱 Up to 70 cm ❀❀ Late spring to early summer ❄❄❄ ✸ 🪣 💧 ❀

Dianthus chinensis hybrid 'Charm Scarlet'

Hybrid pink, Chinese pink

The single-flowered, compact 'Charm Scarlet', one of the Charm series, has brilliant scarlet flowers on sturdy stems, and displays them throughout the entire summer. The numerous hybrids of the Chinese pink look their best when planted en masse in flowerbeds, particularly as borders or edging, or in containers. In a sunny location and a nutrient-rich soil, these biennials will need little care.

🌱 Up to 1.2 m ❀❀ High summer ❄❄❄ ✸ 🪣 !

Dianthus barbatus Sweetwilliam

This splendidly colourful cottage garden plant is a grateful bloomer. However, its beautiful, old-fashioned, romantic look only really comes into effect when planted in a group. A bushy, short-lived plant, cultivated as a biennial, sweetwilliam forms dense, flat clumps, 8 to 10 centimetres across, composed of many small, single or double, sweetly scented, and often also two-coloured flowers in white, pink, salmon pink, or scarlet. *D. barbatus* is an outstanding and long-lasting cut flower, and is very simple to cultivate. Propagate by seed – sweetwilliam tends to self-seed – or young seedlings. A frost protection mulch of brushwood is recommended for the winter. This plant likes a fresh soil rich in nutrients.

🌱 Up to 20 cm ❀❀ Late spring to early autumn ❄❄❄ ✸ 🪣

Digitalis ferruginea subsp. *ferruginea*

Rusty foxglove

The biennial rusty foxglove – in certain favoured locations, it can be a perennial – is one of the largest *Digitalis* species. It develops a truly impressive flowerhead made up of innumerable exotic-looking, golden-brown, bell-shaped flowers, with reddish-brown veining on the inside. In the garden, the rusty foxglove prefers dry and sunny spots with nutrient-rich soil. In the first year after sowing, only a rosette of leaves will appear, but in the second year you can admire the marvellous flowers. This plant self-seeds. **Take care:** all parts of this plant are poisonous.

Up to 1 m	Early to high summer	

Digitalis grandiflora Yellow foxglove

Digitalis is a wonderful plant for borders, often found as *the* classic plant in cottage gardens. Yellow foxglove is distinguished by its large, pale yellow, bell-shaped flowers, all pointing to one side. It looks wonderful in borders of tall plants, together with larkspur or monkshood, or bringing a touch of life to evergreen shrubs. This biennial – in favourable sites, it can be a perennial – likes a sunny to semi-shady location in any well-drained soil. It will self-seed if the seedpods are left in the autumn. **Take care:** all parts of this plant are poisonous.

1–2 m	Early to high summer	

gitalis purpurea subsp. *purpurea*
 rple foxglove

 he conspicuous, bell-shaped, pinkish-
 rple flowers form a loose raceme on the
 per part of the stem. The nodding flowers,
 ich resemble thimbles, turn their pretty
 otted throats upward and all point in one
 rection. **Take care:** all parts of this plant
 e poisonous.

1–2 m	Early to late summer	

Digitalis purpurea f. *albiflora* White foxglove

This elegant foxglove variety displays a dense flower spike of beautiful, pure white flowers, arranged around a sturdy stem. This robust plant, usually biennial, has a strong tendency to self-seed, so that all you need to do is thin out the seedlings at a later stage. It prefers semi-shady to shady sites on any good, well-drained soil and is an ideal plant for brightening up dark parts of the garden. **Take care:** all parts of *Digitalis purpurea* f. *albiflora* are poisonous.

25–80 cm | Spring

Erysimum cheiri syn. *Cheiranthus cheiri*
Aegean wallflower

No spring flowerbed is complete without *E. cheiri*. The numerous racemes of scented flowers appear on the ends of the stems, in many velvety shades of yellow, orange, red, bronze, and brown. Just the thing for adding touches of warm colour. It works well in combination with *Myosotis*, *Primula*, and tulips. The plant prefers moderately fertile, well-drained, alkaline soils.

Hesperis matronalis subsp. *matronalis* Dame's rocket, sweet rocket

This delightful bloomer with the delicate panicles of usually lilac or crimson flowers gives off a sweet violet-like scent in the evenings. Dame's rocket is for the most part cultivated as a biennial, but in a suitable location will produce shoots repeatedly, like a short-lived perennial. It prefers a sunny to semi-shady place with fertile, alkaline, moist soil. As an old cottage garden plant, it is best suited to beds of tall flowers, wild-look or cottage gardens. **Tip:** the flowers can be eaten in salads, and the young leaves can be used like rocket.

Up to 90 cm | Late spring to high summer

Up to 90 cm | Late spring to summer | Summer

Lunaria annua Annual honesty

Let's get this straight from the beginning: annual honesty is cultivated as an annual and as a biennial. As this plant tends toward self-seeding and naturalises quickly, the difference is in any case marginal after a few years. It is, however, well worth paying attention to *L. annua*, because everything about this plant is attractive. The delicate, white to pale violet, scented flowers are followed by conspicuous flat, silvery seedheads, which can be used for flower arrangements and are definitely the most special feature of *L. annua*. The pretty, ovate leaves are roughly dentate at the edges. The scent of *L. annua* attracts bees. The plant likes light, moist soil.

| 15–30 cm | Mid-spring to early summer |

Myosotis sylvatica Woodland forget-me-not

One of the most popular spring flowers is little *M. sylvatica*, usually blue, more rarely white, with its yellow dot in the middle. The plant, cultivated as a biennial, will thrive in all kinds of soils and likes plenty of water. If the weather is very frosty, the plant should be covered with a layer of brushwood. Self-seeds profusely.

| 40–50 cm | Up to 60 cm | Late spring to mid-autumn |

alva sylvestris 'Primley Blue'
gh mallow

e high mallow's distinctive wildflower aracter shows to best effect in natural- k gardens and borders of tall plants. rimley Blue', a biennial or perennial, ows into an upright, bushy plant with und-lobed, dark green leaves. This tstanding repeat bloomer, its attractive, rk-veined blue flowers arranged in ferent levels around the stem, is a real e-catcher. It should have a sunny site moist, well-drained soil. The soil can n be on the poor side. Good companion nts are *Campanula*, flowering grasses, lox, evening primrose, or sage. It tends self-seed.

| 1–1.5 m | Early summer to early autumn |

Oenothera biennis Common evening primrose

Common evening primrose can grow to an impressive size. The tall, erect main shoot of this biennial plant bears large, yellow, cup-shaped flowers at the end. They do not open until it is nearly evening and then have a sweet scent. The plant colonizes well-drained humus, but also dry and stony soils, and because of its wildflower character looks good in natural gardens or rockeries. As it is a profuse self-seeder, it is well suited to naturalising. Evening primrose oil is produced from the ripe seeds.

Up to 3 m | Summer

Onopordum acanthium
Scotch cottonthistle

Well defended, but highly decorative, with silvery-grey hair, you need to be sure of one thing before sowing this plant in your garden: once you plant it, you will have your work cut out to get rid of it. The best place for Scotch cottonthistle, therefore, is a wild garden. It does particularly well in sunny locations with nutrient-rich soil, and will bring butterflies and bees into your garden.

Papaver nudicaule Icelandic poppy

The great attraction of *P. nudicaule* is due to the papery, transparent petals of its flowers, an intense, glowing, strong red or pastel colour. But the leafless, hairy, not quite straight stems add to its appeal. The flowers are short-lived, but new ones keep on coming, followed by decorative seedpods. Icelandic poppies look their best planted in groups, even en masse, where they provide pretty, airy touches of colour in flowerbeds or natural-style. This plant, rarely cultivated as an annual, is extremely undemanding and will grow on any well-drained, fertile soil. **Tip:** the flowers will keep longer in a vase if cut when the buds are still closed. Briefly dip the end of the stem into boiling water.

Up to 30 cm | Summer

Salvia sclarea Europe sage, clary sage

This ancient medicinal and culinary herb is planted mainly because of its upright, bushy stature and the delicate colour of the flowers. Biennial or perennial, clary sage is an impressive solitary plant, bearing spikes of pale purple flowers in the second year, and at the same time developing conspicuous lilac-coloured bracts. It is marvellously eye-catching. The colourful bracts remain on the plant after flowering. The plant likes slightly dry soil moderately rich in nutrients, in full sun. It is self-seeding.

Up to 1 m | Late spring to high summer

| 1.2–2 m | | Summer | | | |

erbascum thapsus subsp. *thapsus*
ommon mullein

he statuesque common mullein is an
sential plant for wildflower borders, herb
nd heath gardens, among thistles, low
asses, sage, or lavender. The decorative
af rosette stays green in the winter.
n the summer, a strong, wooly-haired,
nbranching stem arises from it, bearing
llow cup-shaped flowers at its end. The
owers are short lived, but new ones are
nstantly opening, and they are especially
tractive to bumblebees. Wind-sheltered
tes in full sun, with well-drained dry soil
it can even be on the poor side – are ideal
r this plant. Tends to self-seed.

| 10–25 cm | | Spring and late autumn to winter | | | | |

Viola × *wittrockiana* Imperial series Pansy

The bushy erect plants of the Imperial series, cultivated as biennials,
develop beautiful, large individual flowers in early spring or winter.
The flowers come in a wide range of colours and have contrasting
markings in the centre of the flower. In the gloomiest time of the year,
it brings cheerful splashes of colour into flowerbeds or containers. It
likes sunny to semi-shady locations with humus, fertile soil. If you sow
in the summer, you can count on the first flowers in the autumn. In
winter, protect by covering with a brushwood mulch.

HERBACEOUS PERENNIALS

SOCIABLE EVERGREENS AND INDIVIDUAL CENTREPIECES

First, a brief definition of the herbaceous perennial: this term covers a multitude of flowering plants, architectural plants with magnificent leaves, and foliage plants. What they all have in common is that they are herbaceous – green and sappy – rather than woody perennials. Most of them spend the winter under the ground and send out fresh shoots in the spring. They have a firmly established place in garden design, as it is impossible to manage without these multitalented plants. Whether in formally laid-out beds, semi-natural gardens, dry zones, or moist areas, in light or in shade, they always put on a good show. The spectrum of species and varieties is so diverse that herbaceous perennials can provide something for every location and offer unlimited design options for every season of the year. Finding the right composition is a matter of individual preference and reflects the personal style of the gardener.

One more practical tip to finish with: herbaceous perennials can be propagated by seed – some self-seed – but are usually propagated by division or by cuttings. Most can tolerate being cut back after the first flowering and will then flower for a second time. As a rule, spring and autumn are the typical planting times. For frost-susceptible herbaceous perennials, spring is better, so they have a chance to develop well before the winter.

  Up to 1.2 m Early to late summer

Acanthus mollis Latifolius group
Bear's breech

The fascinating slender flower spikes of *A. mollis*, which stand high above its bushy, flat-lobed, glossy green, attractively-veined foliage, make it an outstanding architectural plant in the herbaceous border or an ornamental feature plant that is emphatically wild in character. The flowers are white, usually tinged with purple, and stand close to the stems, which are up to 1 metre tall. They make very good cut flowers and dry well. Bear's breech is very vigorous and prefers moderately fertile, very well-drained soil. It requires only limited tending. Faded flowerheads and leaves should be removed after flowering. Winter protection is recommended in cool climates. **Tip:** leave a few flowerheads standing over the winter, as they look magical coated with frost.

Up to 1.5 m | Late spring to high summer

Acanthus spinosus Spine acanthus

This statuesque flowering plant with its delicate white and violet flowers is guaranteed a leading role in the dramatic interplay of an herbaceous border. The charm of *A. spinosus* lies not only in its breathtaking tall flower spire, but also in its beautiful dark green leaves, which are deeply incised as far as the midrib and spiny at the edge. The strikingly shaped leaves were often used as models in classical sculpture. Likes well-drained soils moderately rich in nutrients. The flowers attract bees. In areas with a harsh climate, light winter protection is recommended.

Up to 1.2 m | Early summer to early autumn

Achillea filipendulina Fernleaf yarrow

With its umbrella-like, flat cymes on upright stems and its finely pinnate grey-green foliage, *A. filipendulina* is a classic cottage garden plant. Its golden-yellow flowers are so compact that in a group they look like hovering points of colour. They can be accompanied by red and blue flowerbed perennials to produce a picturesque composition. This undemanding perennial likes full sun and will tolerate almost any well-drained soil. If you cut off spent heads, then new flower shoots will form, significantly prolonging the flowering period. Dried-up flowerheads will, however, also keep into the winter. *A. filipendulina* forms vigorous clumps. Contact with the foliage can cause skin irritation.

Achillea millefolium
subsp. *millefolium* 'Feuerland'
Common yarrow

The intensely orange-red, umbrella-like, disk-shaped flowerheads of 'Feuerland' are not only an attractive highlight in the herbaceous or wildflower bed, they also keep well as cut flowers. The fern-like, dark green foliage is noted for its aromatic scent. Has a tendency to spread vigorously, so the plant should be divided every few years in late winter. Thrives in all types of soil; only waterlogged areas should be avoided. Incidentally, the botanical name is derived from Achilles, who is supposed to have used it to heal his wounds.

Up to 60 cm | Early summer to early autumn

| Up to 1.2 m | High to late summer | ❄❄❄ | ☀ | 🐭 | 🏺 | ! |

Aconitum × cammarum 'Bicolor'
Monkshood

The majestic loose flower panicles of 'Bicolor' require first and foremost a position where the delicate blue-white blooms can really come into their own. It fits particularly well into an informal garden or a woodland garden. The shape of the flowers is reminiscent of a helmet or a cap, and they contrast beautifully with the dark green, lobate, glossy leaves. × cammarum prefers a cool spot out of the sun, with moist, rich in nutrients subsoil. It can cope well with a sunny position with regular watering, but the midday sun should be avoided. Otherwise, its requirements are modest. A moist soil is important, so water during dry periods. This upright perennial can be divided if it begins to flower less freely after a number of years. **Take care:** all parts of the plant are highly poisonous. Preferably handle with gloves.

| Up to 1.8 m | Early to late autumn | ❄❄❄ | ☀ | 🐭 | 🏺 | ! |

Aconitum carmichaelii var. carmichaelii 'Barker's Variety'
Carmichael's monkshood

'Barker's Variety' offers a very impressive spectacle. The tall, deep violet-blue flower panicles bring a real touch of colour to the herbaceous bed in the autumn. **Take care:** all parts are poisonous.

| 60–90 cm | Early to high summer | ❄❄❄ | ☀ | 🜄 |

Acorus calamus 'Variegatus' Calamus

The reed-like calamus originally grew on river banks or in swampy areas and it therefore prefers an environment at the edge of a pond, in a bog garden, or in a container set in water. The sword-shaped leaves of 'Variegatus' have white longitudinal stripes. The unprepossessing green flowers only appear after mild winters and in warm summers. They are conspicuously displayed on 5 to 7 centimetres long flower spikes, which grow out laterally between the leaves. This ornamental foliage plant likes sunny positions.

| Up to 90 cm | Late spring to early summer | Late summer | | | |

Actaea alba White baneberry

This woodland plant is particularly happy in damp, shady places. It is therefore ideally suitable for shady borders, woodland gardens, or the banks of streams. Its large, deeply pinnate, toothed leaves and the clusters of white berries which follow on from the flowers make *A. alba* a popular garden perennial. This plant is also very undemanding. **Take care:** the berries are extremely poisonous.

Actaea rubra Red baneberry

Inconspicuous small, white flower spikes turn into dense clusters of gleaming red berries on straight red-green stems, which bring richly decorative splashes of colour to shady areas. This valuable shade perennial is a good partner for shade-loving grasses, ferns, hostas, and insectbanes. This plant also goes under the name 'herb Christopher', after Saint Christopher, protector against illness and death. **Take care:** the berries are extremely poisonous.

| Up to 45 cm | Late summer | | |

Adonis vernalis Spring pheasant's eye

The lovely spring pheasant's eye is a real charmer. Its large, anemone-like flowers, glowing golden yellow, and its finely pinnate, soft green foliage, which forms neat wreaths around the stems, make it a highly sought-after plant for the rock garden. In late summer, its fragile splendour is enhanced with glossy, nut-like fruit, and it is highly attractive to bees. *A. vernalis* prefers a well-drained, alkaline soil moderately rich in nutrients, in full sun. Otherwise it is very easy to look after and if allowed to remain in the same spot for a long time will reward you with beautiful flowers. **Take care:** this little beauty is poisonous.

| Up to 40 cm | Mid- to late spring | Late summer | | | |

Up to 60 cm		High summer to early autumn				

60–90 cm		Late summer to early autumn					

Agapanthus praecox subsp. *orientalis* African lily

Its magnificent structure and Mediterranean aura make *Agapanthus* a popular garden and pot plant. It has long, strap-shaped leaves, which are lush green and highly ornamental, and forms beautiful clumps. From these rise the plant's most attractive feature – long, stalked umbels of trumpet-shaped, mid-blue blooms.

Up to 2 m		Up to 3 m			

apanthus africanus 'Albu
y of the Nile

e elegant white form of the lily of the
le brings a touch of fresh, tropical
arm to the garden. Its trumpet-shaped
ooms, which form round heads, stand
gh on rigid, upright, leafless stems that
e in large numbers from the attractive,
ap-shaped, grey-green foliage. This
agnificent perennial's favourite spot is,
course, in the sun, and it prefers fertile,
oist, but well-drained soil. Where there is
risk that temperatures may autumn below
°F (0°C), however, *A. africanus* is better
own in a pot. It should be overwintered
a cool but frost-free place that is not too
rk. Water generously and feed monthly
til the end of the flowering season. The
ooms make outstanding cut flowers.

Agave americana American century plant

In most areas, *A. americana* needs to be kept in a pot, as this fleshy succulent will not withstand temperatures lower than 41°F (5°C). However, its ability to store water and nutrients means that it can survive a period of drought without any problems. Its primeval, dominant leaf structure makes it an outstanding structural element on terraces, walls, or paths. The American century plant does not flower until it reaches old age, when it produces flowerheads up to 4 metres tall. It then dies, but leaves behind plenty of offsets for posterity.

| Up to 15 cm | 60–90 cm | Late spring to early summer |

Ajuga reptans Common insectle

Within a few years, the common insectle will form a dense evergreen carpet covering semi-shaded bare patches or woodland edges, and will happily do so even in a damp environment. From late spring onwards, the dark green foliage of this wild perennial is covered with short, leafed spikes of dark blue flowers. If this easy-care plant begins to get too invasive, the runners can easily be pulled out of the soil.

| 30–60 cm | Early to late summer |

Alchemilla mollis Lady's mantle

The principal charm of *A. mollis* lies in its extremely decorative, rounded, scalloped leaves, whose cape-like form gives it its common name. This clump-forming perennial readily and unobtrusively fills up gaps in herbaceous borders or light woodland areas. In early summer, numerous tiny, yellow-green, long-lasting flower panicles, perfectly colour-coordinated, form an airy veil over the grey-green foliage. The flowers are suitable for both cutting and drying. This very adaptable perennial is happy in a moist, humus soil and needs no further care. Cutting the plant back after flowering will stimulate a second flush of flowers in the autumn and prevent seeding.

| 60–75 cm | Early summer to early autumn |

Alisma plantago aquatica
European water plantain

The European water plantain is most at home in water 10 to 20 centimetres deep. In summer, this pond-edge plant, with its extremely unusual grey-green, long-stemmed, elliptical leaves, forms tall, whorled panicles of white or pinkish-white flowers, which are also suitable for dried-flower arrangements. It is at its most attractive combined with other bog plants such as pale yellow iris, *Cyprus*, or *Carex*. It propagates by self-seeding, but the rhizome can also be divided in the spring.

Up to 90 cm | Early summer to early autumn

***Anchusa azurea* 'Loddon Royalist'** Italian insectlos

The flowers of 'Loddon Royalist' have an intense deep blue colour that is seldom encountered. This sturdy, upright flowering perennial makes a wonderful companion plant in a sunny herbaceous border. Its stalks bear numerous bristly-haired, elongated leaves. Likes full sun and a moderately fertile soil that is dry in summer.

60–90 cm | High to late summer

***Anemone hupehensis* 'Hadspen Abundance'**
Japanese thimbleweed, Japanese windflower, Japanese anemone

An enchanting, soft-pink, autumn-flowering plant with striking yellow stamens, whose beauty is shown at its best in a position out of the sun. Besides its fine, porcelain-like, cup-shaped flowers, the Japanese thimbleweed is distinguished by its pretty, dark green lobed foliage and its graceful, branching, open habit. This plant is popular in gardens, because it is as undemanding as it is beautiful. It prefers sunny or semi-shaded, or even shady, cool and sheltered sites with moist, humus soil, so it is very happy beneath trees or in the shade of a wall. In areas with harsh, snow-free winters it likes a light covering of leaves in winter.

Up to 1 m | High summer to early autumn

***lthaea officinalis* 'Romney Marsh'**
ommon marshmallow

Romney Marsh' is a multistemmed, upright ant, which puts on a summer display of usters of pale pink, funnel-shaped flowers. he dark green leaves are shallowly lobed nd have slightly toothed edges. It is simply ndispensable in semi-natural plantings, nixed beds, or herbaceous borders. In rder to develop its modest splendour to he full, the common marshmallow needs a unny spot sheltered from wind, with rich in utrients, moist, but well-drained soil.

90 cm–1.2 m | Late summer to mid-autumn

Anemone × hybrida 'Honorine Jobert'
Japanese anemone

The splendid 'Honorine Jobert' is a truly magnificent specimen. Its radiant white flowers with their golden-yellow stamens are shallowly cup-shaped when they open and have a soft pink flush on the undersides. It brings a lightness and playful elegance to semi-shaded beds or woodland edges and will tolerate almost any type of soil. It generally needs a little time to get used to a new location, but once it has, there is no stopping it!

Angelica archangelica Angelica

Angelica, with its majestic upright flower stems soaring upwards, lends the garden a touch of elemental force. From early summer, the stately stems bear umbrella-shaped, broad umbels of greenish-yellow flowers, which later develop into decorative seedheads. The beautiful light green foliage with its deeply cut leaves adds further to the attractiveness of this clump-forming perennial. Having put all its strength into flowering, *Angelica* dies back, but not without first having self-seeded plentifully, so its succession is assured. However, if it is deadheaded before the seeds form, the plant can survive to flower again the following year. This old medicinal plant will tolerate full shade or semi-shaded locations in deep, moist soil. Ideal as a specimen between trees and shrubs, in borders or in the herb garden.

Up to 2 m | Early to high summer

Anthemis tinctoria Golden chamomile

A little unprepossessing at first, the golden chamomile becomes a dense, golden-yellow bush when in bloom. Then, its daisy-like flowers with their yellow centres, reaching up to the sun on thin stems, almost completely cover the delicate, feathery foliage. This short-lived perennial is the ideal gap-filler for sunny, dry herbaceous borders or rock gardens. It is undemanding and is happy with a nutrient-poor, dry soil that is very well drained. Incidentally, its life can be prolonged by cutting it back hard in late summer.

Up to 90 cm | Early summer to early autumn

Aquilegia **'Crimson Star'** Columbine

Particular care needs to be taken when choosing a site for the bicoloured 'Crimson Star', in order to make the most of its pretty flowers. Its loosely arranged, bell-shaped flowers, glowing an intense red and white, hang on slender stalks high above the blue-green foliage. *Aquilegia*'s nodding blooms are particularly popular in semi-natural plantings in cottage gardens or in light shade at the edge of woodland, where its wildflower characteristics come to the fore. All it needs is a fertile, moist, but well-drained soil. As it has a tendency to self-seed freely where it is happy, it should be cut back before the seeds ripen.

nthericum liliago St. Bernard's lily

ne easy-to-care-for, delicate *A. liliago* is e ideal plant for a wildflower bed. In late ring, clusters of lily-like white flowers on ender stems grow above the grassy leaves. uitable for any well-drained soil in a sunny osition.

Aquilegia vulgaris **'Nivea'** European columbine

The innocent-looking white flowers of 'Nivea' hang like full gathered skirts on the fittingly modest pale green shoots. The first impression is deceptive, however, as this fragile flower is extremely vigorous and grows to quite a height. Grown in drifts in semi-shade, it provides cheerful splashes of light and works particularly well next to campanulas, anemones, bleeding hearts, and ferns. Columbines also make good cut flowers.

	Up to 15 cm		Up to 50 cm		Late spring		

Arabis caucasica Rock cress

Mountain rock cress grows outwards far more than it does upwards. In fact, this vigorous, evergreen, cushion-forming perennial is so invasive that smaller species can be swamped by it. Careful thought should therefore go into selecting a site for it. Typical choices are barren, rocky, even dry locations, which it can transform into a dense floral carpet in the spring with its masses of small white, pale-yellow, or pink flowers. This robust plant is totally undemanding.

Armeria maritima Thrift seapink

Despite the similarity in their common names, thrift seapink is not related to the pinks of the *Dianthus* family. As its botanical name suggests, *A. maritima* is indigenous to coastal areas, and this small perennial will tolerate salty sites. However, it has a firm place in the non-maritime garden and is particularly stunning in the spring, when numerous puffy, round flowerheads shoot cheerfully up on slender stems from the grass-like foliage and turn the somewhat unprepossessing green cushion into a strong splash of colour. Its spectrum ranges from white through pale pink to dark pink. Rocky, sandy, barren, well-drained soils are no problem for it, making it an ideal plant for rock or moorland gardens and for planting in paths or crevices. *A. maritima* is very undemanding and is capable of surviving periods of drought.

	Up to 20 cm		Late spring to early summer		

Aruncus dioicus Bride's feathers

Wanted: undemanding, long-lived, attractive flowering perennial, preferably with pretty foliage, for shady, damp areas. Bride's feathers, a clump-forming perennial, meets all these requirements. With its pale, feathery flower panicles, swaying picturesquely above its large, heavily-veined leaves in the summer, it is an indispensable feature plant in shady wooded areas or at the edge of a pond. As a woodland species, it loves rich in nutrients soils and a humid climate. *A. dioicus* is dioecious, so it has both male and female plants. The female flowers develop green stamens, which scatter their seeds freely if the faded flowers are not removed. **Tip:** the young shoots can be prepared as an asparagus-like vegetable.

	Up to 2 m		Early to high summer				

| Up to 1.5 m | | Late spring | | | | |

Asphodeline lutea King's spear

Distinguishing features: blue-green, grassy foliage and tall, slim flower spikes. If King's spear comes to your garden as a seedling, you will need a little patience, as its brilliant yellow, scented flowers will not appear for at least two, possibly even three years. Likes dry, well-drained, moderately fertile soil.

| Up to 90 cm | | High summer to early autumn | | | | | |

clepias tuberosa Butterfly milkweed

e fiery orange-red flower umbels of *tuberosa* are real magnets for butterflies d bees. This tuberous, long-lived, corative perennial is therefore suitable wildflower gardens and summer borders. e seedpods that develop from the flowers oduce long, silky-haired seeds, which dly let the wind disperse them. The terfly milkweed is very undemanding. the right spot, it will flower year after ar and will not annoy its neighbours by eading. It likes well-drained soils rich in trients, in full sun, but will also tolerate rtial shade. It makes a wonderful cut wer. **Take care:** regarded as slightly isonous.

| Up to 90 cm | | Mid- to late spring | | | |

Asphodelus albus Asphodel

Asphodel's slender, leafless flower stalks are crowned with long, delicate clusters of flowers in white or pink. This strikingly beautiful plant is a real asset in a semi-natural garden. It feels at home in warm, very well-drained soils.

▶ *Aster alpinus* **'Dunkle Schöne'**
Alpine aster

The small alpine asters are charming, compact, spring-flowering plants with only one flowerhead per stem, which are best displayed in the rock garden. They like very well-drained, moderately fertile soils. The variety 'Dunkle Schöne' has particularly beautiful, small dark purple flowerheads with yellow centres. Divide every two to three years.

Up to 25 cm | Late spring to early summer

Aster Aster

◀ *Aster amellus* **'Rudolf Goethe'**
Italian aster, Michaelmas daisy

The wild, coarse-haired charm of 'Rudolf Goethe' is accentuated by its large, star-shaped, deep lavender flowers. Likes well-drained, chalky soils in full sun.

Up to 60 cm | High summer to early autumn

Up to 60 cm | High summer to mid-autumn

Up to 1.2 m | Late summer to mid-autumn

▲ *Aster cordifolius* **'Silver Spray'**
Blue wood aster

The strikingly small, pale pink tinted flowerheads of 'Silver Spray' are borne on much-branched panicles. Prefers moist, moderately fertile ground.

◀ *Aster divaricatus* White wood aster

This bushy, free-flowering, robust species forms loose umbellate panicles composed of numerous white-yellow flowers.

The broad spectrum of asters ranges from compact-growing dwarfs for the rock garden to tall-growing showy perennials for the herbaceous border. In cheerful shades of white, pink, blue, and violet, they delight the observer at their various flowering times, from late spring until well into the autumn. Even the first frost will not do them too much damage.

Most species of aster love sunshine and warmth; only a few, such as *A. divaricatus*, can also thrive in partial shade. As regards soil, they are not particularly fussy. Most of them like it moist, well-drained, and not too heavy. Cutting back after flowering is recommended in order to prevent them setting seeds and possibly self-seeding, as they show a marked tendency to spread where they are happy. Dividing plants occasionally is also beneficial for growth and flowering. Asters provide an important food source for insects.

▶ *Aster × frikartii* **'Flora's Delight'**
Frikart's aster

'Flora's Delight' has a bushy, upright habit with lilac-coloured flowers and grey-green foliage. Its captivating features are its large, 5 to 8 centimetre wide flowers and its long flowering period.

Up to 50 cm | Late summer to early autumn

◀ *Aster lateriflorus* **'Horizontalis'**
Calico aster

The widely spreading branches of 'Horizontalis', with their tiny rose-tinged flowers, give it the appearance of a dense flowering bush. Prefers moderately fertile, moist ground in partial shade.

Up to 60 cm | High summer to mid-autumn

▶ *Aster novae-angliae* **'Barr's Pink'** New England aster

'Barr's Pink', a semi-double cultivar, is a tall, large-flowered autumn aster with radiant pink flowerheads. It has coarse-haired leaves and is more drought-tolerant than the other varieties. The *A. novae-angliae* cultivars are some of the most important late-blooming perennials. These tall asters may need to be supported. Tolerates sun and partial shade.

Up to 1.3 m | Late summer to mid-autumn

Up to 60 cm | Late summer to mid-autumn

◀ *Aster novae-angliae* **'Purple Dome'**
New England aster

Its dark purple flowers bring a real splash of colour back to the flowerbed on sunny autumn days. On overcast days, however, the flowers remain closed.

◀ *Aster dumosus* 'Professor Anton Kippenberger'

Rice button aster

The mid-blue flowerheads of 'Professor Anton Kippenberger' gaze studiously skywards. This free-flowering cushion aster prefers fertile, moist soils.

Up to 35 cm · Late summer to mid-autumn

Aster Aster

▶ *Aster pyrenaeus* 'Lutetia'

Michaelmas daisy

'Lutetia' is a robust, large-flowered, purple-pink cultivar, which brings a touch of romantic charm to the semi-natural garden. It has a bushy habit and is remarkably free-flowering. It likes a well-drained site in full sun.

Up to 50 cm · Early to late summer

Up to 45 cm · High summer to mid-autumn

▶ *Aster thomsonii* 'Nanus'

Michaelmas daisy

'Nanus' has what it takes to become a favourite. With its pretty, star-shaped, particularly large flowerheads in an unassuming lilac blue, this long-flowering plant brings colour to semi-shaded areas.

Aster tongolensis 'Wartburgstern'
Summer aster

The informal garden is the place for the low-growing, mat-forming cultivar 'Wartburgstern' with its violet-blue flowers with orange-yellow eyes. Prefers very well-drained, moderately fertile soils.

Up to 40 cm

Late spring to early summer

<table>
<tr><td>80–100 cm</td><td>60–90 cm</td><td>Early summer</td></tr>
</table>

Astilbe × arendsii 'Amethyst' Astilbe

Early summer marks the beginning of the flowering period of the tall-growing garden astilbe 'Amethyst'. It is sure to attract admiring glances when it unfurls its striking, feathery panicles, laden with hundreds of small, pale-lilac flowers like little stars. Even when it is not flowering, however, it has no need to hide away in the shady places it prefers, since it has exceptionally decorative, digitate, dark green leaves. The soil should be very moist and nutritious. The flower panicles are very good in mixed bouquets, but unfortunately they do not last long.

Astilbe chinensis var. pumila Chinese astilbe

With its compact, bushy form, low habit, and preference for the shade of trees, the dwarf astilbe is the ideal choice for planting at woodland edges or in lightly shaded beds. The important thing is that the soil is rich in nutrients and moist. It doesn't mind being in the sun as long as the soil does not dry out. In late summer it produces dense, conical, pink-violet flower panicles, providing an intense splash of colour in dark corners. Once the flowers are over, a green carpet of digitate, toothed, red-green leaves will remain until the foliage dies down. The dwarf astilbe sends out runners.

<table>
<tr><td>Up to 25 cm</td><td>Late summer</td></tr>
</table>

Astilbe 'Sprite' False goat's beard

The loose, delicate flower panicles of the low-growing cultivar 'Sprite', with hundreds of tiny flowers in subdued shell pink (*Astilbe simplicifolia* hybrids), have a light, feathery appearance. However, 'Sprite's' finely-dissected, glossy foliage, in a green so dark it is almost black and with a beautiful bronze tinge when it first emerges, is also particularly attractive. This spreading, clump-forming cultivar is not only a real asset in darker areas of the garden, but is also relatively tolerant of sunny and drier positions. Ideal for small gardens.

<table>
<tr><td>Up to 50 cm</td><td>Up to 1 m</td><td>Early to high summer</td></tr>
</table>

| | Up to 1.5 m | | Up to 1.2 m | | Early to high summer | | |

tilboides tabularis Shieldleaf

hint of the jungle in your own garden. The
agnificent ornamental foliage perennial,
tilboides tabularis, is simply immense. Its
ield-shaped, lobed, long-stemmed leaves
n reach the impressive length of almost
metre. As if that were not enough, in early
mmer white, feathery flower panicles
e above its ornamental foliage. This
tractive perennial is not recommended for
y positions, however. The optimum choice
a waterside location or a site near a pond,
t it will also provide plenty of atmosphere
a sheltered spot at a woodland edge with
mus soil. It will not tolerate waterlogged
dry conditions. The shieldleaf looks best
gether with *Astilbe*, ferns, and other semi-
ade plants.

| | Up to 90 cm | | Early to late summer | | | | |

Astrantia major 'Roma' Greater masterwort

Filigree, pink flower umbels, surrounded by delicate, pale pink bracts,
with palmately divided ornamental foliage. This strikingly beautiful,
lavishly flowering wild perennial is a dependable stalwart for stocking
herbaceous borders and woodland edges. It appreciates plenty of
moisture, but will also tolerate dry soils. Cut it back after flowering if
you do not want it to self-seed profusely.

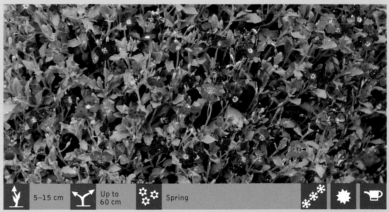

| | 5–15 cm | | Up to 60 cm | | Spring | | |

Aubrieta hybrid Royal blue

The long-lived cushions of the *Aubrieta* hybrids, glowing pink, red,
blue, or violet, are a real eye-catcher in the spring. The flowers are
produced in such numbers that the small, semi-evergreen to evergreen
leaves are almost completely covered. The place for it is in a sunny
rock garden, in crevices in walls or at the edge of a path. The hybrids
are easy to look after, but should be cut back hard after flowering.

| Up to 20 cm | Up to 30 cm | Mid-spring to early summer | |

Aurinia saxatilis Basket of gold

The cushion-forming basket of gold is an unusual, luxuriant spring-flowering plant with masses of yellow flowers and grey-green leaves. Its show of flowers is best displayed in full sun on poor soil in a spot that is not too damp. This robust, low-growing evergreen is very versatile, and is used in rock gardens, as an edging for herbaceous borders, on sunny banks or in crevices in walls. Cutting back after flowering encourages compact growth and prevents unwanted self-seeding.

Baptisia australis Blue wild indigo

With its slender, erect habit, the blue wild indigo brings greater height to the wildflower garden or border. In early summer, this clump-forming perennial bears long, multiflowered clusters of dark blue blooms, which are reminiscent of lupines in their overall appearance. The strikingly beautiful flowers are followed by large, applanate, dark seedpods, which last through to the autumn. The digitate, deep green foliage is also retained well into autumn. *B. australis* prefers a site in full sun on well-drained soil. It is also drought-tolerant.

| Up to 1.5 m | Early summer | |

| Up to 50 cm | Early to late summer | |

Begonia semperflorens hybrid Wax begonia

The small-flowered *Begonia semperflorens* hybrids are among the easiest to care for and are particularly popular for planting in flowerbeds and window-boxes. These evergreen plants have a bushy, compact habit and produce single or double blooms in wonderful strong colours from whites through yellows, oranges, and pinks to rich reds. In frost-free areas they can be treated as herbaceous perennials. In areas subject to frosts they can be overwintered as pot plants if they are dug up before the first frost. They flourish in partial shade but will also tolerate bright positions. Fertile, well-drained, humus soil.

Up to 45 cm | Up to 65 cm | Mid- to late spring

Brunnera macrophylla 'Jack Frost'
Largeleaf brunnera

It has everything it takes to become a favourite perennial. Its large, heart-shaped, fresh green foliage appears early in the spring and forms thick cushions of leaves. Its delicate, light blue flowers look as though they have somehow been scattered loosely on top. On nutrient-rich, moist soils it will form luxuriant stands, completely covering the ground.

10–40 cm | Up to 45 cm | Spring

Caltha palustris Yellow marsh marigold

This plant, with its waxy, golden-yellow, cup-shaped flowers, likes a site that is as damp as possible, ideally at the edge of a stream or pond. It is a popular plant for water gardens, not only because of its striking flowers, but also for its beautiful heart-shaped leaves. If the soil is sufficiently moist, the yellow marsh marigold will also grow well in meadows. It does best left undisturbed.

30–45 cm | Spring and late summer

ergenia 'Morgenröte' Elephant's ear

he spring-flowering 'Morgenröte' may, cool summers, even produce a second ush of the rich pink flowers it holds erect its red flower stalks. *Bergenias* spread gorously and with their large, evergreen liage they are therefore popular as ground ver. It prefers partial shade or shady ots, but will cope in sunny positions if the il is sufficiently moist. As it is happy in ny well-drained soil, it is used in woodland ardens, in flowerbeds, or beside water.

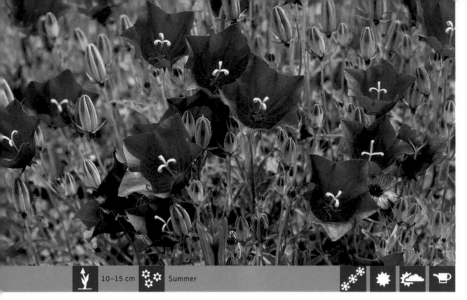

10–15 cm   Summer

Campanula carpatica 'Jewel'
Tussock bellflower

In summer, the low-growing, compact cultivar 'Jewel' extends its long-lasting supply of broad, purple-blue flower bells skywards. This robust cushion plant is favoured for planting in rock gardens or in raised beds. It requires a very well-drained position.

Up to 60 cm   High summer

Campanula glomerata 'Superba' Dane's blood

Simply superb. The almost mystically deep purple-violet, somewhat tubular flowers of 'Superba' are borne in tight clusters at the end of a short stalk. It always catches the eye in an informal garden or a romantic herbaceous border, as its exuberant appearance is really unique. It will tolerate sun or partial shade in moist, but well-drained, fertile soils. Incidentally, its striking flowerheads make extremely decorative cut flowers. Cutting it back after flowering will stimulate the formation of fresh shoots. If you take the trouble, it will repay you all summer long.

Up to 1 m   Early summer to early autumn

Campanula lactiflora 'Loddon Anna'
Milky bellflower

C. lactiflora has masses of star-shaped blooms densely packed on panicles. The delicate, lilac-coloured flowers of 'Loddon Anna' last longest in partial shade. This showy specimen plant is shown off to best advantage in front of trees and shrubs, in herbaceous beds or between rose bushes. It prefers fertile, moist and well-drained soils. 'Loddon Anna' may require support. Once again, cutting it back will prolong the flowering period.

| ⚘ Up to 15 cm | ⚘ Up to 60 cm | ✿✿ Summer to autumn | ❄ ☀ 🐌 ☕ |

***Campanula poscharskyana* 'Stella'** Serbian bellflower

'Stella', a delicate plant with pretty, heart-shaped leaves, forms low-growing cushions. Its small, star-shaped flowers are an intense violet with white centres. Likes sunny to semi-shaded positions on well-drained soil and is perfect for the rock garden or border. It can be rather invasive.

| ⚘ Up to 90 cm | ✿✿ Early to high summer | ❄ ☀ 🐌 ☕ |

mpanula persicifolia
achleaf bellflower

e peachleaf bellflower has very narrow, ight, evergreen basal leaves surrounding n, generally unbranched stems, so when is not flowering, the general impression makes is not exactly one of luxuriance. owever, this impression changes in early mmer, when the cheerfully nodding, urn-aped white or violet blooms appear, three eight per stem. As *C. persicifolia* is a licate little plant, it is better to plant it groups. It is effective placed in woodland rdens or borders, in moist, fertile soils. special care is needed.

| ⚘ Up to 30 cm | ✿✿ High to late summer | ❄ ☀ ☕ |

***Carlina acaulis* subsp. *simplex* 'Bronze'** Carline thistle

This variety of silver thistle forms deep tap roots, so it is better not to transplant it once it has found a suitable home. Thanks to its modest requirements, dry, barren, and even stony sites are fine. Its long-lasting, attractive flowerheads make it a much-sought-after addition to the rock garden, but this bronze-leafed wild perennial also looks pretty in an informal garden. **Tip:** the flowers make long-lasting dried flower decorations.

Centaurea montana 'Parham'
Perennial cornflower

The large, thistle-like flowerheads of 'Parham', in deep lavender blue, brighten the summer for weeks on end. The unobtrusive colour of this mat-forming perennial fits particularly well into semi-natural plantings. It likes warm, sunny spots, but will readily tolerate light shade. It has a definite preference for moderately dry, fertile, well-drained soils. As you can imagine, the flowers of 'Parham' also look beautiful in a vase.

Up to 45 cm | Up to 60 cm | Late spring to high summer

Centranthus ruber Red valerian

In early summer, numerous small red or white flower umbels, emitting a delicate scent, are borne on an abundance of lax stems. This beautiful, branching perennial with its blue-green leaves is much loved by butterflies and bees. Rock gardens, cottage gardens, crevices in plaster and walls, and stony banks are its preferred terrain. There it can really run riot on dry, stony soils in full sun. Red valerian can also be used as a cut flower.

Up to 1 m | Late spring to early summer

Cerastium tomentosum Snow in summer

Although it looks so delicate with its pure white flowers, snow in summer is extremely vigorous and well able to hold its own against any competition its own size. It has all the attributes of an outstanding ground cover plant – it spreads, covers large areas, and is sometimes invasive. In the last case, a well-aimed cut with a spade will reestablish its boundaries. It is very much at home in cracks, crevices in rocks, dry-stone walls, or similarly dry locations.

5–8 cm | Late spring to early summer

| Up to 30 cm | Summer | | | | |

Chamaemelum nobile Roman chamomile

finely-divided, fresh green, aromatic [fol]iage and its daisy-like flowerheads make [th]e Roman chamomile a popular companion [pla]nt in herbaceous beds and herb gardens. [Th]ere is also a non-flowering variety [wh]ich is so hard-wearing that it is used for [cre]ating scented lawns. This short-lived, [ma]t-forming perennial loves sunny, moist [bu]t very well-drained locations. Plants [sho]uld be divided in the spring so that they [re]tain their compact habit. Faded flowers [ca]n be removed.

| 40–60 cm / 60 cm | High summer to early autumn | | | | |

Chelone obliqua Red turtlehead

The curiously shaped, pink or purple flowers of this exceptionally beautiful wild perennial stand on short flower spikes above the toothed, coarsely-veined foliage. This late-flowering plant is extremely robust and prefers moist, even heavy soils. Feels particularly at home at the edge of a pond.

| Up to 60 cm | Autumn | | | |

Chrysanthemum 'Herbstbrokat' Chrysanthemum

These quintessential autumn-flowering plants come in innumerable colour variants and a variety of interesting flower forms. The beautiful 'Herbstbrokat' is brownish red and pompon shaped. Chrysanthemums are displayed to best advantage when planted in groups. As for soil, they need an open, damp, nutrient-rich, chalky substrate, preferably in a sheltered, sunny position. If after a number of years it begins to flower less freely, it should be divided and one part placed in a different spot. Light winter protection is recommended, preferably using the spent flower stems.

Cimicifuga racemosa var. *racemosa*
Black insectbane

Black insectbane seems to bring an air of weightlessness to darker areas of the garden. This upright perennial produces conspicuous, slender white flower spikes, sometimes slightly curved, which may be up to 60 centimetres long. The small flowers give off a scent which not everyone finds pleasant. It should be put in a somewhat sheltered position, as it is not always firmly anchored. It is happiest in a cool, moist area of the garden, preferably under trees.

1.2–2 m   High to late summer

Clematis integrifolia 'Olgae' Solitary clematis

The queen of climbing plants also comes in a non-climbing version. The dizzy heights attained so eagerly by its relatives have absolutely no attraction for *C. integrifolia*, which shows a clear preference for staying close to the ground. 'Olgae' is a particularly successful example of this variety, with sweet-smelling, purple-blue flower bells and attractive long leaves. Its soft stems do, however, require support. It fits superbly well in herbaceous beds or between other summer-flowering plants, but appears at its best when planted between roses. It is especially happy in sun and a nutrient-rich soil, but will also tolerate partial shade, although this has an adverse effect on its flowering.

60–90 cm   Summer

Up to 40 cm   Late spring to high summer

Coreopsis lanceolata 'Sterntaler'
Lanceleaf tickseed

Without a care in the world, 'Sterntaler' opens its masses of golden-yellow, not quite cup-shaped flowers, all adorned with a striking reddish-brown ring in the centre, and spreads summer cheer with its free-flowering habit. One single bloom per stem is the motto of this model border perennial, which, as it turns out, is a totally straightforward contemporary plant. It will be happy with any well-drained soil in a warm and sunny spot.

Up to 30 cm | Mid- to late spring

Corydalis flexuosa 'China Blue' Fumewort

The slender, tubular flowers of 'China Blue' are a truly electric blue in colour. They appear in spring in dense clusters above the fern-like, pinnate, fresh green foliage. A woodland perennial, it prefers locations in partial shade with high humidity and a moderately fertile, humus, moist, well-drained soil. It thrives best in a planting of wild perennials or at the edge of woodland. This easy-going plant has a tendency to self-seed.

Up to 75 cm | Up to 60 cm | Early summer

Crambe maritima Sea kale

C. maritima loves extremes. It copes equally well with full sun and drought and with partial shade and poor soil. Being a coastal plant, sea kale can even withstand salty air and wind with no problems. The best place for it in the garden is in a wild herbaceous border with well-drained soils. There, the imposing appearance of this plant, with its blue-green, wavy-edged, cabbage-like leaves and its branching flower stems, means that it could almost be employed as a feature plant.

60–80 cm | Early to high summer

reopsis verticillata
horled tickseed

is variety can be distinguished from hers by its attractive, needle-like foliage ranged in whorls. It flowers all summer ng, with loose panicles of numerous llow, star-shaped flowers.

Cynara scolymus **group** Globe artichoke

This structural plant makes an extremely attractive addition to herbaceous beds or mixed borders. Its striking, grey-green leaves, together with its bold, thistle-like flower buds, give it a very impressive, slightly archaic appearance. The heads are edible as a vegetable. They open to reveal a spectacular, large, purple flower. In cold winters, this beautiful perennial should be given a light mulch for protection. Likes well-drained, moderately fertile soils. The flowers can be dried.

Up to 2 m　Up to 1.2 m　Early autumn

Darmera peltata Indian rhubarb

This large and imposing structural foliage plant requires plenty of space, as its spread can reach over 1 metre. Its heavily-veined, dark green leaves, which can reach a diameter of up to 60 centimetres, are impressive in their own right. However, before this gigantic, long-stemmed foliage emerges, *D. peltata* puts on a show of white or pink flower umbels, which appear to shoot straight out of the ground on their sturdy stems. The foliage takes on an attractive red hue in the autumn. Indian rhubarb can be incorporated into shady, damp herbaceous borders, but it is just as suitable as a feature planting in a waterside location.

Up to 2 m　Late spring

Delphinium 'Ariel' Elatum group
Candle larkspur

Broad, light blue blooms with a white eye. Growing to a height of around 1.3 metres, 'Ariel' is one of the smaller cultivars in the Elatum group.

| Up to 1.3 m | | Early to high summer | | | | | |

Delphinium Larkspur

◀ **Delphinium 'Butterball'** Elatum group

The small 'Butterball' differs from the – admittedly very pretty – blue standard, with its mass of semi-double, creamy-white flowers with yellow centres.

| Up to 1.5 m | | Early to high summer | | |

| Up to 1.6 m | | Early to high summer | | |

| Up to 2 m | | Early to high summer | | | |

▲ **Delphinium 'Faust'** Elatum group

The long, semi-double flower spikes come in a magical dark cornflower blue, lightly tinged with purple.

◀ **Delphinium 'Finsteraarhorn'**
Elatum group

The single, gentian-blue blooms with their mysterious black centres are enchanting in every way. The flower stems are not susceptible to wind damage.

During its flowering period, the larkspur, with its distinctive, long, dense flower spikes, is right at the centre of events. This 'blue classic' comes in a variety of different shades, from creamy-white and light yellow through pink to various tones of blue and violet. As well as the wild varieties, which are suitable for informal and rock gardens, there are three distinct groups of hybrids. The largest and most important group is that of the Elatum hybrids, which has produced particularly robust, long-lived plants. Belladonna hybrids have a relatively low habit, up to around 1 metre and loose flower panicles. The short-lived Pacific hybrids have a short flowering period, but large, semi-double blooms.

Larkspurs love sunny places, preferably sheltered from the wind, and a fertile, deep, well-drained soil. They are typically planted at the back of an herbaceous border. If you cut them back after the first flowering, they will flower again in late summer. Tall varieties require support. **Take care:** seeds and leaves are poisonous.

▶ *Delphinium* **'Polarnacht'** Elatum group
Candle larkspur

A rigidly upright-growing, small Elatum hybrid with spikes of violet flowers with white centres. It produces a very strong impact at a distance and makes a beautifully decorative cut flower.

◀ *Delphinium* **'Skyline'** Elatum group
Candle larkspur

The large, white eyes, lightly tinged with blue, contrast beautifully with the semi-double, sky-blue flowers.

Up to 1.5 m | Early to high summer

Up to 1.5 m | Early to high summer

▶ *Delphinium grandiflorum* **'Blue Butterfly'**
Siberian larkspur

D. grandiflorum is larkspur's miniature version. This loosely branching perennial is extremely short-lived, and so it is often treated as an annual or biennial, but it does self-seed. The brilliant blue flowers of 'Blue Butterfly' contrast beautifully with the finely-lobed, dark green foliage. This plant's low-growing habit makes it suitable even for exposed situations.

20–50 cm | Early summer to early autumn

Delphinium **'Astolat'**
Pacific group

The American hybrid can be propagated by seed. This variety has very large-bloomed flowerheads with densely-packed, semi-double, pink to lilac blooms. Outstanding cut flower.

Up to 1.8 m | Early to high summer

| Up to 15 cm | Up to 40 cm | ✿✿ Summer | | ✳✳ ✴ ⌣ |

Dianthus gratianopolitanus 'Badenia'
Cheddar pink

D. gratianopolitanus forms attractive, compact, blue-green leaf cushions and finds its ideal living conditions in dry, well-drained soils poor in nutrients, in full sun. Its large, saucer-shaped, long-lasting flowers appear in summer on short, sturdy stems. The strong scarlet flowers of 'Badenia' provide cheerful splashes of colour in rock gardens or make a colourful edging to a bed. After flowering, cut back by one-third to encourage new shoots.

Dianthus plumarius hybrid Feathered pink

The *D. plumarius* hybrids form robust, loose, evergreen cushions with branching stems that are slightly longer than those of *D. gratianopolitanus* and create a more airy effect. However, they have the same requirements as *D. gratianopolitanus* and can be used in a similar way. In high summer, it produces numerous fragrant, fringed, single or double, pink, red, white, or salmon-coloured flowers above its blue-green foliage. When flowering diminishes, the cushion can be divided.

| 25–30 cm | ✿✿ High summer | | ✳✳ ✴ ⌣ |

Diascia 'Sydney Olympics' Twinspur

Cutting back after initial flowering also works wonders with 'Sydney Olympics', as in late summer it then produces a second very dense flush of lovely apricot-coloured flowers. This perennial is perfect for planting at the edge of beds, underplanting roses, or in the rock garden. Likes moist, but well-drained soils. *Diascia* is not fully hardy.

| Up to 25 cm | Up to 45 cm | ✿✿ Summer | | ✳✳ ✴ ⌣ |

| ↓ 40–90 cm | ✿✿ Early to high summer | ❄❄❄ ✹ 🍃☁ 🚿 ◐ |

ctamnus albus var. *albus*

asplant, burning bush

s well as its captivatingly beautiful pink, casionally white, flowers, which are borne ymmetrically on long, rigidly upright, nbranched flower stems, burning bush oduces vast amounts of essential oils with lemon fragrance. This old cottage garden erennial obviously gets its common name om the fact that it gives off these essential ls: in the heat of summer, one spark is nough to set the plant on fire. However, it at much less risk from conflagrations in ne garden than in the wild. The attractive owerheads of this clump-forming wild plant re most effective at the edge of woodland, large rock gardens or in herbaceous eds. The prerequisite is a well-drained soil noderately rich in nutrients. No special care necessary. **Take care:** contact with the eaves can cause skin to become sensitive o light.

| ↓ Up to 70 cm | ✿✿ Late spring to early summer | ❄❄❄ 🍃☁ 🍵 ! |

Dicentra spectabilis Bleeding heart

This old cottage garden perennial evokes a sense of nostalgia and kitsch. Its heart-shaped flowers hang like rows of beads on the gently arching flower stems. The digitate, soft green foliage rounds off the image of transitoriness conjured up by bleeding heart. Left undisturbed in the right location, this little plant can live for many years. It prefers a site out of direct sunlight or in partial shade, with nutrient-rich, fresh, humus soil. The young shoots are susceptible to late frosts, so it needs protection in areas with harsh winters. Bleeding heart looks most beautiful against a dark background. **Take care:** despite its beguiling charm, all parts of the plant are poisonous.

| ↓ Up to 40 cm | ✿✿ Mid- to late spring | ❄❄❄ ✹ 🍃☁ 🍵 |

Dodecatheon meadia Pride of Ohio, shooting star

The flowers of Pride of Ohio look very much like cyclamen, although the petals of the magenta-coloured flowers, that hang in voluptuous umbels from the arching stems, are strongly swept back, almost as though the flowers were trying to point down to the ground. In summer, after flowering, the long, broad leaves die back, leaving behind the stems with their seedpods, which remain until the autumn. This period is used for self-seeding. The edge of a woodland garden is an ideal location.

Doronicum orientale Leopard's bane

Leopard's bane stretches out its flowers toward the spring sun really early in the spring. The yellow, double, or single blooms sit on individual stems up to 30 centimetres long. This long-lasting, undemanding plant is one of the first hardy perennials to flower each year. The bright, radial composite flowers fit particularly well into woodland gardens and herbaceous beds. There, in moist, well-drained soil, they can run wild and form flower cushions of considerable size.

Up to 60 cm	Up to 90 cm	Mid- to late spring			

Echinacea purpurea 'Kim's Knee High'
Eastern purple coneflower

Knee-high. As you can tell from the name, this pretty-as-a-picture, intensely pink cultivar is a low-growing variety of Eastern purple coneflower. Its low habit makes it an ideal foreground plant for herbaceous beds, where its large flowerheads provide one more wonderful, long-lasting show of colour as the summer draws to a close. This upright, undemanding, but very short-lived perennial likes a fresh, nutrient-rich soil, but has no other particular requirements. *E. purpurea* is enormously attractive to bees and butterflies.

Up to 55 cm	High summer to early autumn			

Up to 70 cm	High to late summer			

Echinacea hybrid 'Harvest Moon'
Coneflower

The large, scented blooms of 'Harvest Moon' sit on really sturdy stems, making them very good cut flowers. The fine crown of golden-yellow petals which surrounds the orange-gold, gently-domed cone stands vertically initially, but droops when in full bloom. This hardy cultivar will tolerate drought once it is settled. It will go on flowering if faded flowers are removed.

| Up to 60 cm | | High summer to early autumn | | | | |

Echinacea purpurea 'White Swan' Eastern purple coneflower

Last but not least, a white version of the popular *E. purpurea*. 'White Swan' bears gleaming white petals, neatly arranged around a fascinating orange-bronze centre. A valuable addition to any sunny herbaceous bed. The seedheads make a beautiful sight in winter.

| Up to 1.2 m | | High to late summer | | | | |

Echinops bannaticus 'Taplow Blue'
Globe thistle

A dream in blue. The extremely undemanding, tall-growing cultivar 'Taplow Blue' flowers continuously through to late summer, with its bright blue, spherical flower balls. The flowerheads remain attractive right through to winter. Its grey-green foliage, with silvery hairs on the undersides, is particularly handsome, though prickly. This interesting plant with its wild appearance fits well into the wildflower garden, but it also looks stunning planted in groups in the herbaceous bed and will be happy with any well-drained soil. It is very sturdy and self-seeds a little. Popular with bees and butterflies.

| Up to 80 cm | | High summer to early autumn | | | | | |

chinacea purpurea 'Razzmatazz'
astern purple coneflower

Razzmatazz' is celebrated by its fans s a minor sensation for its fully double, ee-flowering pompons. The wonderful urplish-red flowers really are an extremely npressive eye-catching feature, and on top f this they also emit a lovely fragrance. his cultivar, too, is very hardy and drought-olerant, but thrives best in sun and a moist, ell-drained, soil rich in nutrients.

Epimedium grandiflorum 'White Queen'
Barrenwort, bishop's hat

The low-growing *E. grandiflorum* should not be overlooked when planning shady areas of the garden. This pretty, deciduous ornamental foliage plant has prickly-edged, light green, glossy leaves, which are tinged with bronze when they first emerge. 'White Queen' also has large, spurred, pure white flowers in spring. This undemanding plant will be satisfied with a humus, moist soil in partial shade or shade.

| Up to 30 cm | | Mid- to late spring | | | | |

Epimedium × versicolour 'Sulphureum'

The heart-shaped, veined leaves of this valuable evergreen ornamental foliage plant are copper brown when they first emerge and later are shaded mid-green. In the autumn, the red veining takes on a bold, glowing deep red hue. The stems of the young foliage are also tinged red. In spring, small sulphur-yellow flowers appear. Once it settles in, 'Sulphureum' soon covers the ground with a dense carpet of foliage. Planted in drifts, this ground-covering plant looks beautiful between woodland grasses and ferns. Remove dead leaves in spring.

| Up to 30 cm | Up to 1 m | Mid- to late spring | | | |

Erigeron hybrid 'Quakeress'
Fleabane

Cutting 'Quakeress' back hard after flowering encourages a second flush of single, pinkish-white radial flowers. This *Erigeron* hybrid is a particularly rewarding and unfussy cut-flower perennial, suitable for any well-drained soil. The heavily branching bushes are most effective planted in groups. This popular companion perennial will tolerate even salty winds, so it is a good option for coastal gardens.

| Up to 60 cm | | Early to high summer | | | |

Eryngium alpinum 'Superbum' Alpine sea holly, alpine eryngo

The bizarre shape of its feathery flowerheads and its steel-blue stalks make 'Superbum' an extremely striking plant that should on no account be omitted from the herbaceous border. In winter, in particular, the skeletal structure of this sturdy cut-flower plant is a real highlight. Likes deep, barren soils.

Eupatorium maculatum 'Atropurpureum' Spotted joe-pye weed

Spotted joe-pye weed has showy, wine-red flowerheads on red-coloured stems. This autumn-flowering plant is not only a fantastically eye-catching feature at the back of an herbaceous border, it also makes a good show in waterside plantings. This stately plant is very effective planted together with grasses at the edge of woodland. It is most at home in nutrient-rich, moist soils.

inus alpinus Alpine balsam

ain characteristics: undemanding cushion nt, evergreen, and short-lived. The small, shy _E. alpinus_ will adorn rock gardens d crevices in walls and colonise cracks in ving. In summer, its white, pink, or violet wers appear in clusters. The soil should chalky. Light protection is recommended winter.

Euphorbia cyparissias 'Fen's Ruby'

Cypress spurge

This vigorous, spreading perennial with its fine, feathery foliage, red when the shoots emerge in the spring, and its greenish-yellow flowers certainly deserves a place right at the front of the herbaceous bed.

| Up to 45 cm | Up to 60 cm. | Late spring to high summer | | | |

Euphorbia Spurge

▼ *Euphorbia griffithii* 'Fireglow'

'Fireglow' really lives up to its name. The pretty, dark green foliage, which has a striking red central rib on each leaf, takes on red and yellow hues in autumn. As if that weren't ornament enough, in summer it has long-lasting, brick-red flowers. It needs light winter protection for the first few years.

| Up to 75 cm | Up to 1 m | Early summer | | |

Their highly original, sculptural structure makes these plants look somehow rather bizarre. Common to them all are the peculiar, tiny, yellow-green flowers which appear in loose clusters at the ends of the stems. We are, of course, talking about that wonderful, illustrious family of plants, the euphorbias.

The family is enormous, with something to suit every taste. One of them even finds its way into our living rooms every Christmas – the poinsettia (*Euphorbia pulcherrima*). In general, euphorbias require little attention. They can sometimes even cope with less-than-favourable site conditions and short-term drought. Most of the species shown here, with the exception of *E. palustris*, like a dry, light, well-drained soil. All the species mentioned are fully hardy.

Take care: the stems exude a milky sap, which is poisonous.

◄ *Euphorbia myrsinites*
Myrtle spurge

The prostrate, slightly pendulous, evergreen myrtle spurge reaches a spread of up to 60 centimetres. With its fleshy, blue-green leaves, it makes an enchanting ground cover plant. It bears greenish-yellow flowers.

| Up to 20 cm | ✿✿ | Spring | ❋❋❋ | ✸ |

▶ *Euphorbia seguieriana* Siberian spurge

The semi-evergreen *S. seguieriana* features glaucous bluish-green, long, narrow leaves and lime-green flowers. Its small size makes it an ideal companion plant in the herbaceous bed.

| Up to 50 cm | ✿✿ | Late summer to early autumn | ❋❋❋ | ✸ |

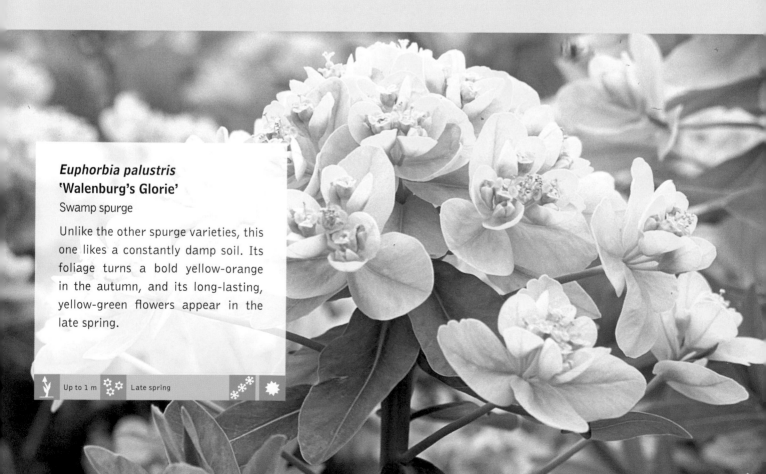

Euphorbia palustris 'Walenburg's Glorie'
Swamp spurge

Unlike the other spurge varieties, this one likes a constantly damp soil. Its foliage turns a bold yellow-orange in the autumn, and its long-lasting, yellow-green flowers appear in the late spring.

| Up to 1 m | ✿✿ | Late spring | ❋❋❋ | ✸ |

| | 1.2–2 m | | Up to 1.2 m | | Early to high summer | | | | | | |

Filipendula rubra 'Venusta'
Queen of the prairie

This species of meadowsweet has a very spreading, almost bushy habit, so it requires a certain amount of space. It does best in a semi-shaded position, perhaps in front of a group of trees, near tall grasses or beside water, preferably with moist, well-drained soil. In summer, 'Venusta' produces fluffy, deep pink, scented flower panicles above its prettily pinnate foliage. As they age, the flowers fade to a delicate pink.

Fragaria 'Frel' Strawberry

The delicate flowers of 'Frel', also known under the name 'Pink Panda', shine out in a rich, truly radiant pink. The colourful flowers contrast beautifully with the dark foliage with its reddish-green stems. This plant flowers absolutely non-stop and has a tendency to spread rapidly. Because of this, 'Frel' seems predestined to be used as ground cover, suppressing weeds in a most charming way and suiting any well-drained soil. The ornamental strawberry also does a good job edging beds or borders, in cracks in paving or in hanging baskets. However, this semi-evergreen perennial produces strawberries only extremely rarely. Will tolerate sun or partial shade.

| | 10–15 cm | | Mid-spring to mid-autumn | | |

Gaillardia hybrid Blanket flower

Thanks to the richly-contrasting colours of the blanket flower's daisy-like flowers – which also act like a magnet to bees and butterflies – this utterly straightforward plant brings cheerful highlights to sunny beds and mixed borders. Depending on the variety, there are many different colour combinations, but the main ones available are in shades of yellow, carmine red, orange, or copper brown. This long-flowering plant likes a well-drained, humus soil rich in nutrients. It is essential to cut it back hard in the autumn so that it can form new shoots for the following season. It is a short-lived plant and requires winter protection in areas with hard winters.

| | 30–80 cm | | Early to late summer | | | | |

| Up to 80 cm | Late spring to early autumn | |

Gaura lindheimeri 'Siskiyou Pink' Lindheimer's beeblossom

The loose, airy habit of 'Siskiyou Pink' is shown to particular advantage in semi-natural areas of the garden. The delicate flowers, tinged with pink, are short lived, but are continually replaced with new ones. This species of *Gaura* prefers a moist, sunny spot, but will also tolerate dryness and semi-shaded sites. It should be cut back hard after flowering. Winter protection is recommended in areas with harsh winters.

| Up to 1.5 m | Up to 90 cm. | Early summer to early autumn | | |

...lega 'Candida'

...andida' blooms in summer and autumn, its ...uriant white flower spikes exuding elegant ...endour. Another attraction of this robust ...d undemanding, long-flowering plant is ... beautiful, bushy, vigorous habit, which ...kes it an imposing flowerbed perennial ...t also naturalises well. It welcomes any ...ist, well-drained soil in sun or partial ...ade. Because of its exceptional height, ...andida' needs to be supported.

| Up to 10 cm | Up to 30 cm | Late spring to early summer | | |

Gentiana acaulis
Gentian

Gentian blue – the *Gentiana* genus, with its deep blue trumpet-shaped blooms, has given its name to an entire shade of colour. The mat-forming, evergreen *G. acaulis* is one of these bewitchingly blue, instantly recognisable plants, and seems to sprout directly from the ground. As an alpine plant, the stemless gentian is ideally suited to the rock garden, where it can gradually make itself at home between vigorous cushion plants. It can tolerate sun only in areas with cool, damp summers, otherwise it is better protected from the sun. The ideal soil for it is loamy, thoroughly moist, and humic.

▶ *Geranium* 'Johnson's Blue'

Cranesbill

With its loosely bushy, slightly spreading habit, 'Johnson's Blue' can be used as an unusually attractive ground cover plant. Its lavender-blue, cup-shaped flowers, up to 5 centimetres across, which become tinged with grey over time, combined with its elegantly divided, mid-green foliage, are a highlight in cottage gardens and summer flowerbeds or as an underplanting for climbing roses. Rich in nutrients, fresh, well-drained soil.

| | 30–45 cm | | 60–75 cm | | Summer | | | | |

Geranium Cranesbill

| | Up to 20 cm | | 75–90 cm | | Early to high summer | | |

| | Up to 15 cm | | Up to 30 cm | | Late spring to early summer | | |

◀ *Geranium* × *cantabrigiense* 'Biokovo'

'Biokovo' is distinguished by its rounded, glossy, light green leaves and rose-tinged white flowers with lightly turned-back petals. The compact habit of this evergreen plant makes it particularly suitable for rock gardens with a moderately dry, well-drained soil.

◀ *Geranium cinereum* subsp. *subcaulescens*

This dwarf-growing, very vigorous plant bewitches people with its bold magenta-coloured flowers with penetrating black eyes at their centres. It is evergreen in mild winters. Needs a poor, very well-drained soil, preferably in the rock garden. Grey-green foliage. Requires little water.

The popular cranesbill is an extremely varied and easy-to-care-for perennial, which comes in a huge number of different colours and forms. Varieties differ in the colour and pattern of their flowers as well as in their habit and in their foliage, which is often decorative.

The spectrum of colours it comes in ranges from pure white through all sorts of shades of pink and red to an intense blue. Even purple-black flowers are available. There are evergreen varieties as well as the deciduous ones, some of which take on lovely attractive colours in the autumn. While the smallest varieties only grow to around 20 centimetres tall the Armenian cranesbill reaches up to 1.2 metres. Their many possible uses in the garden vary according to habit, vigour, and site requirements: small varieties are suitable as dense ground cover; tall ones bring wonderful colour and natural charm to herbaceous borders or rock gardens as well as to shadier areas of the garden. All species of cranesbill have one thing in common — they are at their most effective planted in drifts.

Up to
60 cm

Early summer
to early autumn

Up to
50 cm

Early to late summer

▲ *Geranium clarkei* **'Kashmir Purple'**

Planted at the edge of woodland, the large, intensely purple-blue blooms of 'Kashmir Purple' are guaranteed to catch the eye. This variety tends to spread rapidly. Decorative, mid-green leaves.

▲ *Geranium endressii* **'Wargrave Pink'**

In summer, 'Wargrave Pink' produces absolutely masses of small, intense salmon-pink flowers. This undemanding ground cover plant is a good solution for a wooded area or for large open sites. Likes moderately dry soil. 'Wargrave Pink' is very vigorous, reaching a spread of up to 90 centimetres. Evergreen in mild winters.

Geranium himalayense **'Gravetye'**
Himalayan cranesbill, lilac cranesbill

Its radiant blue flowerheads, with purple markings leading to the centres, can be up to 7 centimetres wide. The foliage turns a beautiful colour in the autumn. Likes sunny to semi-shaded, cool positions. Flowers for a second time in early autumn. Up to 60 centimetres spread.

Up to
30 cm

Early summer

◀ *Geranium macrorrhizum* 'Spessart'
Bigroot cranesbill, bigroot geranium

In early summer, 'Spessart' produces an abundance of unassuming, white to light pink flowers. The bigroot geranium forms dense carpets, making it a brilliant ground cover plant, although it is very competitive. It tends to prefer a dry, moderately rich in nutrients soil.

20–30 cm   Early summer

Geranium Cranesbill

▶ *Geranium × magnificum*
Showy cranesbill

Although the violet-coloured showy cranesbill has a tendency to be very vigorous, it combines outstandingly well with other hardy perennials in a sunny position. Its mid-green foliage turns an attractive colour in the autumn. Cutting back encourages a second flush of flowers.

Up to 60 cm   Up to 60 cm   High summer

▶ *Geranium phaeum* Dusky cranesbill

G. phaeum differs in a number of respects from other *Geranium* species. Its purple-black, turned-back flowers, unusual for the genus, hang in large numbers on stems sprouting from the soft-green foliage. The lobed, large-leafed foliage is flecked in places with purple-brown. *G. phaeum* will tolerate even shady locations.

Up to 80 cm   Up to 45 cm   Late spring to early summer

◀ *Geranium pratense* **'Plenum Caeruleum'**
Meadow cranesbill

The beautiful, violet-blue variety 'Plenum Caeruleum' has long-lasting double flowers on long stems and is enticingly wild in appearance. Prefers nutrient-rich soils. Tolerates sun and partial shade.

60–90 cm | Early to high summer

▶ *Geranium psilostemon* Armenian cranesbill

The Armenian cranesbill's closely-packed, magenta-coloured blooms, with a black eye to each flower, makes it look really good from a distance. This, combined with its size, makes it an ideal plant for the herbaceous border. The mid-green foliage is tinged with carmine red in the spring, and in the autumn it takes on wonderful red hues. Cutting it back after the first flush of flowers encourages it to shoot again. Provide light winter protection in areas with harsh winters.

60–120 cm | Early to late summer

Geranium sylvaticum **'Mayflower'** Woodland cranesbill

'Mayflower' is a low-growing variety notable for its early flowering. In the late spring, it produces large numbers of large, lightly-veined, violet-blue flowers with white centres. Prefers a moist soil.

Up to 50 cm | Late spring to early summer

| | Up to 45 cm | | Late spring to high summer |

Geum rivale 'Leonard's Variety'
Purple avens

This gorgeous purple avens cultivar cheers up the late spring with huge quantities of old-rose coloured, semi-double flowers, nodding gracefully on brown stems above the attractive, deep green carpet of foliage. It sometimes flowers again in late summer if the faded flowers are removed. 'Leonard's Variety' likes fertile, moist soil in herbaceous beds or light spots at the edge of woodland and is also happy beside water.

Gillenia trifoliata Bowman's root

Bowman's root, an upright, loosely branching plant, creates a wonderfully delicate, light, and airy impression, thanks in particular to its elegant oval, finely-toothed foliage, which takes on an attractive reddish colouring in the autumn. From late spring onward, it produces loose panicles with lots of small, star-shaped, white to pink flowers, which look almost as though they had been scattered over the bronze-green foliage. The place for *G. trifoliata* is in a light spot at the edge of woodland or in an herbaceous border with fertile, moist, slightly acid soil. This pretty plant, which also makes an outstanding cut flower, needs no special attention. However, it can take two to three years to develop fully.

| | Up to 1 m | | Late spring to late summer |

Gunnera manicata Giant rhubarb, giant gunnera

At first glance, the gigantic *G. manicata* looks totally oversized and at the same time unbelievably spectacular. Everything about this perennial is XXL, starting with the decorative rhubarb-like leaves, which can grow to up to 2 metres long, on through the hefty leaf-stalks, which reach a length of up to 2.5 metres, to the flowerheads, which themselves can be up to 1 metre across. The really amazing thing about it is that the leaves only need about two months to reach their full size – and they do it all over again every spring. Given these dimensions, it soon becomes obvious that this moisture-loving, large-leafed structural plant requires a special location appropriate to its needs. It needs a sunny to semi-shady position in deep soil with plenty of moisture. The ideal place is a pond or along a stream, but it can also develop to its full glory in front of a wall or in a lawned area. In winter, it is imperative that the rhizome be protected with a layer of leaves and brushwood.

| | Up to 2.5 m | | 3–4 m | | Early summer |

	Up to 1.5 m		Late summer to early autumn

Helenium 'Chipperfield Orange'
Sneezeweed

The orange-yellow flecked 'Chipperfield Orange' is a tall-growing *Helenium* variety, which definitely needs staking. However, it is worth the trouble, as this beautiful plant brings glorious colour to the herbaceous bed late in the year. **Take care:** poisonous.

	1.5–1.8 m		Late summer to early autumn

Helenium 'Die Blonde' Sneezeweed

'Die Blonde' flowers tirelessly, with small, daisy-like blooms in, as its name suggests, a magnificent, radiant yellow. *Helenium* cultivars are definitely among the most popular flowering plants of late summer. If you pinch out the tall-growing varieties soon after the shoots appear, they will grow more bushy and be more likely to stand firm during the flowering period, though the flowers will appear later. **Take care:** poisonous.

10–15 cm	Up to 50 cm		Late spring to high summer

ypsophila repens 'Rosa Schönheit'
reeping baby's breath

s pink veil of star-shaped flowers brings lour and fragrance to a rock garden or y-stone wall in an especially beautiful way. . *repens* is very well known and popular ove all as a cut flower, its romantic anicles adding lightness to any bunch of wers. Prefers a light, well-drained soil in sunny position.

Up to 1.2 m | Late summer to early autumn

Helenium 'Flammendes Käthchen'
Sneezeweed

'Flammendes Käthchen' sets off a firework display of colours with its sea of scarlet flowers, each ornamented with a fine yellow ring in the centre. The warm red flowers contrast particularly beautifully with the mid-green foliage. This fiery, upright cut-flower perennial brings bold splashes of colour to the herbaceous bed or the water's edge. **Take care**: contact with the leaves can provoke skin allergies.

Helenium 'Kupferzwerg' Sneezeweed

Helenium gets its name from the Greek word '*helios*' meaning sun, and that is precisely what it needs, as well as lots of nutrients and plenty of moisture. Anything that works so tirelessly at producing new flowers is entitled to expect some standards! So the maintenance schedule is as follows: water freely when dry, feed in spring, divide regularly, and support tall varieties. It is not really a lot of effort in return for this magnificent showy perennial, which provides wonderful cut flowers and is at the same time an important source of food for bees. Now a few words about 'Kupferzwerg'. Its name, which means 'copper dwarf', says it all: it is a small variety – well, relatively small for an *helenium* – and flowers in the most beautiful copper red.

Up to 70 cm | High to late summer

90–110 cm | Late summer to early autumn

Helenium 'Rubinkuppel' Sneezeweed

'Rubinkuppel' has particularly appealing flowers, ruby red with a light yellow flush. An absolute must for lovers of sensuous red flowers.

Helianthus decapetalus
Thinleaf sunflower

The perennial sunflower is a relative of the annual *Helianthus annuus*. Though somewhat more retiring, it compensates for this by returning every year. Its flowers remain about the size of a side plate and are borne on sturdy, branching stems. The fresh, lemon-yellow flowers of 'Capenoch Star' acquire a real luminous quality in the sunlight. This long-lasting feature plant therefore makes an impressive eye-catching feature in the cottage garden or mixed herbaceous border. To promote the formation of new buds, regular deadheading is recommended. Prefers a moist, rich in nutrients, deep soil.

Up to 1.3 m | *Late summer to autumn*

Heliopsis helianthoides var. *scabra* 'Goldgrünherz' Smooth oxeye

The smooth oxeye, with its tall, branching, upright stems, has definitely earned a place in the herbaceous border, thanks to the luxuriant abundance of its sunny flowers. Not only is it a long-flowering plant that provides long-lasting cut flowers, but it also makes minimal demands. Give it a warm place in the sun and a well-drained soil rich in nutrients, and it will be more than happy. 'Goldgrünherz' has lemon-yellow double flowers which are green in the centre until they are fully open.

Up to 90 cm | High summer to early autumn

Helleborus 'Mrs. Betty Ranicar'

The lovely 'Mrs. Betty Ranicar' has large, dark green foliage. However, its special feature lies in its exquisite white flowers. These little wonders are double and they are significantly larger than those of other hybrids.

| Up to 40 cm | Early to mid-spring | | | | | ! |

Helleborus Hellebore

| Up to 1.2 m | Late winter to early spring | |

◀ *Helleborus argutifolius* Corsican hellebore

With its prickly leaves, the early-flowering *H. argutifolius* has a somewhat bizarre appearance. It is robust, has overwintering leaves and bears cup-shaped, hanging, pale green flowers on upright flower stems. Its stature approaches that of a shrub. Ornamental foliage plant. Will tolerate partial shade.

| Up to 80 cm | Mid-winter to mid-spring | | |

◀ *Helleborus foetidus*

Stinking hellebore, bear's foot

The stinking hellebore gets its name from its unpleasant-smelling, leathery, dark green leaves. This long-flowering, evergreen plant is otherwise a delight, with its mass of pale green to greenish-yellow, pendent, slender flower bells. Will tolerate partial shade.

| Up to 30 cm | Early winter to early spring | |

◀ *Helleborus niger*

Black hellebore

The fabulous white flowers, sometimes tinged with pink, are borne on sturdy, purple shoots. The name 'black hellebore' derives from its black roots. Evergreen. Will tolerate partial shade.

The numerous *Helleborus* species and hybrids provide exquisite and enchanting flowers in the winter garden. Hellebores flower in all shades of white and yellow through pink to deep purple tones and even in a delicate, understated green.

This genus is also characterised by its leathery, fan-shaped, digitate leaves, evergreen in some species, which make the plant attractive even when it is not flowering. In any case, the dark green foliage provides a pretty contrast with the fine flowers.

The ideal location is in partial shade, although some species will also tolerate sun. The soil should always be chalky and damp. After flowering, the old leaves should be removed, so that the plant can put its energy into the new shoots. It can take a few years before it produces flowers, but *Helleborus* can live for 50 years or more. **Take care:** all parts of the plant are extremely poisonous.

▶ *Helleborus orientalis* hybrid
Lenten-rose

The white flowers, flecked with pink, nod shyly from their stems. In mild winters, the colossal, highly decorative, glossy, dark green foliage is evergreen. Will tolerate partial shade.

Up to 45 cm | Mid-winter to mid-spring

◀ *Helleborus purpurascens* Purple hellebore

Flowering begins at soil level even before the first foliage appears, and only later do small stems begin to grow. Bears numerous purple-grey flowers. Will tolerate more sun than the other species. Will tolerate partial shade.

5–30 cm | Mid-winter to mid-spring

▶ *Helleborus* × *sternii* 'Boughton Beauty'

'Boughton Beauty' has leathery, veined, mid-green foliage, which is evergreen in mild winters. It produces pink flowers, coloured a pale green inside, hanging on purple-pink shoots. This spectacular perennial will tolerate full sun or light shade.

50–60 cm | Late winter to mid spring

Helleborus viridis
Green hellebore

This low-growing, green-flowering species is shown to its best advantage planted in a group. The pretty, pendent, cup-shaped flowers are among the darkest of the green-flowering species. Will tolerate partial shade.

20–40 cm | Late winter to early spring

Hemerocallis 'Children's Festival'

The extremely attractive and popular small-flowered variety 'Children's Festival' bears slightly ruffled peach-pink flowers with an apricot throat. Looks especially fine in a group.

Up to 60 cm | Early to high summer

Hemerocallis Daylily

Up to 80 cm | Early to high summer

Up to 50 cm | High summer

◀ Hemerocallis 'Ed Murray'

The magical red-black ruffled flowers of 'Ed Murray' stay open for up to 16 hours. That should be enough time to appreciate adequately this beautiful small-flowered daylily with its green-yellow throat.

Up to 1.2 m | High to late summer

▲ Hemerocallis 'Frans Hals'

The radiant rust-red and yellow flowers of 'Frans Hals' open in the shape of a star with median stripes. This large-flowered daylily will bring warm colour to a sunny bed.

◀ Hemerocallis 'Green Flutter'

A rich canary yellow and a slightly ruffled star-shaped flower with a green-tinged throat characterise the small-flowered 'Green Flutter', which is scarcely discreet, but all the more splendid for it. Night-blooming.

Each of the enchanting, velvety individual flowers of the daylily is unfortunately allotted the very short life span of just one day. These beautiful blooms will fade overnight, and by the following morning the next new buds will already have opened to replace them and begin their own perfect performance. This cycle of death and rebirth can last many weeks, so although the plant's flowers are short-lived, it is actually a long flowerer.

There can scarcely be a perennial that has a wider colour range than the daylily: only blue and pure white are not represented in the spectrum. They also come in heights ranging from just under 0.5 to 1.5 metres and in many different flower sizes. The miniature-flowered varieties have a diameter of up to 7 centimetres, while the small-flowered varieties reach between 7 and 10 centimetres and the large-flowered varieties measure 12 centimetres or more. Their flowers are smooth-edged, ruffled, or striped; some have a glowing throat, while others are multicoloured. There seems to be no limit to the variety of forms and colours.

▶ *Hemerocallis* 'Light the Way'

This cool beauty bears large white flowers with a pale yellow throat. Semi-evergreen foliage.

| Up to 95 cm | Early to high summer | ❋❋❋ | 🝫 |

◀ *Hemerocallis* 'Mauna Lowa'

The large triangular flowers of 'Mauna Lowa' shine out in a warm amber gold with a light green throat. Fragrant.

| Up to 55 cm | Early to high summer | ❋❋❋ | 🝫 |

▶ *Hemerocallis* 'Pardon Me'

There is nothing to apologise for here. The miniature-flowered 'Pardon Me' features round red flowers which have a green throat at their centre. This evergreen is remontant, which means that it blooms again in the autumn.

| Up to 45 cm | Early to high summer | ❋❋❋ | 🝫 |

Hemerocallis 'Pink Damask'

With its radiant salmon-coloured flowers with their fine pale median stripes, the large-flowered 'Pink Damask' brings vibrant colour to the summer border. Looks particularly good together with blue flowers.

| Up to 90 cm | High to late summer | ❋❋❋ | 🝫 |

Hemerocallis 'Prairie Blue Eyes'

The semi-evergreen, large-flowered 'Prairie Blue Eyes' bears majestic, lavender-blue flowers with green throats and finely ruffled edges. Prolific flowerer.

| | Up to 75 cm | | Early to high summer | | | | |

Hemerocallis Daylily

Hemerocallis 'Stafford'

The evergreen, small-flowered variety 'Stafford' displays scarlet star-shaped flowers with yellow stripes and yellow throats.

Hemerocallis 'Summer Wine'

The rounded pink-magenta flowers with yellow throats are heavily ruffled. 'Summer Wine' is a large-flowered variety.

| | Up to 70 cm | | High summer | | |

Daylilies are considered to be extremely straightforward to grow. The plants prefer warm sunny beds or water margins, but will also cope with semi-shaded garden areas, say on a woodland edge, although they will flower less profusely there. The fertile, moist and well-drained soil should neither get too wet nor dry out too fast.

| | Up to 65 cm | | High to late summer | | | |

Hemerocallis citrina
Citron daylily

The fragrant lemon-yellow flowers of *H. citrina* are ideal for night owls, as the small flowers do not open until late afternoon and bloom through the night.

| | Up to 1.2 m | | High summer | | |

Heuchera 'Crimson Curls' Alumroot

Definitely too good to be a gap-filler, 'Crimson Curls', with its unassuming nature, really deserves to be noticed. The unusual aspect of this clump-forming ornamental foliage plant is the somehow creased appearance of its evergreen foliage, which is purple brown with a heavily ruffled and veined leaf structure. Delicate panicles full of coral-coloured, bell-shaped flowers dance above the leaves in late spring. In addition to its appealing looks, it can be used in a whole range of possible locations, from sun to shade, all depending on the soil moisture. Most of all, it prefers moist, fertile, well-drained ground. It provides a softening contrast in front of evergreen trees and shrubs, but can also be used as edge planting in beds and at water margins. Water adequately during dry periods.

30–45 cm   Late spring to high summer

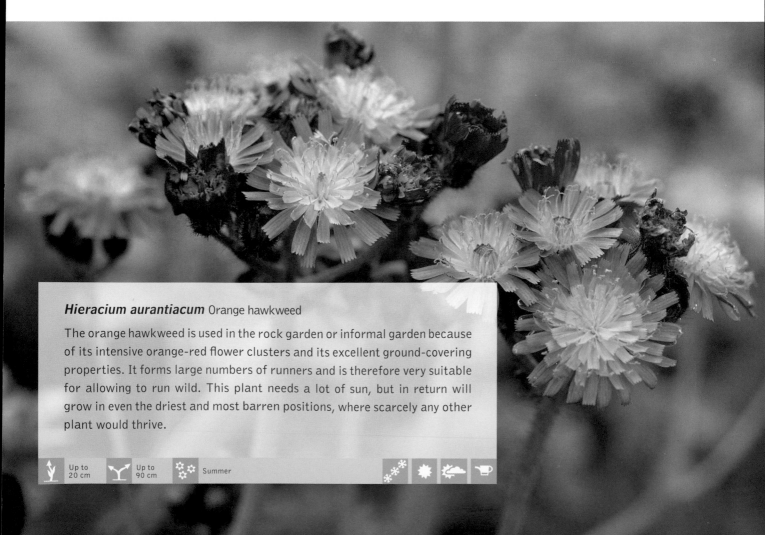

Hieracium aurantiacum Orange hawkweed

The orange hawkweed is used in the rock garden or informal garden because of its intensive orange-red flower clusters and its excellent ground-covering properties. It forms large numbers of runners and is therefore very suitable for allowing to run wild. This plant needs a lot of sun, but in return will grow in even the driest and most barren positions, where scarcely any other plant would thrive.

Up to 20 cm   Up to 90 cm   Summer

◀ *Hosta* 'Crispula'

The radiant one. Its matt green, heart-shaped leaves have an irregular wavy white edge. Since 'Crispula' has such an exuberant character, it can tolerate the company of plants which are altogether more subdued. Its long flower stems bear lavender-white funnel-shaped flowers.

| Up to 50 cm | Up to 1 m | ✿✿ Early summer | | | | |

Hosta Plantain lily

◀ *Hosta* 'Gold Standard'

The golden one. One of the most popular yellow *hostas* is 'Gold Standard'. Its ovate to cordate leaves change from yellow-green through yellow to creamy-white and are embellished with a narrow green margin. Lavender-blue flowers.

| Up to 65 cm | Up to 1 m | ✿✿ High summer | |

| 35–40 cm | Up to 70 cm | ✿✿ Summer | |

◀ *Hosta* 'Halcyon'

The cool one. 'Halcyon' is a particularly attractive blue-leafed specimen. The medium-sized glaucous leaves convey cool elegance, which in summer is playfully interrupted by lavender-blue flower panicles. Works well in a shady spot.

Hostas, those classic, popular ornamental foliage perennials, are the specialist plants for shady corners of the garden. Each year in spring, large numbers of initially inconspicuous, but nonetheless strong, shoots emerge from the soil and uncurl into leaves that range from heart-shaped to lanceolate. The most interesting aspect of these is the variation of colours, patterns and textures: green, blue, or yellow leaves, some glaucous, with a coloured centre or tinged margin, ribbed or wavy. The plant's sometimes very large and dense screen of leaves graciously conceals its surroundings, weeds included. These perennials bloom only for a short period in summer, but when they do, the flower is a bonus adding to the already very attractive appearance of the foliage. The light shade under trees and shrubs or at the water's edge is ideal for *Hostas*, because they retain their leaf colour better there. However, they also thrive splendidly in plant containers. They are robust and easy to care for and are long lasting. Their greatest adversaries are slugs. Where these are a problem, blue *Hosta* varieties are recommended, as their leaves have natural protection.

▶ *Hosta* 'June'

The beautiful one. 'June' comes in exciting glaucous tones of green and blue. Its leaves have a green-yellow hue at their centres and occasionally also on the margins.

| | 35–40 cm | | Up to 70 cm | | Summer |

◀ *Hosta fortunei* 'Aurea'

The bright one. The young foliage is a radiant bright yellow which becomes steadily greener as the season progresses. Brings light to darker areas of the garden.

| | 50–70 cm | | High summer | | |

▶ *Hosta sieboldiana* 'Elegans'

The great one. The elegant, large, grey-blue, glaucous foliage of 'Elegans' is truly magnificent. With its spreading habit, it is one of the largest of its species. Pale lilac flowers.

| | Up to 60 cm | | Up to 1.25 m | | High summer | | |

Hosta ventricosa 'Aureomarginata'
Blue plantain lily

The versatile one. The leaves are a glossy dark green and broadly veined with an irregular wide margin which is initially coloured yellow and later creamy white. Purple bell-shaped flowers with white stripes on the inside appear in late summer.

| | Up to 50 cm | | Up to 1 m | | Late summer | | |

Iberis sempervirens
Evergreen candytuft

Iberis sempervirens has richly dark green foliage, with which it covers the soil completely from view, providing fresh green cushions even in winter. Small white flowers in dense flowerheads appear in late spring. This evergreen loves warmth; a sunny position, ideally in a rock garden or at the edge of a bed, is therefore the best choice for it. Add to this a moderately dry, well-drained soil and protect it from drying out in winter with some brushwood. Trimming will maintain the plant's compact form.

Up to 30 cm | Up to 40 cm | Late spring to early summer

Inula hookeri
Hooker's inula

With its fine, slender, ray flowers in a cheerful yellow with yellow-toned centres, this *Inula* species gives the summer garden another brief period of grace before the autumn finally sets in. This heavily flowering perennial with its hairy shoots and fine foliage is best raised in semi-shaded, moist, well-drained and fertile soil. It goes together very well with other summer perennials to make a colourful bed.

60–75 cm | Late summer to mid-autumn

Iris Iris, sword lily

Extravagantly beautiful, noble and in magnificent colours, *Iris* reign supreme in the garden in late spring. Not without reason are their flowers sometimes known as the orchids of the North.

Among the most frequently cultivated irises are the bearded irises, in which standards and falls are well defined and which typically bear a line of hairs, the beard, on the throat of the falls. However, there are also some magnificent flowering perennials among the beardless irises. Common to all is the long, slender foliage.

As regards their site preferences, the species and varieties differ significantly from one another. Some require a sunny, moderately dry, and rather sandy position so that water can run off well. These include the bearded irises. Others, such as *Iris pseudacorus*, *Iris sibirica*, or *Iris versicolour*, like to be close to water, love damp, wet or boggy conditions and will also tolerate lightly shaded sites.

Iris 'Warrior King' Germanica hybrid

The deep red flowers, up to 15 centimetres in size, of the stately evergreen 'Warrior King' have a beautiful velvety sheen. Eight to nine flowers grow on each stalk. Rhizomatous bearded iris.

Up to 95 cm | Late spring to early summer

Iris Iris, sword lily

Up to 45 cm | Late spring to early summer

90–150 cm | High to late summer

◀ Iris japonica Crested iris, fringed iris

Though the pale lavender-blue flowers, which are adorned with purple markings and orange crests, are small, they are finely ruffled. Has dark evergreen foliage. Rhizomatous crested iris.

◀ Iris pseudacorus Pale yellow iris, yellow flag

The pale yellow iris, with its gloriously colourful yellow flowers which carry purple markings, puts on a proud display. Suitable for pond edges or wet soils. Rhizomatous beardless bog iris.

▶ *Iris setosa* Beachhead iris

Bristle-like standards and blue falls characterise the usually small-growing *I. setosa*. Rhizomatous beardless iris.

| ⇡ 15–90 cm | ✿✿ | Early spring to early summer | ❋❋ | ✦ |

◀ *Iris sibirica* 'Sparkling Rose' Siberian iris

Free-flowering and colourful. The effect that the pink-mauve flowers with their yellow bases produce is positively electrifying. To complement its luxuriant flowers, this beardless iris bears narrow grass-like leaves. Will tolerate sites with little sun. Likes moist, muddy soils rich in nutrients close to ponds or in moist herbaceous beds.

| ⇡ Up to 1 m | ✿✿ | Mid- to late spring | ❋❋❋ | ⚱ |

▶ *Iris* 'Fort Ridge' Spuria hybrid

This robust beardless iris has vigorous broad foliage. This is complemented in early summer by the appearance of blue-violet flowers with a yellow signal.

| ⇡ Up to 1.2 m | ✿✿ | Early and high summer | ❋❋ | ✦ |

| ⇡ 20–50 cm | ✿✿ | May to June | ✦ | ⚱ |

◀ *Iris versicolour* 'Kermesina'
Harlequin blueflag

This bog iris variety is most at home in marshy areas and areas of shallow water. It has long leaves and wonderful red-purple flowers with a conspicuous white signal. Beardless bog iris.

60–80 cm | Up to 45 cm | High to late summer

Knautia macedonica Knautia

A short-lived but enchanting wild plant for the wildflower or cottage garden. The full-to-bursting flowers, in rich cherry red, also make valuable cut flowers. This long-blooming perennial prefers a site in full sun with well-drained, moderately fertile soil. It self-seeds prolifically, thereby ensuring its own continued survival.

Kniphofia 'Goldfinch' Red-hot poker, torch lily

The extravagant yellow flower spikes of 'Goldfinch', which reach a length of at least 15 to 20 centimetres, seem to shine with a fluorescent glow and, with their conspicuous flowering habit, provide a profusion of special effects in the summer garden. A quiet, dark background is the most suitable setting for this magnificent feature plant, which sends up several of these fascinating flower stems – which incidentally also make excellent cut flowers – from the evergreen clump of foliage. Outside the flowering period, it could almost be confused with a grass, because of its reed-like foliage. Warm, protected sites in sun or partial shade and a fertile, sandy soil will help it to blossom. Good winter protection is important, so bind the foliage in order to protect the plant.

Up to 1.2 m | Early to high summer

Lamium galeobdolon Yellow archangel

L. galeobdolon looks like a stinging nettle, but since it does not have any stinging hairs, you don't need to be afraid of touching it. The really decorative feature of this easy-care perennial is its pretty, ovate, slightly-toothed leaves, which occasionally have splashes of silver. The picture is rounded off by a whorled yellow flower. This ground-covering plant is suitable for use beneath shrubs and herbaceous perennials, suppressing even troublesome weeds. However, it can itself be troublesome to neighbouring plants which you want to keep.

Up to 60 cm | Summer

| Up to 20 cm | ⚘⚘⚘ | Late spring | | ❄❄❄ | ✾ | ☕ |

Leontopodium alpinum Edelweiss

The mountains send their greetings. Its alpine origins make the edelweiss a favourite for a sunny spot in the rock garden, where it is particularly attractive next to stone. It can thrive wonderfully in a chalky, well-drained and nutrient-poor soil and needs no further tending, except that the soil should not be allowed to dry out completely.

| Up to 90 cm | ⚘⚘ | Early summer to early autumn | | ❄❄❄ | ✾ | 🌿 | ☕ | ⚱ |

Leucanthemum × *superbum* 'Phyllis Smith' Shasta daisy

The white and yellow flowers of 'Phyllis Smith' are old-fashioned and somewhat tousled in appearance, but they are indispensable long-flowering plants. The unusual feature of this variety lies in its slightly twisted and recurved rays. The picturesque flowerheads sit on long, robust stems which need no additional support. It thrives in fertile, moist but well-drained soil, ideally in a white bed or else in semi-natural areas of a garden.

| Up to 20 cm | ⚘⚘ | Up to 1 m | ⚘⚘ | Summer | ❄❄❄ | ☁ | ☁ | ☕ |

...*ium maculatum* 'Beacon Silver'
...ted henbit

...acon Silver' is useful as an outstanding ...attractive ground cover plant, which ...time forms closed mats. Its extremely ...dsome silver leaves, which are framed ...ly by a narrow light green margin, bring ...immer of brightness to shady areas. In ...mer, light pink whorls of flowers appear. ...y-care *L. maculatum* prefers rich in ...ients, light, fresh to moist soils.

| Up to 30 cm | Up to 25 cm | ✿✿ | Late spring to early summer | ❄❄❄ | 🐌 | 💧 |

Lewisia cotyledon Siskiyou lewisia

The name does not necessarily conjure up a captivating flower. Yet as early as late spring, compact panicles containing large numbers of pretty, delicately-striped flowers in rose purple, more rarely in white, cream, or yellow, sprout from its evergreen rosette. The dark green foliage is faintly glaucous. *L. cotyledon* will feel particularly at home in rock gardens or crevices in walls, in a location out of direct sun.

Liatris spicata '**Kobold**' Dense blazing star

When you consider that *L. spicata* can attain the stately height of 1.5 metres, then 'Kobold' is a really small, but nonetheless select, example of this species. The intensive dark purple flower spikes, which stand on rigid flower stalks, exhibit an interesting peculiarity: they flower from the top downward. 'Kobold' is a pretty little perennial for the front of the flowerbed, which can be planted singly or in small groups, preferably in fertile, moist, well-drained soil in full sun. The flowerheads are sought out eagerly by bees and they also make good cut flowers.

| 40–50 cm | ✿✿ | Late summer to early autumn | ❄❄❄ | ✸ | 💧 |

| Up to 1 m | ✿✿ | High summer to early autumn | ❄❄❄ | 🐌 | 💧 |

Ligularia dentata '**Desdemona**'
Summer ragwort

With shoots about 1 metre long, 'Desdemona' is among the smallest of this species. In mid-summer, this free-flowering plant with a bushy habit produces brilliant orange, umbrella-like flowerheads and accompanies these with large, highly decorative, rounded leaves in a dark red-brown. *L. dentata* thrives on moist to wet soils and is therefore suitable for woodland or pond edges and other damp spots. On soils that dry out, it should be watered regularly. Protect against slugs.

| 30–90 cm | | Late spring to autumn | | | |

Linaria vulgaris Butter and eggs

On dry sites at the front of semi-natural borders or in the rock garden, *L. vulgaris*, with its needle-shaped leaves and dense clusters of pale yellow flowers, looks almost like a small snapdragon. A lovely, long-flowering companion perennial.

| Up to 2 m | Up to 1 m | | High and late summer | | |

...ularia przewalskii Ligularia

...th its large, deeply cut, digitate leaves
...d slender, magnificent yellow flowerheads
... their purple-green stems — what a
...trast — *L. przewalskii* very definitely
...erves its own special place. In any event,
...s imposing giant perennial will assume a
...minant position wherever it is sited, since
...will attract the eye of the observer even
...m a distance. Ideal locations are pond
...nks, stream and woodland edges, or moist
...ders, as it likes a very moist and fertile
...l. *L. przewalskii* is easy to cultivate and,
...the right location, needs no tending.
...erates sun and partial shade.

| 10–60 cm | | Early to high summer | | | |

Linum perenne Blue flax

As a companion perennial, *L. perenne* will grace dryish semi-natural open sites, rock gardens, or borders. The blue flax works to maximum effect when planted in groups. The loosely, arranged shoots with their pretty blue cup-shaped flowers then appear wonderfully compact. The flowers do, though, have very strict opening times: only if it is sunny and only up until midday. Nonetheless, it is well worth granting this short-lived perennial a spot in the garden, as it flowers for weeks on end.

Up to 90 cm · Summer to early autumn

Lobelia cardinalis 'Queen Victoria'
Cardinalflower

Red, as everyone knows, is a colour used for creating highlights. And the richly scarlet flower-spikes of 'Queen Victoria', together with the beautiful metallic-bronze foliage, are truly unmissable in the garden. This great plant prefers relatively moist and deep soils in a sheltered position, so it fits perfectly into bog gardens or other damp areas. It should be supported if required and needs a dry winter mulch. **Take care:** all parts of the plant are poisonous.

Lupinus 'The Page' Lupine

The luxuriant, dense flower spikes of lupines, closely packed with pea-like flowers, come in many wonderfully colourful versions. 'The Page', with its wonderful carmine-red flower clusters, is particularly striking. Lupines are among the most popular of all flowering perennials. Features typical of them are the digitate foliage, hairy on the underside, and the densely-haired bean-like pods which follow the flowers. If lupines are cut regularly, for example to obtain cut flowers, then they will flower again right into the autumn. This stately perennial is happiest on moderately dry, moderately rich in nutrients, open soils.

Up to 90 cm · Early to high summer

Up to 1 m · Early spring

Lysichiton americanus
American skunkcabbage

The good points first. The American skunkcabbage is a really unusual, colourful marsh perennial, with glossy dark green ovate leaves which can grow up to 1.2 metres long. The attractive flowerhead consists of a flower spadix which is sheathed by a brilliant yellow spathe. It appears in the early spring, even before the leaves. After flowering, berries form on the spadix. One minor disadvantage: the plant exudes an unpleasant, musky odour.

| Up to 1 m | High to late summer |

Lysimachia punctata Large yellow loosestrife, circle flower

The yellow loosestrife, also known as the circle flower, is an acknowledged long flowerer with a very marked inclination to spread. Its star-shaped, golden-yellow, cup-like flowers, which emerge in large numbers from the leaf axils, are as effective at the edge of water as they are as a cheerful underplanting beneath large trees and shrubs. This easy-to-tend perennial grows in tall, dense clumps, preferably in a fertile and moist, but well-drained soil. Its invasiveness needs to be kept somewhat in check.

| Up to 90 cm | High to late summer |

~~Ly~~simachia clethroides
~~Go~~oseneck loosestrife

~~Co~~ol extravagance best describes the ~~ex~~tremely attractive flower spikes of ~~th~~e gooseneck loosestrife. The tapering ~~flo~~werheads initially point elegantly ~~do~~wnwards, but as the small white flowers ~~bl~~oom, they slowly right themselves to ~~po~~int upwards, forming a gooseneck shape. ~~L.~~ clethroides is a good, easy-going wild ~~pe~~rennial for damp sites rich in nutrients ~~su~~ch as can be found on woodland edges or ~~w~~ater margins. It is particularly effective ~~w~~hen planted in drifts. It will even put up ~~w~~ith damp areas of a border. Sunny positions ~~pr~~esent no problem, as long as there is an ~~a~~dequate supply of water.

| Up to 1.2 m | High summer to early autumn |

Lythrum salicaria Purple loosestrife

The purple loosestrife's very colourful, slender purple-red flower spikes shine out unmistakably above its foliage base. The best place for this moisture-loving perennial is at the edge of the garden pond or, provided it is sufficiently moist, in a semi-natural herbaceous border.

Up to 2.5 m | High to late summer

Macleaya cordata Plume poppy

The plume poppy, which grows taller than the height of a person, is anything but inconspicuous. It is one of the most striking, light, and airy ornamental foliage plants which the garden has to offer. While the long, plume-like flower panicles tend to be rather inconspicuous, the large, lobate, silver-green foliage provides indispensable highlights at the back of a border and in front of walls or fences. It is extremely easy to look after and loves a rich in nutrients and moderately dry soil. It does, however, have one bad habit, of which it can be cured only with difficulty – its tendency to spread vigorously.

Malva moschata 'Rosea' Musk mallow

The hibiscus-like, delicate pink, cup-shaped flowers and the foliage that smells faintly of musk make 'Rosea' a welcome guest in any herbaceous border. Its bushy wildflower style also fits wonderfully in a semi-natural garden. Cutting back after the first flowering is a great encouragement to the plant to flower again. While this robust beauty is most likely to thrive in a moist, well-drained soil, it has also shown itself to be fairly drought-tolerant. It is inclined to self-seed.

60–90 cm | Early summer to early autumn

Up to 1.2 m | Early summer

Meconopsis betonicifolia Blue poppy, Tibetan blue poppy, Himalayan blue poppy

M. betonicifolia is one of the most sought-after treasures, without which no gardener's life is truly fulfilled. Its incomparable, sapphire-blue, silkily shimmering flowers, with yellow powder-puff stamens at their centres, are unique in the impact they produce. They appear singly or in groups in early summer on tall flower stalks rising from a rosette. The captivating effect of this feature plant, which sadly is only short lived, is best enjoyed against the green backdrop of a woodland edge, particularly where there are rhododendrons.

| Up to 90 cm | | High summer to early autumn | | | | |

Monarda 'Mahogany' Beebalm

The spider-like, exotic-looking flowerheads of 'Mahogany' have an excitingly bizarre appearance. Its tall, vigorous habit and wine-red flowers make it wonderful for providing splashes of colour in the late summer bed. The free-flowering beebalm also has an aromatic scent and attracts masses of bees to the garden. Likes moist, well-drained soils.

| Up to 70 cm | | Early summer to early autumn | | | | |

Nepeta × faassenii 'Walkers Low' Catnip

Low is not quite the appropriate word for the bushy 'Walkers Low' as it reaches the impressive height of no less than 70 centimetres, and is thus clearly one of the taller varieties of catnip. With its dark violet-blue flowers, this tireless long-flowering plant has outstanding impact from a distance. Another characteristic feature is the beautiful, silvery grey-green foliage. Allegedly, this variety is largely left untouched by cats, although it is extremely popular with bees and bumblebees. It favours open, moderately dry, well-drained soils not too rich in nutrients. A versatile border perennial.

| Up to 30 cm | Up to 60 cm | Late spring to summer | | |

mulus luteus Yellow monkey-flower

is easy-to-cultivate and long-flowering mmer perennial provides a colourful show flowers in the water garden. With its g yellow flowers, very similar to those of e snapdragon, the yellow monkey-flower lly brings darker areas of the garden to e. Combining it with the formal structure ornamental grasses accentuates its orous spreading habit especially well. erates sun and semi-shade.

| Up to 20 cm | Up to 30 cm | Spring | | | |

Omphalodes verna

Creeping navelwort, blue-eyed Mary, creeping forget-me-not

Omphalodes verna is one of those indispensable spring flowering plants for which a space should be made in every garden. The lovely loose sprays of brilliant sky-blue flowers are reminiscent of forget-me-not, but flower significantly earlier than the latter. Its dense, carpet-like habit, lightened up beautifully by the ovate, pointed, fresh-green leaves, makes this semi-evergreen, easy-care perennial a good ground cover plant.

Ophiopogon planiscapus '**Niger**' Black mondo grass

Black is 'in'. With plants, too. Any plant whose leaf colour differs from the green norm is assured plenty of attention. Given this trend, 'Niger', with its sword-shaped, deep black-violet foliage and its ground-covering qualities, could become an unrivaled leader. Its dark waxy foliage is joined in spring by wonderfully contrasting clusters of pale purple-white, bell-shaped flowers, from which spherical black berries develop. These remain on the stems even through to the first night frost. Used sparingly, this evergreen plant fits in well with ornamental foliage perennials with green-yellow or variegated leaves, but it also produces an elegant effect combined with grasses. It likes moist, well-drained soils.

| Up to 20 cm | Late spring to high summer | | | |

Pachysandra terminalis

Japanese pachysandra

Anyone searching for a shade-loving, evergreen ground cover plant will be making the right choice in *P. terminalis*, which is rewarding and easy to look after. This perennial rapidly spreads to form a dense carpet of glossy, dark green, coarsely-serrated leaves. The leaves sit in bright whorls at the tips of the fleshy stems. It grows particularly vigorously in a moist soil and where humidity is high.

| Up to 20 cm | Early summer | | | | |

75–80 cm | Early to high summer

Paeonia lactiflora hybrid 'Krinkled White' Chinese peony

The cup-shaped, white, slightly-crinkled flowers of 'Krinkled White' with their radiant golden-yellow centres produce a delicate effect, almost as though they were assembled from thin tissue paper. This long-lived hybrid perennial prefers to grow undisturbed in full sun and on rich in nutrients, moist soil. Waterlogged soil should definitely be avoided. Water during dry periods and feed occasionally.

Up to 90 cm | Late spring to early summer

aeonia 'Coral Charm' Peony

oral Charm' is captivating, with its credibly enchanting flowers in a coral-ach tone which is considered extremely re in peonies. The gardener's heart will e gladdened all the more by the fact that e magnificent semi-double 'Coral Charm' so comes with a large, full flowerhead. s unusual colouration has earned 'Coral harm' a place as a feature plant. This gorous hybrid prefers a rich in nutrients, oist, well-drained soil and likes to be left ndisturbed.

65–90 cm | Late spring to early summer

Paeonia mlokosewitschii Caucasian peony

The Caucasian peony has a rather modest appearance, but is very reliable and robust. The cream to lemon-yellow single flowers, which open cautiously and for a short period only in late spring, rise up beautifully from the bluish-green, slightly hairy, divided foliage, which in the sun takes on a red tinge. The mature seed capsules are particularly handsome. Also tolerates positions out of direct sun.

Paeonia officinalis 'Rubra Plena'
Common peony

The expressive carmine-red double flowers of 'Rubra Plena', with their slightly crinkled edges, are a really valuable addition to the early summer garden. Sufficient space should be allowed from the outset when planting this beautiful flowering plant, as later transplanting will not do this slow-growing perennial any good. It will thrive increasingly from year to year in a deep, rich in nutrients, and moist but well-drained soil, preferably in the sun. Lovely cut-flower perennial.

70–75 cm | 70–75 cm | Early to high summer

Papaver orientale **'Patty's Plum'** Oriental poppy

The captivatingly beautiful plum-purple flowers of 'Patty's Plum' offer a genuine alternative to the typical standard red of the oriental poppy. The inimitable appearance of its large, parchment-like flowers, with striking crosses of black stamens in their centres, earns it a prominent, sunny and warm spot in the garden. The main thing is that the soil should be deep and well-drained. The short-lived flowers are continuously replaced by new ones, followed by its characteristic decorative seed capsules.

70–80 cm | Late spring to high summer

Paris quadrifolia Herb Paris

What makes *Paris quadrifolia* such an attractive, eye-catching plant is not so much the inconspicuous flower as the bizarrely-positioned spherical blue-black berry which matures from it and the four voluptuous leaves. But that's enough drama. As a woodland plant, it is best suited to semi-natural sites beneath trees and shrubs, in partial shade to full shade, and to a moist acidic soil. The plant will require you to be patient for a few years until it appears. Keeping it moist and mulching with coniferous needles may help. **Take care:** the berry which the plant appears to be handing you nicely wrapped is poisonous.

15–40 cm | Late spring to early summer

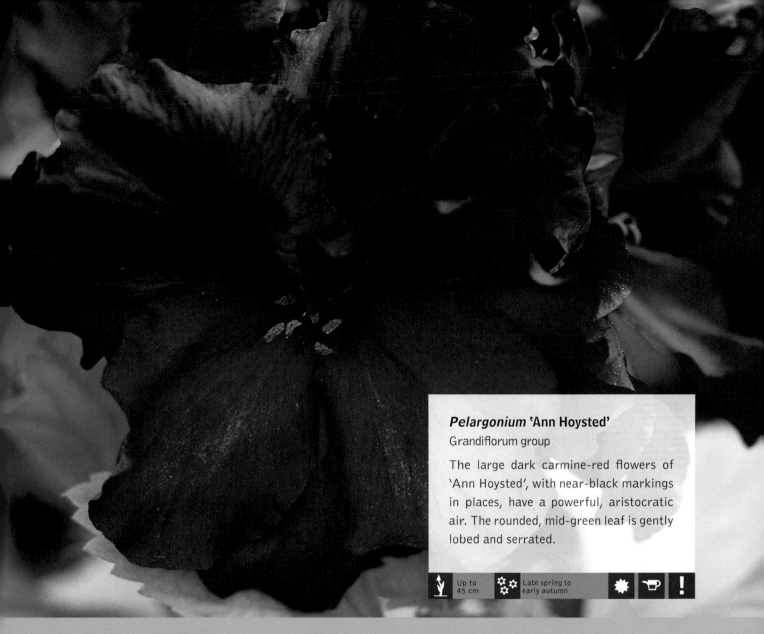

Pelargonium 'Ann Hoysted'
Grandiflorum group

The large dark carmine-red flowers of 'Ann Hoysted', with near-black markings in places, have a powerful, aristocratic air. The rounded, mid-green leaf is gently lobed and serrated.

Up to 45 cm	Late spring to early autumn			

Pelargonium Geranium, pelargonium

The choice of pelargonium hybrids is enormous. The reason for this is the overwhelming diversity not merely of their flowers, but also of their leaves: these come in a great variety of shapes and sizes, some being multicoloured and others having an intensive aroma of citrus or rose. Some are impressive, upright bushy perennials while others tend toward a pendulous habit. Their differing growth habits determine where they are planted: in a bed, in a tub, or in a hanging basket. However, they all have one thing in common, namely their frost susceptibility, which is why they are predominantly kept as pot plants, balcony plants, or hanging-basket plants in areas where there is a risk of frost.

Pelargoniums love a rich in nutrients, well-drained soil. Depending on the variety, they prefer a bright, sunny, or semi-shaded position. The sumptuous splendour of the flowers can be improved still further by regular feeding and by regularly removing faded parts of the plant. **Take care:** contact with the leaves can lead to skin irritation.

▶ *Pelargonium* 'Arctic Star' Zonal group

Like glittering crystals, the simple, star-shaped, white flowers sit massed in umbels on their flower stalks. 'Arctic Star' is an upright, bushy evergreen perennial with pointed lobed leaves. For summer beds or containers.

25–30 cm | Late spring to early autumn

Pelargonium Geranium, pelargonium

50–60 cm | Late spring to early autumn

◀ *Pelargonium* 'Barbe Bleu'
Peltatum group

The vigorous, hanging ivy-leafed pelargoniums are so called because of their ivy-like foliage. The free-flowering 'Barbe Bleu' bears double purple-black flowers which in sunlight fade to a brilliant wine red. Good for hanging baskets, boxes, or for growing over the edges of walls.

Up to 30 cm | Late spring to early autumn

▲ *Pelargonium* 'Catford Belle'
Angel group

The numerous lilac-rose-coloured flowers of 'Catford Belle' are marked with dark red blotches on the upper petals. Angel pelargoniums have a very bushy habit.

▶ *Pelargonium* '**Delli**' Grandiflorum group

The bushy 'Delli' is a miracle of plant breeding. The large, frilled flowers combine a discreet pink tone with elegant white.

30–40 cm	Late spring to early autumn	

◀ *Pelargonium* '**L'Elégante**' Peltatum group

Flower and leaf are equally enchanting in this chameleon-like, trailing ivy-leafed pelargonium, as the evergreen 'L'Elégante' bears grey-green leaves whose cream-coloured edges turn rose pink if kept dry. To go with these, it has simple white flowers with a small red tattoo.

20–25 cm	Late spring to early autumn	

▶ *Pelargonium* '**Mrs. G. H. Smith**' Angel group

The compact 'Mrs. G. H. Smith' is adorned with white rose-tinged flowers with a carmine-red marking superimposed on the upper petals. This angel pelargonium has slightly lemon-scented leaves.

20–25 cm	Late spring to early autumn	

Pelargonium capitatum
Rose-scented pelargonium

The superb *P. capitatum* is one of the most heavily rose-scented pelargoniums. Pretty, pink, umbelliferous flowers, coupled with rounded, slightly divided, dark green leaves. This spreading and vigorous perennial is not only an ideal ground cover plant but also, thanks to its somewhat overhanging habit, a decorative hanging-basket plant.

Up to 40 cm	Late spring to early autumn	

Penstemon 'Alice Hindley' Beardtongue

Until the first frost, the large-leafed, bushy 'Alice Hindley', with its numerous, tall, erect flower panicles, provides the garden with radiant, enchanting blooms. It neatly extends its foxglove-like, lilac-coloured, bell-shaped flowers, with their white throats, horizontally. The beardtongue is an extremely rewarding flowerbed perennial, which loves a rich in nutrients and very well-drained soil. Since the beardtongue is not very frost-hardy, it needs winter protection with brushwood. Support with stakes where plant is insufficiently sturdy.

Up to 90 cm | High summer to autumn

Penstemon 'Beckford' Beardtongue

'Beckford' has large, cream-coloured, bell-shaped flowers with a delicate rose tint. The beardtongue hybrids are among the finest end-of-summer flowering perennials. In order to obtain as long a flowering period as possible, the beardtongue's flower stalks should be removed completely after flowering. They can be used for compost or winter protection. The lifespan of beardtongue hybrids is generally only short, but they can easily be propagated by taking tip cuttings. Fertile, very well-drained soil in sun or partial shade.

50–90 cm | High summer to autumn

Up to 60 cm | High summer to autumn

Penstemon 'Sour Grapes' Beardtongue

The metallic sheen of its elongated bell-shaped flowers, in blue grey with a strong hint of purple, makes 'Sour Grapes' a colourful, eye-catching highlight in the perennial flowerbed. 'Sour Grapes' blossoms most happily in a very well-drained soil rich in nutrients.

Phlomis russeliana
Sticky Jerusalem sage

Tall-growing, hairy *P. russeliana* is one of the most valuable flowering perennials, displaying its decorative qualities throughout the year. The large, pastel yellow, labiale flowers occur from late spring onwards in dense whorls arranged neatly in layers around the sturdy stem. These develop into bizarre fruit clusters which stay in place throughout the winter and make a particularly beautiful sight when covered in hoar frost. The foliage is reminiscent of sage: elongated, oval, mid-green, slightly felty leaves. This robust, heavily-flowering wild perennial is, moreover, long lived and easy to look after. It tolerates sunny or semi-shaded positions and also copes well on dry, well-drained, fertile soils. The sticky Jerusalem sage looks very attractive planted in groups in the perennial flowerbed or on the edge of woodland. Popular with bees.

Up to 90 cm | Late spring to early autumn

▶ *Phlox adsurgens*
'Wagon Wheels'
Northern phlox

From late spring onwards, this creeping, semi-evergreen perennial produces a large number of salmon-pink, light-centred flowers which are deeply incised like wagon wheels. Wonderful in rock gardens or slope plantings. Prefers partial shade.

Up to 30 cm | Up to 30 cm | Late spring to early summer

Phlox Flame flower, phlox

Up to 20 cm | Late spring to early summer

◀ *Phlox douglasii* **'Boothman's Variety'**
Douglas phlox

This small, compact cushion plant has pretty, needle-like leaves and during the flowering period is covered with rose-violet flowers with dark centres. For rock gardens or edging beds. Likes sun or partial shade.

From spring right through to autumn, the various representatives of the *Phlox* family, with their luxuriant and sometimes also wonderfully fragrant blooms, immerse the garden in a colourful sea of flowers. While the flat individual flowers appear delicate, even fragile, their exhilarating abundance transforms them into an impressive, eye-catching sight.

Phlox reaches heights ranging from 5 to 140 centimetres. An appropriate plant can therefore be found for every use, as an impressive feature plant, as a decorative accessory in a flowerbed, as an addition to the rock garden or as a pretty ground cover plant.

Up to 60 cm | Late spring to early summer

◀ *Phlox maculata* **'Natasha'**
Wild sweetwilliam, meadow phlox

The cheerful, bicoloured flowers in rose pink and white are arranged on long, upright, slightly conically-shaped panicles. Ideal for cut flowers. This showy perennial belongs in the summer perennial bed. Tolerates sun and partial shade.

60–80 cm | Late spring to early summer

◀ *Phlox maculata* **'Reine de Jour'**
Wild sweetwilliam, meadow phlox

'Reine de Jour', with its cream-white flowers and mauve-rose eyes, feels happiest in sun or partial shade. This variety is extremely sturdy.

The *Phlox* species mentioned need a deep and moist but well-drained soil – for *P. subulata*, moderately dry – with an ample supply of nutrients and, depending on the species concerned, sun or partial shade. *Phlox* must be watered adequately in dry conditions. In the case of the tall species, remove shoots after flowering in order to prevent them setting seed.

▶ *Phlox paniculata* **'Blue Paradise'**
Autumn phlox

P. paniculata is one of the most impressive representatives of the flame flower. 'Blue Paradise' produces blue flowers with dark centres and is without doubt one of the most beautiful of the blue varieties. The disk-shaped flowers form a dense dome.

| | 70–100 cm | | Summer to early autumn | | |

◀ *Phlox paniculata* **'Utopia'** Autumn phlox

'Utopia', a delicate rose-coloured variety, reaches a truly impressive height. It will tolerate sun and partial shade.

| | Up to 1.5 m | | Summer to early autumn | | |

| | Up to 20 cm | | Early summer | | |

▶ *Phlox stolonifera* **'Home Fires'** Creeping phlox

With its stolons, the creeping phlox grows rapidly to form a mat. It is an enchanting ground cover plant for semi-shaded sites such as woodland edges. To accompany the long, slender, dark green leaves, 'Home Fires' produces masses of dark purple flowers in early summer.

Phlox subulata **'Candy Stripes'**
Moss phlox

This cushion-forming *Phlox* is a talented all-rounder. It rapidly forms dense carpets without becoming rampant, and it is therefore an excellent ground cover plant. It is an easy-care, evergreen plant that tolerates sun or light partial shade. Its unique white-rose colour combination gives it the appearance of a delicious candy.

| | Up to 20 cm | | Late spring to early summer | | |

	60–75 cm		Up to 90 cm		High summer		Autumn				

Physalis alkekengi var. franchetii
Strawberry groundcherry

Anyone fortunate enough to have a strawberry groundcherry plant in their garden will be provided with a most beautiful show in the autumn. The rather inconspicuous cream flowers of this very vigorous perennial develop in the autumn into berries which are enveloped by vividly-glowing, lantern-like red calyces. It is inclined to spread rapidly in soils rich in nutrients and in doing so can sometimes overwhelm neighbouring plants. Regular thinning out is therefore recommended.

Physostegia virginiana 'Summer Snow' Obedient plant

Mid-summer sees the start of the 'Summer Snow' show. It is then that this industrious late-summer flowerer displays its elegant, funnel-shaped white flowers, tightly packed on upright, pointed spikes. As if hanging on hinges, they can be turned to face any direction without breaking. This delicate, free-flowering plant not only produces good cut flowers but is also a valuable companion plant for borders and flowerbeds. In places with harsh winters, it should be covered with a light winter protection of brushwood. Likes moist, nutrient- and humus-rich soils.

	Up to 1.2m		High summer to early autumn			

Platycodon grandiflorus Balloon flower

When it first appears, *P. grandiflorus* is not very large and rather delicate in stature. However, what distinguishes it, as its botanical name suggests, are its fascinating, wide-open, brilliantly blue, bell-shaped flowers, in which a clearly visible, beautifully decorative network of veins stands out. The large-flowered balloon flower is a little gem, which without question has earned its place in the rock garden or the border. The flower buds of this stocky perennial, which puff up like small balloons, are also delightful. It likes a relatively moist, well-drained soil which should be rich in nutrients.

	Up to 60 cm		High to late summer					

Up to 90 cm | Late spring

Polygonatum multiflorum Solomon's seal

This undemanding and impact-providing woodland perennial is the ideal choice for the woodland garden. The curved stems of Solomon's seal arch gently to one side. Three to five tubular white flowers, each with a small green tip, emerge in late spring from the axils of the lily-like leaves, and these are followed by spherical berries. A moist, open, preferably chalky soil and some water during dry periods are *P. multiflorum*'s only requirements.

Up to 90 cm | Spring to late summer

‎lemonium 'Sonia's Bluebell'

‎cob's ladder

‎is the elongated, pinnate foliage, which ‎s a ladder-like appearance, that has ‎ven the genus *Polemonium* the name ‎cob's ladder. The pretty flowering ‎rennial 'Sonia's Bluebell' forms rosettes ‎m which upright shoots with cup-‎aped, scented blue flower panicles, ‎nich are much loved by bees, rise in ‎rly spring. The somewhat short-lived ‎rennial is extremely undemanding, needs ‎well-drained, moist soil and should be ‎equately watered during dry periods. A ‎onderful plant for the wildflower garden.

45–60 cm | 60–90 cm | Early summer to early autumn

Potentilla nepalensis 'Ron McBeath' Pink cinquefoil

In a sunny location – no great demands are made in terms of the soil – the striking, cheerful, richly rose-coloured, cup-shaped flowers of 'Ron McBeath' will continue to appear all summer long. The red shoots of this loosely growing perennial bear five-fingered, mid-green leaves, which are reminiscent of those of strawberry plants. However, they are not related. Most suitable for areas of open land or light woodland edges or for planting in a flowerbed.

◀ **Primula bulleyana** Candelabra primrose

This exceedingly striking, semi-evergreen candelabra primrose, with up to seven tiers, opens its whorled flowers from bottom to top. The flowers are initially red orange, but later fade to a warm yellow tone. Likes semi-shaded, moist, slightly acid soils.

Up to 60 cm		Summer			

Primula Auricula, primrose, cowslip

◀ **Primula denticulata** Drumstick primrose

The spherical, violet flower umbels of the drumstick primrose, whose flower stems can grow up to 30 centimetres high above the leaf rosettes, are truly enchanting. The drumstick primroses prefer a semi-shaded site with moist humus soil.

Up to 45 cm		Mid-spring to summer		

Up to 25 cm		Late spring to early summer		

Up to 30 cm		Spring to summer		

▲ **Primula elatior** Oxlip

P. elatior, also known as the oxlip, bears umbels of two to twelve yellow flowers on upright stems. Likes moist, humus-rich soil. Semi-evergreen.

◀ **Primula farinosa** Birdeye primrose

The lilac-coloured flower umbels of *P. farinosa* are covered with a white 'flour', hence the botanical name. Prefers moist, slightly acidic, humus soil.

Everyone knows the small, pretty *Primula* hybrids which, with their vivid, brightly-coloured show of flowers, herald the start of spring very early in the year. The word 'primula' does after all come from the word for 'first'. Besides these popular, mainly cushion-forming, classics, there are also a large number of other *Primula* species which bloom in a truly astounding variety of forms: in layers, umbels, globes, and even in elongated spikes.

Most of the species love semi-shaded positions, but some will also tolerate sun, provided that the soil is adequately moist, as *Primulas* appreciate a moist, cool site. For this reason, care must be taken to ensure that the soil is kept constantly moist without causing waterlogging. A little fertiliser in the spring will promote flowering. In places with very harsh weather conditions, a protective blanket of spruce branches or a fairly thick layer of foliage will help with overwintering. The diversity of forms means that they can be used in different ways: as woodland-edge or water-edge plantings, in beds and rock gardens, or even as pot plants.

◀ *Primula florindae* Giant cowslip

The scented, sulphur-yellow flowers of this large primula species stand tall. Moist, humus soil in sun or partial shade.

Up to 1.2 m | Summer

▶ *Primula japonica* Japanese primrose

Rising from the pale green leaf rosette are conspicuously large flowerheads containing flat, purple to white flowers. This robust plant likes nutritious, humus soil retaining moisture, in a sunny to semi-shaded position.

Up to 45 cm | Late spring to early summer

Primula 'Schneekissen' Juliae group

The evergreen variety 'Schneekissen' grows up to 20 centimetres wide and can thus almost be used as a ground cover plant. Bears wonderful pure white flowers with a yellow eye. Moist, humus-rich soil in sun or partial shade.

8–10 cm | Spring

Primula × pubescens

The flowers of this evergreen *Auricula* hybrid, which are slightly old-fashioned looking but have extremely pretty markings, last for a long time and form an attractive eye-catching feature in the rock garden. Moist, humus-rich soil in sun or partial shade.

Up to 15 cm | Spring

Primula Auricula, primrose, cowslip

▶ **Primula pulverulenta** Candelabra primrose

The tubular red-purple flowers are enthroned high up on their sturdy, white farina-coated flower stems, making them easy for everyone to see. They have a darker eye at the centre. Humus-rich, moist, slightly acidic soil.

Up to 1 m | Late spring to early summer

Up to 25 cm | Mid- to late spring

◀ **Primula veris** Cowslip primrose

Some of this plant's earlier common names refer to keys, reflecting the fact that its flower umbel resembles a bunch of keys. This perennial flowering plant bears scented, dark yellow flowers. Moist, humus-rich, slightly acidic soil.

Primula vialii Poker primrose

This unique primula species differs markedly from its relatives. Its small red flower buds are held on a pointed spike. When they open, they are a radiant purple violet. Unfortunately, the plant is short-lived. Partial shade.

30–60 cm   Summer

Up to 20 cm   Spring

◄ *Primula vulgaris* 'Miss Indigo'
English primrose

The fantastic, deep purple, double flowers of this cushion primrose are adorned with a discreet cream-coloured edge. 'Miss Indigo' blooms and blooms and blooms.

Prunella grandiflora 'Carminea' Large selfheal

This plant's most significant characteristic includes its outstanding quality as a totally easy-going ground cover plant. It will soon cover borders, rock gardens, or entire areas of open ground with its hardy mats. Pretty, purple-rose, labiate flowers massed on compact spikes appear in summer. The large selfheal needs no tending at all and is also resistant to drought.

Up to 25 cm | 1 m and more | Summer

Pulmonaria angustifolia Blue lungwort

The lungwort likes it shady, rich in nutrients, and moist, making it a really good candidate for areas of the garden, such as woodland edges, that are spurned by other flowering perennials. With its pretty, long, dark green foliage, *P. angustifolia* is a very appealing ground cover plant which also spreads well by means of its rhizomes. The masses of delicate, rich blue flowers which appear early in the year in small clusters above the leaves are really delightful. No special care is required.

25–30 cm | Up to 45 cm | Early to late spring

Pulmonaria saccharata Bethlehem lungwort

The funnel-shaped, red-violet, or white flowers of the Bethlehem lungwort, which is characterised by decorative white flecks on the mid-green foliage, emerge even earlier than those of *P. angustifolia*. It is best suited for plantings in light shade and for semi-natural plantings or for greening up shaded areas in front of walls. It prefers fresh to moist sites on well-drained, humus soils rich in nutrients.

Up to 30 cm | Late winter to late spring

Pulsatilla vulgaris European pasqueflower

Its splendid violet flower, with radiantly yellow stamens, seems somehow much too large for this striking small plant. This flower, together with its finely pinnate, light green foliage and conspicuous feathery seedhead, definitely makes *P. vulgaris* one of the most beautiful perennials for the rock or alpine garden. Leaves and buds are covered in silvery hairs. No dominant plants should be positioned close to it, as the pasqueflower does not tolerate competition well. Its other requirement is a very well-drained, sandy, poor soil. **Take care:** all parts of the plant are strongly poisonous.

10–20 cm | Early spring

| Up to 1.2 m | Up to 75 cm | High to late summer | | | | |

Rodgersia pinnata 'Superba'

Featherleaf Rodgersia

This impressive showy foliage species, with large, pinnate, glossy green, and heavily-veined leaves, which are purple-coloured when they first shoot, is an extremely beautiful ornamental foliage perennial for the woodland edge. From mid-summer onward, the reddish-green buds of 'Superba' bear up to 70 centimetres long panicles packed with star-shaped, bright rose-coloured flowers. They should be grown in deep, fertile, moist soil. Water profusely in dry periods.

| Up to 60 cm | Late summer to autumn | | | | | |

| Up to 10 cm | Late spring to early autumn | | | |

odohypoxis baurii

is pretty, small perennial from South rica has very hairy, narrow, strap-like aves and in addition produces reddish-nk, star-shaped flowers on short individual ems. For rock gardens or tubs. Protect om wetness in winter.

Rudbeckia fulgida var. *sullivantii* 'Goldsturm' Orange coneflower

When the summer has passed its zenith, the coneflower comes into its prime. Then, the bushy-habited variety 'Goldsturm', which has wonderful large golden-yellow flowers and a domed black-brown eye, attracts the last rays of the sun, week after week. This magnificent free-flowering perennial likes a moist, well-drained and fertile soil. Remove faded flowerheads.

1.6–2 m | High summer to early autumn

Rudbeckia nitida 'Herbstsonne'
Shiny coneflower

This variety is regarded as very wind-resistant, which in a plant that reaches up to 2 metres in height is not an insignificant plus factor. As well as its turned-back, light yellow radial flowers, the fruiting heads are also attractive, and these can still be very decorative in winter, with their bright, conical button-heads coated with hoar frost. *R. nitida* is particularly happy as a specimen perennial in a border. It can be planted alone, or in small groups with perennials of equal merit, such as autumn asters, salvias, or ornamental grasses.

Up to 50 cm | Summer to autumn

Salvia nemorosa 'Blauhügel' Perennial sage

Not only is sage a popular and effective medicinal plant and herb, but this genus also includes robust, scented ornamental perennials which are suitable for summer flowerbeds and cottage gardens. 'Blauhügel' has pure blue flower clusters, which are much visited by bees during the flowering period. This strongly branching, upright plant has elongated, rough, mid-green leaves. Makes a dream combination with oriental poppies, evening primroses, coneflowers, or even roses. Needs fertile, well-drained, moderately dry soils in a warm, sunny spot. Cut right down after flowering, then it will flower for a second time.

Up to 60 cm | Up to 60 cm | High to late summer

Sanguisorba obtusa Japanese burnet

The bottlebrush-like flower spikes, covered in tiny, feathery, pink flowers, look really odd. These unusual flowerheads, borne on wiry, upright shoots, form a highlight in the summer border. Besides the flowers, this perennial, known as Japanese burnet or Japanese bottlebrush, has grey-green, pinnate leaves up to 40 centimetres long. Suitable for sunny to semi-shaded positions. Ideal for moist, humus soils.

nguisorba officinalis 'Tanna'

ficial burnet

e oval, glowing brownish-red 'cones',
d high on branching stems, appear in
uriant quantities the whole summer long.
anna', a robust plant with a refreshing
pearance, brings a loose structure to
tland meadows and wildflower gardens.
ry suitable for naturalising, and also as
ut flower.

Saponaria ocymoides Rock soapwort

In the summer, the rock soapwort can finally begin to spread out
its cushions in the rock garden or on slopes. Over the years, it will
form long-lasting, flat carpets, which during the flowering period are
covered with a cloud of small, cute, pink, star-shaped flowers. This
undemanding, vigorously-spreading cushion plant thrives in dry to
fresh, preferably lime-rich, soils in sunny positions. To preserve this
plant's compact form, it can be cut back after flowering.

| Up to 15 cm | Up to 20 cm | ❀❀ | Summer to early autumn | ❄❄❄ | 🐟 | 🪣 |

Saxifraga aizoides Yellow mountain saxifrage

The yellow mountain saxifrage has evergreen, fleshy, shiny, dark green leaves. These are joined in summer by small, orange, star-shaped flowers. A valuable addition to any rock garden. Likes moist, but well-drained, humus ground.

Saxifraga × arendsii Mossy saxifrage

Path edges, steps, rock gardens, or lightly-shaded borders are the preferred terrain of the mossy saxifrage. There, this flat, evergreen cushion plant can find its niche and spread itself out comfortably, like moss. Mossy saxifrages appear in the spring, with masses of white, pink, red, or even yellow flowers, and transform their surroundings into a huge floral carpet. *S. × arendsii* likes a site in partial shade best, with well-drained, humus soil.

| 5–20 cm | ❀❀ | Mid- to late spring | ❄❄❄ | 🐟 | 🪣 |

Scabiosa caucasica **'Clive Greaves'** Caucasian pincushion flower

Sun worshipers like the magnificent, lavender-blue 'Clive Greaves' definitely belong in the best position in the herbaceous border or in cottage gardens or informal gardens. Its graceful, scented flowerheads stand on finely haired stems with few branches. They attract bees and butterflies to the garden and make excellent cut flowers. This showy perennial likes well-drained soil rich in nutrients. The flowering period can be prolonged by cutting back the stems after the flowers have faded.

Up to 60 cm

High to late summer

Sedum 'Herbstfreude'

Telephium hybrid

The glowing colours of the large, dark red flowerheads of 'Herbstfreude', which turn a subdued copper red, are very impressive. This upright, tall-growing variety has fleshy, dark green, waxy leaves.

| Up to 60 cm | Late summer to early autumn | | | |

Sedum Stonecrop

◀ *Sedum* 'Matrona' Matrona stonecrop

With its dark, grey-green leaves, wine-red stems, and soft pink flowers, 'Matrona' is a late-summer highlight in the garden. Its striking fruiting heads remain attractive even in winter.

The innumerable species of *Sedum*, with their attractive, fleshy leaves, provide a great diversity of forms and structures. The taller-growing ones, with their voluptuous flower umbels, provide attractive, eye-catching features in late summer borders, while the shorter-growing varieties develop into dense carpets of flowers.

The *Sedum* genus belongs to the succulents. These dry-loving plants use their thickened leaves as a water reservoir and are thus well prepared to survive in dry locations. Moderately rich in nutrients, sandy soils, from which water drains away quickly, are ideal for them, preferably in full sun. Otherwise, these perennials are very easy to look after and modest in their requirements.

| 40–70 cm | Late summer to early autumn | | | |

▲ *Sedum* 'Strawberries and Cream'

As befits its name, this tall variety displays small, red- and cream-coloured flowers, carried in dense flowerheads above the purple-tinged foliage.

◀ *Sedum acre* Goldmoss stonecrop

The evergreen, fleshy leaves form small mats, on which star-shaped, yellow-green flowers tumble in the summer.

The low-growing species fit well into rock gardens, crevices in walls, or paving cracks, and are also suitable for green roofs. The tall *Sedum* species will fit into any herbaceous border, in dry areas around walls or in the rock garden.

| 45–60 cm | Late summer to early autumn | | |

| Up to 5 cm | Up to 60 cm | Summer | |

▶ *Sedum album* White stonecrop

The white-flowering, evergreen *S. album*, also known as white stonecrop, is excellently well suited for greening-up large areas rapidly. Tends to naturalise.

| 10–25 cm | ✿✿ | High to late summer | ❋❋❋ |

◀ *Sedum reflexum* Jenny's stonecrop

In summer, the pendent buds of *S. reflexum* open into upright, yellow flowers. It forms evergreen carpets with a spread of up to 60 centimetres.

| Up to 10 cm | ✿✿ | Summer | ❋❋❋ | ✦ |

▶ *Sedum spectabile* Showy stonecrop

Its star-shaped, pink flowers attract large numbers of bees. The showy stonecrop – its relatives, too, are outstandingly showy – prefers sites in full sun with a dry soil. The upright stems bear fleshy, grey-green foliage.

| Up to 45 cm | ✿✿ | Late summer | ❋❋❋ | ✦ |

| Up to 15 cm | ✿✿ | High to late summer | ❋❋❋ |

Sedum spurium 'Fuldaglut' Tworow stonecrop

'Fuldaglut', an attractive, evergreen, ground cover plant, is one of the red-leafed varieties of *S. spurium*. In summer, it displays bold, carmine-red star-shaped flowers. Will tolerate sun or partial shade. Prefers dry, nutrient-poor soils.

| 45–60 cm | ✿✿ | Late summer to early autumn | ❋❋❋ |

Sedum telephium subsp. *maximum* 'Atropurpureum' Witch's moneybags

'Atropurpureum' is an unusual variety: it has dark purple foliage and in late summer bears pretty, pink flowers with an orange-red centre. Likes sunny positions.

Sempervivum tectorum Common houseleek

This primeval succulent, with its attractive rosettes of fleshy leaves, is particularly decorative in extreme locations such as crevices in rocks, roofs, cracks in walls, rock gardens, and troughs. It combines happily with *Sedum*. Its spectacular, evergreen charm is enhanced in summer by the addition of pretty, purple-red flowers, which appear on hairy stalks. *S. tectorum*, known popularly as the houseleek, likes warm, even hot, dry sites. No additional care is necessary.

Up to 15 cm | Up to 50 cm | Summer

Silene chalcedonica
Maltese cross, Jerusalem cross

Maltese cross, with its star-shaped flowers arranged in a flat umbel, brings a thrilling, temperamental, scarlet red to the garden. Red stands for burning passion and adds bold accents of colour. This strong colour is particularly effective next to white, yellow, or blue flowering perennials in a sunny border or in a cottage garden with a fresh, rich in nutrients soil. This tall-growing plant needs supporting to prevent it from flopping. If cut back hard, it will flower again in the autumn.

90–120 cm | Early to high summer

Up to 20 cm | Early summer to early autumn

Sisyrinchium 'Californian Skies'
Blue-eyed grass

'Californian Skies' provides lively contrast in the rock garden or gravel garden, with its delicate flowers in a mix of sky-blue shades and its open, grass-like foliage. This long-flowering plant prefers a poor but moist soil in a sunny position.

Up to 30 cm | Early spring

Soldanella montana Alpine snowbell

The lavender-blue, bell-shaped flowers, with their lightly fringed edges, nod charmingly from the tops of their rigidly upright stems, softly enveloped by kidney-shaped, evergreen foliage. This beguiling plant is the rising star of the rock garden and will thrive only on an extremely well-drained, moist, humus-rich soil in full sun. In warm regions it can tolerate a little partial shade.

Up to 75 cm | Late summer to early autumn

Solidago 'Goldenmosa' Goldenrod

In late summer, 'Goldenmosa' provides one more golden-yellow flower spectacle in the garden. This stocky wild perennial is ideally suited to the wildflower garden or a sunny border. It will also tolerate semi-shaded positions, but the flowers will be less vigorous and luxuriant. In terms of soil, goldenrod is not demanding: a straightforward, well-drained soil is all it needs. Remove faded flower stalks.

Up to 90 cm | Early to high summer

yrinchium striatum
ow-eyed grass

ow-eyed grass has numerous panicles
masses of creamy-white flowers, with
purple-brown stripes, and long, iris-
leaves. This long-flowering plant likes a
ny location with well-drained soil.

Stachys byzantina Wooly hedgenettle

This wonderfully old-fashioned wild perennial, with its fine, silver-grey, furry foliage, will form dense, light-coloured carpets wherever relatively small open sites with well-drained, moderately fertile subsoil need covering. In early summer, hairy stems thrust up from the rosettes of leaves and produce woolly, pink-purple flowers. This undemanding, attractive ornamental foliage plant has many uses – in front of trees and shrubs, on banks, in the cottage garden or herbaceous bed, and as a reliable ground cover plant that is not too invasive.

| Up to 45 cm | Up to 60 cm | Early summer to early autumn | | | | |

Strelitzia reginae Bird-of-paradise flower

The bizarre, beak-like orange, yellow, blue flowers of *S. reginae* are reminiscent of the heads of exotic birds, which is where it got its common name, the bird-of-paradise flower. It is not just the flowers that are decorative, but also the blue-green, long-stemmed, oval leaves, elongated towards the tips. This extremely attractive and easy-going exotic – in cold regions traditionally grown as a pot plant – can spend the summer outside. However, as temperatures below 50°F (10°C) should be avoided, it needs to overwinter in a protected, cool and bright spot.

| Up to 2 m | Winter to spring | | | |

Symphytum grandiflorum syn. S. ibericum 'Hidcote Blue'
Comfrey

The incredibly vigorous, rather coarse-looking wild perennial *S. grandiflorum* is a good ground cover plant for areas of the garden where other plants find it hard to cope: humus, rich in nutrients, shady borders or beneath trees which don't let much light through. 'Hidcote Blue' has attractive, veined foliage and beautiful, tubular, pale blue flowers, which open from red buds in the spring.

| Up to 45 cm | Mid- to late spring | | | |

Up to 80 cm | Late spring to high summer

Tellima grandiflora Bigflower tellima

The restrained beauty of this shade-loving perennial is apparent only at second glance. From the late spring, long clusters develop, on which hang numerous delicate, small, greenish-white flower bells. The pretty, heart-shaped, scalloped foliage, bearing hairs on the underside, is evergreen. This woodland plant fits in well beneath trees and shrubs or as ground cover in borders. It likes a damp soil, but will also tolerate dryness. Tends to self-seed.

30–40 cm | Early summer to early autumn

Teucrium hircanicum Caucasian germander

In early summer, the tall-growing, veronica-like Caucasian germander develops large, very attractive reddish-pink flower panicles, which are very popular with bees and bumblebees and are also good used as cut flowers. It has beautiful, finely-toothed, mid-green foliage. All in all, a highly individual addition to rock gardens or herb gardens. Spreads by means of runners. Likes well-drained soils.

Up to 60 cm | Early summer

acetum coccineum syn. rysanthemum coccineum mes Kelway' Pyrethrum daisy

e scarlet-red flowerheads, with their spicuous, radiantly yellow centres, look though they have been painted. With its ly pinnate foliage, this upright, evergreen ennial is a real asset to any border and o makes a wonderful cut flower. Select unny location for it, with well-drained . **Take care:** contact with skin may cause tation.

Up to 90 cm | Early summer

Thalictrum aquilegifolium 'Purpureum'
Columbine meadow rue

The overall effect produced by tall-growing *T. aquilegifolium* is one of delicate slenderness: the delicately slender stems bear finely pinnate, columbine-like leaves. The fluffy, airy, lilac-coloured flowers seem to float like clouds on tall stems above the blue-green foliage. The beautiful columbine meadow rue likes damp, cool summers, so it is perfect for moist, shady, and sheltered spots in semi-natural gardens as well as for lower plantings between shrubs and trees. In the right site, it can grow very old and will need no further tending.

Thalictrum flavum subsp. *glaucum* syn. *T. speciosissimum*
Yellow meadow rue

The soft, creamy-yellow flower-balls form a highly unusual contrast to the blue-green, glaucous foliage. The cheerful, fluffy flower clusters of this upright perennial bring brightness to dark areas of the garden. A totally reliable and robust cultivar for background plantings in shaded borders, wild gardens, and woodland areas. Likes damp, well-drained ground.

Up to 1 m | Summer

10–30 cm | Up to 30 cm | Mid- to late spring

Tiarella cordifolia Foamflower

In spring, the heart-shaped foliage is covered with clusters of creamy-white flowers. *T. cordifolia* combines several agreeable and practical attributes which make it a valued garden perennial. This shade-loving plant is not only free flowering and undemanding, it also turns out to be genuinely early flowering. Its creeping habit makes it a valuable ground cover plant, whose foliage turns a highly decorative bronze red in the autumn. Is happy in open, moist, humus soil.

Trollius asiaticus Asian globeflower

The tall-growing *T. asiaticus* is really at home in a lightly shaded spot in a wetland meadow, at the edge of woodland or a pond, or in a bog garden. Filamentary-divided leaflets peep out like little brushes from the centres of the splayed orange-yellow petals. The palmate, dark green foliage dies back shortly after flowering. This moisture-loving perennial is very undemanding. After flowering, the shoots should be cut back, then it will flower again.

Up to 70 cm · Late spring

Up to 75 cm · Early to mid-spring

40–60 cm · 45–60 cm · Early summer to early autumn

adescantia 'Purple Dome' ndersoniana group) Spiderwort

th its long, narrow leaves arching eways from its heavily-branching stalks, urple Dome' looks a bit like a reed. In rly summer, flat flowers, in an amazing ectric purple, appear in the leaf axils. ese pretty flowers only last for a short ne, but are continually replaced. In mixed rders, perhaps together with grasses, or the water's edge, this cultivar makes a ntastic eye-catching feature. Likes moist, h in nutrients soils.

Uvularia grandiflora Large-flowered bellwort

Wherever a shady spot needs brightening up with a splash of yellow, the delicately slender woodland plant *U. grandiflora* is an obvious choice. This is a rewarding plant, which flowers continuously in the spring. The soil should contain plenty of humus and be fertile and moist. Otherwise, it makes few demands and spreads rapidly if it is happy with its location. Beneath trees or rhododendrons – together with *Viola*, anemones, small ferns, or *Trillium* – it can show off its vividly radiant flower bells to really good effect. It should be planted in the autumn. Can be propagated by division of the rhizomes after flowering.

Up to 2 m — High summer to early autumn

Verbena bonariensis syn. *V. patagonica*

This South American plant has really quite special charms: its lavender-pink flowerheads, on their long, rough stems which branch like antennae, bloom the whole summer long and make for a relaxed atmosphere in the herbaceous border. Verbenas prefer a humus, well-drained soil in full sun. In areas where there is a risk of frost, it should be protected in winter with a layer of mulch.

Veronica teucrium 'Shirley Blue'

Broadleaf speedwell, Hungarian speedwell

Low-growing 'Shirley Blue', with its numerous flower spikes in a breathtaking, radiant blue shows up well from a distance and thus makes a marvellous focal point in the garden. Broadleaf speedwell's sturdy flower stalks, which can be up to 25 centimetres tall, and its beautifully-shaped grey-green, deeply-serrated leaves make it excellently well-suited for the edge of a sunny herbaceous border or rock garden. Its radiant blue colour works particularly brilliantly when planted immediately alongside yellow flowers such as evening primroses or tickseeds. Prefers a poor, well-drained soil.

Up to 25 cm — Late spring to early summer

Up to 1.5 m — High summer to early autumn

Veronicastrum virginicum syn. *Veronica virginica* Culver's root

From mid-summer onwards, Culver's root sends up from its leaf axils numerous rigidly upright, slender flower spikes in elegant white, delicate pink, or magical blue. It is one of the tallest of the veronica-like speedwells and, thanks to its height, creates a truly magnificent impression in the herbaceous border. *V. virginicum* likes a humus-rich, moist, but well-drained soil in full sun or partial shade.

Viola 'Etain' Violet

The aristocratic, prettily-shaped flowers of 'Etain' are creamy yellow with a purple-blue edging and a yellow eye. This cultivar has a compact habit and flowers continuously.

| Up to 20 cm | ✿✿ | Spring to autumn | ❋❋❋ | 🝢 |

Viola Pansy, violet

Tempting shades of violet blue from really pale to deep and dark. To these can be added purple, glowing yellow, elegant cream, pure white, and orange. Bicoloured, even tricoloured flowerheads. Expressive faces or very simple shades of colour. Stripes, speckles, and edgings. Any combination seems feasible.

Most violas like positions in light to partial shade – and it is often only here that they develop in their full glory – as well as a fertile, slightly humus, well-drained soil which retains some moisture. The main flowering periods are generally in the spring and autumn. However, it is impossible to persuade these unorthodox plants to stop flowering outside these usual periods as well if they feel like it, indefatigable perpetual flowerers that they are.

Their uses are as diverse as their looks. Whether they are used outside in the rock garden, in a sheltered window-box, against a dark woodland background, or as an industrious ground-covering plant, members of the *Viola* family will always do their job perfectly. Often evergreen and fragrant.

Viola 'Jackanapes'

Beautiful but short lived, 'Jackanapes' is a classic. Its small flowers are purple violet around the top, while the lower three petals shine out a golden yellow. Evergreen.

Up to 20 cm | Spring to summer

Viola Pansy, Violet

Up to 20 cm | Spring to autumn

▶ *Viola cornuta* hybrid

With their enchanting wildflower charm and numerous colours and combinations, these hybrids of the cute horned violet bring a long-awaited breath of spring. These small-flowered representatives of the *Viola* genus are very robust, long-flowering plants, which appreciate cool, bright locations. Many varieties have an intense fragrance. Evergreen.

◀ *Viola* 'Rebecca' Violetta hybrid

'Rebecca' is an out-and-out beauty. The scented, cream-coloured flowers have delicate violet markings on the slightly wavy edges. Long flowering period. Creeping perennial.

Up to 15 cm | Spring to autumn

▲ *Viola* 'Roscastle Black'

The velvety, purple-black blooms, with their pale, white-yellow eyes, seem to look right through you.

15–25 cm | Spring to autumn

◀ *Viola odorata* Sweet violet

With its small, blue or white flowers and a seductively sweet scent, the evergreen *V. odorata* is a harbinger of spring. Forms a marvellous scented carpet. Evergreen.

| Up to 20 cm | | Late winter to early spring | |

▶ *Viola riviniana* Wood violet, dog violet

The semi-evergreen, cluster-forming wood violet is the ideal variety for shady areas in wildflower gardens. It has very natural-looking, pale blue-violet flowers.

| 10–20 cm | 20–40 cm | | Late spring to early summer | | | |

Viola tricolour

Johnny-jump-up

The very pretty flower-heads of *Viola tricolour* display a fresh colour mix of purple, lavender blue, white, and yellow. The lower petals generally have dark streaks. Evergreen, short-lived perennial. Self-seeds.

| 8–12 cm | | Spring to autumn | | |

Waldsteinia geoides

This valuable wild perennial is a robust, evergreen ground cover plant, which forms clumps and therefore does not run wild. A shade-lover, *W. geoides* is the ideal underplanting for perennials, shrubs, or trees. Once its strawberry-like, evergreen leaves have formed a dense cover, they do not let any weeds through. In late spring, it produces a cheerful mass of small, yellow flowers, followed by brilliant red berries. As a woodland plant, it needs an open, humus, moderately rich in nutrients soil. Will also tolerate dry soils.

Up to 20 cm | Late spring

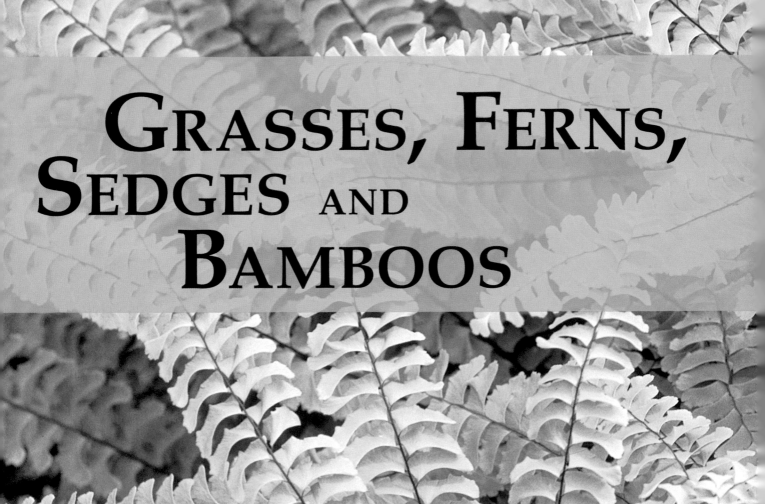

GRASSES, FERNS, SEDGES AND BAMBOOS

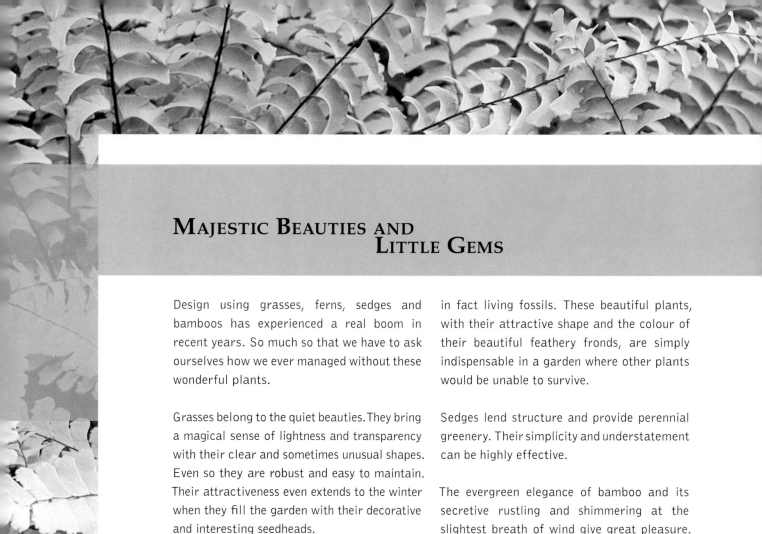

Majestic Beauties and Little Gems

Design using grasses, ferns, sedges and bamboos has experienced a real boom in recent years. So much so that we have to ask ourselves how we ever managed without these wonderful plants.

Grasses belong to the quiet beauties. They bring a magical sense of lightness and transparency with their clear and sometimes unusual shapes. Even so they are robust and easy to maintain. Their attractiveness even extends to the winter when they fill the garden with their decorative and interesting seedheads.

Ferns are ideal for shady gardens and are the most ancient of all plant life: they are in fact living fossils. These beautiful plants, with their attractive shape and the colour of their beautiful feathery fronds, are simply indispensable in a garden where other plants would be unable to survive.

Sedges lend structure and provide perennial greenery. Their simplicity and understatement can be highly effective.

The evergreen elegance of bamboo and its secretive rustling and shimmering at the slightest breath of wind give great pleasure. Despite its movement, it has a calming influence in the garden. Added to that it has superb screening quality.

 30–40 cm

Adiantum pedatum
Five-fingered maidenhair fern,
American maidenhair fern

A. pedatum derives its graceful filigreed charm from its delicate, finely-textured, divided foliage. Its tender, light green fronds turn a beautiful ochre colour in autumn. Old brown foliage should not be cut back until early spring so that it can protect the plant over winter. This fern prefers a cool shady location with high humidity and moist but well-drained soil moderately rich in nutrients. It thrives when grown under trees or ornamental shrubs but can also be used as a pretty complement to higher-growing ferns, grasses, or herbaceous perennials. Propagate it by division in spring or from spores. **Tip:** suitable as ground cover. Plant about six to eight per square metre.

1.5–3 m · Late summer to autumn

Arundo donax 'Versicolor'
Variegated giant reed

The imposing, white-striped giant reed brings a touch of tropical charm to the garden. Planted alone or in a small group, it will enhance larger perennial borders or pond edges. It is important to plant it in a sunny and warm location protected from wind. A plant that is suitable for most types of soil as long as it is moist. Water plentifully and in spring cut back a few inches. Due to frost tenderness, it is best kept in tubs or containers in cool climates. Should be kept frost-free in winter. Only expect it to bloom in warm climates.

Asplenium scolopendrium Hart's tongue fern

This is surely one of the most beautiful ferns in the garden. This low-growing species is striking for its brilliantly green, undivided evergreen fronds that can grow up to 40 centimetres long and resemble tongues. Typically for a woodland plant, it prefers partial shade. The soil should be humic, moist, well drained, and alkaline. It is at its most beautiful and effective when planted in woodland borders or on its own among shrubs. During wet winters it has a tendency to suffer from rust. If this occurs, all that is needed is to remove the fronds with brown patches. Otherwise it is very easy to maintain and can be propagated by division or from spores.

45–70 cm

Asplenium trichomanes
Maidenhair spleenwort

Small but striking, this rock-loving fern is worthy of any garden. Its evergreen or semi-evergreen fronds are made up of opposite pairs of divided leaflets and grow to a length of 10 to 20 centimetres. A low-growing species, it is ideally suited to growing in walls, rock gardens, or containers. It has a more luxuriant effect planted in small groups than planted on its own. It thrives best in moist, humus, alkaline soil in semi-shade. Requires little maintenance and is long-lasting. This applies in general to all ferns.

10–20 cm

20–50 cm

Blechnum spicant Deer fern

This is an extremely reliable and versatile fern that produces slender dark green fronds. The evergreen fronds associate well with woodland herbaceous perennials, heathers, clumps of grasses, and bulbous plant varieties such as *Leucojum vernum* and *Erythronium*. This plant is in its element in acid, moist, and humus-rich soil in shady areas. It should be sheltered from winds and winter sun to prevent drying out. For this reason it is recommended that, from late autumn, a mulch of foliage and brushwood should protect it. Propagate in spring by division of the rhizome runners or from spores.

50–60 cm   High summer to early autumn

20–120 cm

ayrium filix-femina Common lady fern

deciduous fern with two- to three-times-
ided fronds. Should be protected from
d and planted in shady areas. It needs
ist, fertile soil, neutral to acid, enriched
h compost. Goes well with hellebores,
ges, and rhododendrons.

Bouteloua gracilis Blue grama

The cheerful protruding flowerheads, at right angles to their delicate stems, have a curious appearance of small flying brushes. This unusual plant looks dramatic in a rock garden or at the front of a border. A clump-forming durable grass that loves full sun, and fresh to dry well-drained ground, rich in nutrients. It is essential to protect it in winter in harsh climates. Cut back in early spring before new growth appears. Propagate in spring by division.

Briza maxima Big quaking grass

Pendulous yellowish-gold flower spikes on slender, straight stems bring a touch of light movement to the garden as soon as the lightest of breeze touches this delicate grass. This tufted annual does best in full sun and well-drained soil. It needs very little care; even occasional drought does it no harm. It looks just as good in rock gardens or herbaceous perennial borders as it does in open spaces in wild gardens. **Tip:** the large egg-shaped flowerheads look lovely in dried flower arrangements; even fresh growth gives a very distinctive look to floral decorations.

40–60 cm   Spring to late summer

Calamagrostis × acutiflora 'Karl Förster'
Feather reed grass

This masterpiece of a grass with its richly-blooming, feathery-flowering panicles is a wonderful eye-catcher when planted in borders between low shrubs and perennials. It is also the ideal choice for planting in open spaces in wild gardens. 'Karl Förster' is absolutely beautiful in the autumn when its blossoms and stems take on a warm ruddy to tan glow. This striking grass makes an attractive guest in the garden until long into winter. Wait till spring to cut back the flowering stems, as they remain extremely decorative, otherwise further maintenance is unnecessary. This luxuriant grass prefers sun or light shade with moist, humus-rich soil. Propagate this generous all-rounder in spring by division. Grows in compact clumps so it is unlikely to spread. **Tip:** the flowers last well in dried arrangements.

120–180 cm   Spring to summer

▶ *Carex comans* 'Bronze Form'
Bronze sedge

This evergreen perennial has bronze-chocolate foliage that looks like a mop of tousled hair. It does well in moist earth, in sun or partial shade.

25–35 cm   High to late summer

Carex Sedge

60–90 cm   Early to high summer

90–110 cm   Late spring to early summer

◀ *Carex dipsacea* Green sedge

Ideally suited for water gardens. Arching bronze-green foliage. Can be planted in sun or partial shade.

50–70 cm   Late spring to early summer

▲ *Carex elata* 'Aurea'
Bowles' golden sedge, tufted sedge

Golden-yellow foliage with narrow green margins that is just right for brightening dark corners of the garden. This deciduous perennial needs fertile boggy soil.

◀ *Carex flagellifera* Weeping brown sedge

This sedge is almost identical to *C. comans* but is markedly taller and has broader foliage. An evergreen perennial that tolerates sun or partial shade and moist soil.

Sedges make their home in the damp dark corners of the garden, where other grasses are not keen to establish themselves. Many varieties of this species-rich genus prefer shady locations and moist or even wet soil that, depending on the species, may be more or less fertile.

The charm of these grass-like perennials lies in the shape of their foliage – long, slender, softly-arching leaves as well as their colour and patterns. Some produce stunning flowers such as *C. greyi* or *C. pendula*. The different species are suitable for almost all uses in the garden, whether as specimens or in groups, under trees, by water, or in perennial borders.

Once they are established the *Carex* species mentioned here need no special care. The deciduous species should be cut back in spring and the evergreens should have old foliage removed in summer. Sedges should be propagated in spring by division.

▶ *Carex greyi*

Grey's sedge, mace sedge

A deciduous perennial that is most notable for its star-shaped prickly seedheads, which appear after flowering. Plant it in sun or partial shade in a moist to boggy location.

50–75 cm	Summer	

50–75 cm	Early to late summer	

▲ *Carex muskingumensis* 'Oehme'

Variegated palm sedge

Green foliage with yellow stripes along the margins. A robust deciduous perennial that is easy to cultivate. Plant in moist to wet soil in sun or partial shade.

Carex pendula

Drooping sedge, hanging sedge

Evergreen *C. pendula* can be used as a decorative design element. Its numerous decorative, drooping flower spikes are charming. It likes fertile, moist to boggy soil in sun or partial shade, making it ideal for planting by the pond.

100–140 cm	Late spring to early summer	

80–100 cm / Late summer to early autumn

Chasmanthium latifolium
Northern sea oats, Indian woodoats

This tufted, bright green, broad-leafed ornamental grass is highly effective for its attractive inflorescence. The pretty, flat, nodding flower spikes on their long panicles emerge green, turning to bronze later in the season. A dense long-lasting tussock grass that tolerates sunny to relatively shady locations, which gives it a fairly wide range of planting options – from herbaceous borders, to rock gardens, to open planting spaces. The soil should be moist, well-drained, and fertile. Cut back in late winter. Propagate by division or allow to self-seed.

Cortaderia selloana Pampas grass

C. selloana is one of those striking and imposing plants that quickly puts other pretenders into the shade when it makes its entrance. For this reason, the giant is frequently used as a specimen plant; it decorates lawns, ponds, or seating areas with its long bushy fronds. Its silvery-white to delicate pink flowering plumes appear to light up in full sun. The soil should be deep and nutrient-rich, moister in summer than in winter. It requires attention as well as admiration; in late autumn tie together the lush foliage and protect over winter with either a mulch of brushwood or a strong foil cover. In harsh climates planting in tubs is advisable. In spring, divide the clumps and plant them directly into the garden or tubs. Cut back the brown growth in late winter or spring. **Take care:** mind the sharp leaf edges.

2.5–3 m / Late summer

Cyperus eragrostis Tall flatsedge

This rough-leafed cyperus grass grows in loosely-bunched, dense tussocks. Its pretty yellowish-green clusters of spikes that emerge from mid-summer onward resemble fine extended upside-down umbrellas and are especially distinctive. *C. eragrostis* tolerates most soils, but they should be moist. This plant is very sensitive to frost and can only be kept outside long term in frost-free zones. Alternatively it can be kept in a conservatory or greenhouse.

60–90 cm / High summer to early autumn

1.2–1.5 m   Early to late summer

Deschampsia cespitosa Tufted hair grass

D. cespitosa is a delicate but striking grass. In summer its shimmering panicles of silvery flowers shoot up from the dense ornamental evergreen grass that has stiff mid-green leaves, giving the grassy hummocks below the impression of being considerably taller. Tufted hair grass is most effective when planted against a dark background so that the airy flowerheads stand out as a light contrast. However, they can also brighten up marshy spots and perennial borders. It loves deep, humus soil rich in nutrients and moist, but better still, wet earth. Cut back and tidy up in spring to make space for new leaf growth. Does well when divided in spring. **Tip:** this grass is a real good looker in winter when the leaves are glazed with frost. Flowerheads can be left over winter, as the tan colouring still looks great.

1–2 m   High summer to early autumn

yperus papyrus Papyrus

vacious, slender, brush-like heads of
liage sit on top of a long weighty stem.
apyrus is the classic marsh-loving plant
d thrives in moist soil close to the water's
ge. It is frost tender as is *C. eragrostis*.
his plant was used in ancient Egypt to
ake paper.

Dicksonia antarctica
Tasmanian tree fern

2–4 m

This fascinating exotic's tree-like shape and striking foliage make a real impact. Long pale green fronds, which can grow up to 3 metres long in the right conditions, sprout from its trunk-like stem, which can grow up to 60 centimetres wide. It requires humus-rich, acid soil in partial shade or shade. In hot dry weather the stem must be watered daily. The stem and fronds should be well covered in winter. Any brown fronds should be removed in spring. *D. antarctica* is a slow-growing specimen plant.

40–80 cm

Dryopteris erythrosora
Japanese shield fern

Surely this must be one of the most beautiful of all ferns in the garden. The flat outstretched new fronds emerge a startling copper-red colour that later fades to a glossy dark green. In milder zones this species may even keep its green fronds over winter. This fern is suitable for planting in borders or as a specimen and likes moist, loose, nutrient-rich soils in light shade, protected from wind. Divide the mature plants in autumn or spring. **Tip:** in winter, protect the base with foliage from direct winter sunlight and cold drying winds so that it does not dry out. A favourite foliage for use in fresh arrangements.

Dryopteris filix-mas Male fern

D. filix-mas is like a relic from another geological era, strange and fascinating at the same time. This deciduous vigorously growing fern forms powerful rhizomes; therefore, it has a tendency to run wild. It will flourish tirelessly for decades in moist shady borders, beneath trees, or by water and in return requires very little care – a little tidying-up in spring or watering in dry periods and it will be completely satisfied. It will spread if left alone; however, planned propagation can be done by division in spring or early autumn and also by spores. D. filix-mas was once widely used in folk medicine as a cure for worms. However, as it frequently caused poisoning, its medicinal use came to an end.

60–100 cm

Up to 4 m

Fargesia murieliae syn. Sinarundinaria murieliae, Thamnocalamus spathaceus
Umbrella bamboo

Three characteristics make this plant the ideal bamboo for the garden: its year-round, light, evergreen foliage, its hardiness, and its bushy growth. It has a distinctive umbrella-shaped crown with culms that change colour from pale green to powdery white when growing and eventually mature to yellow. It prefers sunny and partially shady positions in fertile water-retaining soil and is ideal as a privacy screen or windbreak.

80–100 cm | Early to high summer

Festuca mairei Atlas fescue

Atlas fescue is an evergreen grass with slender grey-green arching leaves. In summer, airy sprays of flowering panicles soar above the foliage. It is an undemanding plant that tolerates most soils. Cover lightly in winter to give protection.

20–30 cm | Early to high summer

stuca glauca Blue fescue

ue fescue's striking steel-blue slender liage can compete with that of any other ass species. Its small blue tufts are ideal r creating interesting colour contrast. e tolerant nature of this grass should not overlooked either; it withstands drought tremely well and will quickly form long-sting ground cover on poor soil. It looks od partnered with heathers or rock rden plants and is suitable as edging ong borders. The main requirement is that should be planted in a sunny location. In mmer, panicles emerge with violet-tinted ue-grey spikes. To maintain colour and owing power, divide every two to three ars in spring.

5–15 cm | Early to high summer

Festuca scoparia 'Pic Carlit' Bearskin fescue

This miniature version of the bearskin fescue forms an almost perfect moss-like, grass-green carpet. An ideal plant for rock gardens.

60–90 cm · High to late summer

Glyceria maxima 'Variegata'

Variegated manna grass, reed manna grass,
reed sweet grass

Ideal for planting in any problematic damp soils
or for use in garden pond design. 'Variegata'
is striking for its attractively coloured foliage
– its slender leaves are tinted pink in spring,
turning to green and white stripes later in the
season. In summer, green flowering panicles
emerge atop a reed-like stem. Use a planting
basket placed directly into the ground for this
vigorous grower, as it can run wild. Generous
and frequent watering is required during dry
periods. Can be divided in spring.

Hakonechloa macra Hakone grass

The inviting, almost round tufts of this native Japanese grass are
reminiscent of comfortable wide cushions. It is one of the prettiest
grasses suited to partial shade and will brighten up any dark corner
of the garden with its light green softly arching leaves. It can also
be planted in sunny locations if well watered. Its flowers are not
particularly bold; however, in autumn the green leaves of summer take
on a delightful orange to russet-brown tint. The leaves survive into
winter and often keep their colour. It needs nutrient-rich soil enriched
with organic material. Old foliage should be cut back in autumn or
winter. Propagate by division in spring. An attractive ornamental
grass for containers.

30–50 cm · Late summer to mid-autumn

Helictotrichon sempervirens

Blue oat grass

In-rolled grey-blue stems of blue oat grass
seem to spread to all sides like rays of
sunlight. In early summer, delicate purple
spikelets emerge, nodding gracefully, soaring
high above the dense foliage below. This grass
is a real classic in rock gardens or terraces,
either grown as a specimen or, as a contrast,
partnered with silver-leafed plants. It likes
limy, well-drained, humus-rich soil and a
sunny location. Cut back old and withered
foliage in spring.

1–1.4 m · Early to high summer

1–1.5 m

Indocalamus tessellatus Large-leafed bamboo

An evergreen low-growing broad-leafed bamboo, especially suited to deep-shaded areas in the garden, terraces, or courtyards. It needs fresh, fertile soil and the restraint of a container, as the rhizomes are invasive. In harsher zones it should be covered with a substantial protective mulch of foliage in winter.

20–40 cm   Early to high summer

Koeleria glauca Koeleria, large blue hair grass

This dense, blue-green, mound-shaped grass looks very effective in the light moderately nutrient-rich soils of a rock or heather garden. In summer, numerous closely-packed flowering panicles, which turn to a buff colour on fading, rise high above the low foliage. Remove the flowers in the autumn; otherwise no other care is required. Propagate by division from spring to early summer.

40–60 cm   Early to high summer

ordeum jubatum Foxtail barley

his pretty relative of cereal barley with silky, fluffy spikes gives a fresh green cent to the summer garden. In autumn, en the nodding panicles turn reddish to delicate shade of straw, they really do ok like fine shimmering hair. It is usually annual; however, in warmer regions can last several years. It will grow in ost soils but does like a sunny location. longer dry periods it should be watered gularly. Otherwise its outstanding feature its ability to survive and to spread ncontrollably by self-seeding. Do planned wing in spring or autumn in the chosen cation. If required for dried bunches, cut fore the flowers are fully mature.

20–30 cm   Late spring to late summer

Lagurus ovatus Hare's tail grass

This plant produces enchanting fluffy, round, creamy-white flower tufts that emerge from green foliage on delicate wiry stems. Its filigreed upright shape looks good either planted as a single specimen or in drifts and is especially appealing in summer beds or rock gardens. This annual needs little care apart from occasional watering. Sow in spring directly onto open ground or, in autumn, into containers. Ideally locate in a warm sunny spot with light sandy soil.

Matteuccia struthiopteris Ostrich fern

The striking fronds of this fern are almost archaic and especially curious in spring when the tight erect fronds with their furled tips sprout from the ground in abundance. Later in summer the smaller fertile fronds emerge from its centre. It can be invasive and will form whole colonies from its creeping rhizomes. Give it plenty of space to grow, as its size is impressive, and keep it under control as necessary. Ideal planted under trees or by water or as a stimulating contrast to flowering plants. It cannot tolerate prolonged dry periods so liberal watering is essential to protect it from withering. Otherwise give it plenty of compost in spring. Propagate in spring by division or from spores.

80–150 cm

90–150 cm   High summer to autumn

Miscanthus sinensis 'Kleine Fontäne'
Silver grass, Chinese silvergrass

A striking early-flowering variety with splendid reddish flower spikes early on, turning later to silvery white. They arch softly, fountain-like, above the plant in all directions, hence its name which means 'little fountain'. The slender, lightly-arching, blue-green foliage turns a tawny shade in autumn. Requires protection over winter with foliage in harsher zones. Cut back the foliage before new growth appears. It should be watered in dry periods and planted in nutrient-rich, moist, well-drained soil.

60–200 cm ❄ High summer to early autumn

Molinia caerulea subsp. *arundinacea* 'Karl Förster'
Purple moor grass

This tall ornamental grass looks stunning in summer with its lacy panicles growing on top of elegantly-arching stems. In autumn, it has a warm ochre-yellow hue that even outdoes its own spectacular summer appearance. 'Karl Förster' not only lights up any wild garden or pond edge with its spectacular structure and colour but also commands a dominant role in perennial borders. As its autumn colouring is so eye-catching, give it a location in the garden where it can really be enjoyed. Otherwise this plant is easy to maintain. Needing deep, humus-rich, damp soil, it should be watered well in prolonged dry periods.

50–60 cm

Onoclea sensibilis Sensitive fern

This deciduous fern with unusually deeply etched, almost triangular fronds is lovely to look at but tends to be invasive if planted in favourable locations. It is perfect for planting in small groups beneath shrubs such as rhododendrons, as it likes moist, humus, nutrient-rich, preferably acid soil. In harsher zones, newly sprouted fronds should be protected from late frosts in spring.

1.5–2 m ❄ Late summer to autumn

scanthus sinensis 'Roter Pfeil'
er grass, Chinese silvergrass

wers soar into the sky like arrowheads. iage turns a lovely ruddy colour in umn. Very attractive planted as a cimen in open spaces or near paths and ting areas. Plant this tall-growing grass ong ground cover for a great contrast.

`1.5–2 m` | Summer

Osmunda regalis
Royal fern, Flowering fern

Osamunda regalis must surely be one of the most beautiful of all ferns. Its outstanding feature is its spore-bearing fertile fronds that quickly turn orange brown, rising like sceptres above the green foliage below. In autumn the green fronds take on a luminous golden-yellow hue. Mature royal ferns need plenty of space – they can spread up to 4 metres wide – so they should preferably be planted to provide structure, for example, at pond edges or at the edge of woodland. It likes weakly acid, moist, humus-rich soil and should be watered well in dry periods. Propagation from spores takes time but division is not recommended.

Panicum virgatum 'Rehbraun' Switch grass

A classic among ornamental grasses with long, flat, blue-green, upright leaves, which turn a lovely shade of sienna in autumn, it really grabs the limelight. In mid-summer up to 50 centimetre long flowering panicles emerge, floating like a fine veil above the foliage. They look glorious in floral arrangements. Switch grass loves a warm location and fresh, well-drained, moderately fertile soil. Unique and versatile, switch grass – preferably planted in drifts – can be used in either heather gardens, perennial borders, or at the edge of woodland gardens. Wait until spring to cut back the growth and flowering panicles, as they remain decorative right into winter. Propagate from seed or by division.

`80–100 cm` | High summer to early autumn

Pennisetum alopecuroides 'Weserbergland'
Fountain grass, Chinese fountain grass

Fluffy slender flower spikes make this grass a real feast for the eyes in the late summer garden. The flaxen yellow, decorative blooms on their long stems dangle softly above formal, pointed, dark green foliage. This variety is suitable for planting in mixed late-flowering perennial borders in a sunny position with moist, well-drained, light soils. Old foliage can be left to spring before cutting down. A dry, thick, protective winter mulch of foliage and brushwood is essential in zones where there may be a risk of frost.

`50–80 cm` | High summer to autumn

Phalaris arundinacea var. *picta*
Reed canary grass, gardener's garters, ribbon grass

An exuberant grass, its reed-like, highly decorative, green and white striped leaves are anything but formal. To show the long-lasting beauty of its foliage colour to its best advantage, it should be planted in a sunny spot, as in darker locations the distinctive white markings on the leaves are less pronounced. This brightly coloured grass can be planted either as a specimen or in groups in boggy areas, at the edge of woodland or in semi-wild herbaceous perennial borders, where it will provide variety and catch the eye. Its robustness also makes it suited to more extreme gardening demands such as stabilising pond and stream banks. Consider using a soil barrier at the time of planting to contain the rhizomes that have an enormous urge to spread. If the leaf colour fades, it can be trimmed back to 20 centimetres above the ground and it will produce fresh foliage. Propagate by division in spring. The leaves look stunning in bouquets.

80–100 cm · Early to high summer

◀ *Phyllostachys aurea* 'Albovariegata'
Golden bamboo, fishpole bamboo

This is a colourful variety of 'aurea' with striped green and white variegation and greenish-yellow culms. It tolerates dry periods but is not sufficiently hardy for all locations. It should preferably be planted in milder zones.

3–5 m

Phyllostachys Phyllostachys

▼ *Phyllostachys bambusoides* 'Castillonis' Giant timber bamboo

'Castillonis' looks very handsome with its powerful golden-yellow to light orange culms that have green stripes when fully grown and can grow up to 4 centimetres in diameter. The leaves are a glossy green, occasionally lined with fine white stripes. It prefers mild to hot zones but well-established plants are hardy. Plant it as a specimen. Not really suitable for containers.

3–6 m

It is not only its delicate form – grooved, elegant, and attractively coloured culms and sleek leaves – that makes this medium-tall to tall bamboo species so extraordinarily popular, but also its many and varied options for use in the garden. These long-lasting evergreen bamboos have become an important element in garden design. They are always the right choice, whether used as a solitary stunner, planted as a hedge to provide a windbreak or privacy screen, or in containers and shrubberies. Phyllostachys belong to the genus of running bamboos; therefore, to prevent unlimited spreading, physical root barriers may be required, especially when planting hedges and in smaller gardens. Incidentally a bamboo culm grows to its full height within two months and when the shoots emerge from the ground, the culm has already achieved its final diameter – there will be no further growth. They prefer sun or partial shade and fertile, humus-rich, moist but well-drained soil. They will not tolerate waterlogged soil. Propagate by division in spring.

▶ *Phyllostachys bissetii*

A real jack-of-all-trades, this bamboo is the hardiest and most resilient of its genus and suited for harsh climatic zones. It grows masses of dense, shiny, dark green leaves. The culms are green early on but with age take on a light yellowish tone. *P. bissetii* is suitable for planting either as a specimen or is effective as a wind or privacy screen. It forms dense groves.

3–5 m *** ✳

4–7 m ✳

▲ *Phyllostachys nigra* Black bamboo

This bamboo has stunning dark, almost black culms. The vibrant green, dense, slender leaves keep their colour right through winter. It looks stunning as a specimen but can also be planted in groves. Grows vigorously in hot regions.

Phyllostachys vivax 'Aureocaulis'

With its buttery-yellow culms with random green stripes, 'Aureocaulis' grows very vigorously and can reach heights of up to 8 metres while the culms can be between 5 and 9 centimetres in diameter. It looks stunning grown as a specimen or in groups; however, it is less suitable than other bamboos for use as a privacy screen.

5–8 m *** ✳ 🥄

50–200 cm

Pleioblastus auricomus syn. *Arundinaria auricoma, P. viridistriatus*
Dwarf green stripe

This bamboo is very hardy but the leaves are only semi-evergreen. That said, its sulphur-yellow, green-striped leaves are a real highlight among dwarf bamboo varieties and it is perfect for brightening up shady areas of the garden. It looks especially impressive when planted against a background of evergreen trees, although the leaf colour really comes alive when planted in full sun. It has one further advantage in that it is less invasive than other bamboos of its species. Give it a good cut in spring to maintain its desired height.

Pleioblastus humilis var. *pumilus* Dwarf bamboo

This dwarf variety has slender culms with long, medium-broad leaves that are tinted light red when budding. It is the ideal plant for darker spots in the garden and is especially suited for ground cover or to be planted under trees. It can also be partnered with strong growing herbaceous perennials. A rhizome barrier should be constructed at the time of planting to prevent spreading, as it is an aggressive runner and can be very invasive. Dwarf bamboos prefer a location in humus-rich, fertile, moist but well-drained soil and should be planted out of the wind to prevent drying out. It will not tolerate waterlogged ground but it can withstand cutting and shaping. Propagate by division in spring.

50–120 cm

30–40 cm

Polypodium vulgare Common polypody

The unusually-structured evergreen fronds of the common polypody fulfill two gardening requirements at once: first, they offer a pleasing sight right into winter; second, their creeping growth keeps weeds down making it ideal ground cover. This fern flourishes wonderfully well in walls and crevices. The species also belongs to the few ferns that can tolerate sun and, to a certain degree, drought. It needs reasonably fertile, humus-rich, gravelly soil. Propagate by division in late summer.

1–1.2 m

Polystichum setiferum Soft shield fern

This fern has a truly elegant look; its twice-divided filigreed fronds setting it apart as a jewel of the garden. It really is magnificent and is perfect for planting as a majestic solitary specimen. Wherever it is planted – in rock gardens, in front of trees, or in perennial borders – this fern looks a real stunner. The pretty fronds will remain green right through winter in milder zones. The red to light brown scales on the midrib of the fronds make an attractive contrast to the matt green of the leaflets. With regular watering it can even tolerate a sunny position; however, if planted there, it requires a mulch of brushwood to protect the leaves from drying out in winter. This fern loves near neutral, humus-rich, fresh soil. Any decayed fronds should be removed before new growth occurs.

30–60 cm

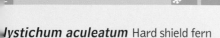

40–60 cm

Polystichum aculeatum Hard shield fern

is reliably evergreen fern looks narkably similar to its counterpart the *setiferum*; however, it is much smaller. It ociates beautifully with rhododendrons d evergreen grasses and likes stony, nus, evenly moist soil.

Polystichum tripteron Trifid holly fern

At first sight this medium-sized fern with its light green fronds does not particularly look as if it belongs to the shield ferns. Unlike most other ferns of the *Polystichum* species this one is not evergreen. It does well in dappled shade in humus, moist soil. Sensitive to sun and drought, it should be planted in a sheltered location to afford some protection from wind.

4–6 m

Pseudosasa japonica syn. Arundinaria japonica Arrow bamboo

This bamboo has very slender, upright, olive-green culms that grow in clumps. Compared with the culms, the leaves are relatively large and are distinctive for their rich, glossy, dark green colouration. They look majestic as solitary specimens or planted in groups and enjoy sheltered spots in moist, humus soil. Apply a thick layer of mulch for protection in winter. Arrow bamboo is liable to form dense thickets. **Tip:** cut back flowering plants right down to ground level and give plenty of mulch and compost.

Sasa tsuboiana

Regular, almost spherical growth and unusually large deep green leaves make *Sasa tsuboiana* a welcome guest in any garden. In addition, this dwarf bamboo species is an extremely robust grower. It will tolerate sunny or shady locations – anywhere where its sturdy, randomly-outstretched leaves can catch enough light. It will also tolerate most soil types; however, if it is planted in full sun, the ground should be moist. Plant in sheltered locations where it will not be dried out by the wind and where leaves will remain green right through winter. This dwarf species is suited for planting by water, on embankments, or even for low-hedge planting. Plant it into containers to prevent it getting out of hand. Propagate by division in spring.

1–1.5 m

Spartina pectinata 'Aureomarginata'
Prairie cord grass

A grass that has truly elegant architectural contours with its lightly arching, shiny green leaves striped with golden yellow at the margins. The whole ensemble is crowned with slender spikes that hang in long clusters when flowering. Its luminous tawny hues during autumn also promise to bring decorative accents to the garden. It enjoys boggy, nutrient-rich soils in sunny or lightly shaded locations; therefore, its ideal setting is by the pond or in wild gardens. Cut back in spring to just above ground level.

70–180 cm   High summer to early autumn

80–100 cm | Summer

Stipa calamagrostis Spear grass

A blue-green grass that shows its true qualities as a garden design element in summer when its feathery panicles with numerous creamy-yellow, shimmering flowerheads emerge. It brings a touch of graceful movement to rock gardens or perennial borders with its cheerfully swaying flowering plumes and is a great plant for softening and covering up any harsh landscaping lines in the garden. In autumn, its lustrous yellow colour remains enchanting. This deciduous, tufted ornamental grass grows, quite slowly, in sunny locations in well-drained soil moderately rich in nutrients. To display it at its best, *S. calamagrostis* needs plenty of space; therefore, neighbouring plants should not be planted in too close proximity. Otherwise, it is very easy to maintain. It can also tolerate longer dry periods. Cut back in early spring before new growth begins. Propagate by division in spring.

40–60 cm | Early to high summer

50–130 cm | High summer to early autumn

...pa brachytricha
...ean feather reed grass

...dely-branching, violet-red, shimmering ...wer panicles on upright stems give a ...nderfully decorative display right into ...ter. Vibrant green foliage turns a lovely ...de of bronze in autumn. Protect during ... winter months in colder locations.

Stipa tenuifolia Pheasant grass

In summer, this deciduous, wispy, pale green ornamental grass develops a real mass of blonde hair which sways gracefully to and fro at the slightest touch of breeze. It is well suited for sunny gravel gardens, or for planting at the edges of herbaceous perennial borders or even in containers. *S. tenuifolia* can also be used extensively for green roof planting. It tolerates dry, well-drained soil.

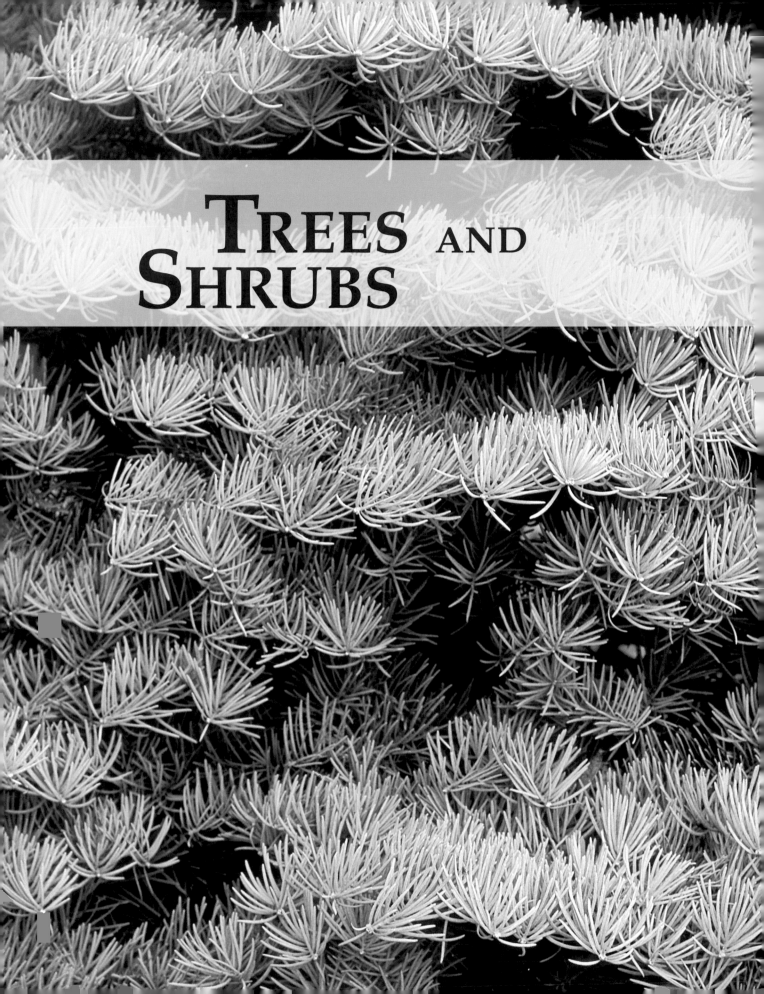

TREES AND SHRUBS

Anything but 'Wooden'

Trees and shrubs are the garden's framework. They create structure, define different spaces and are excellent either as specimen plants or simply as a green backdrop for the other main players. Summer-green deciduous trees and shrubs inspire with their varied repertoire, ranging from fresh leaf shoots through luxuriant blossoms and delicate fruit to blazing autumnal colours, giving the garden a new look for each season. Even the bare branches in winter can have a strikingly ornamental effect, letting the light in again. Conifers and evergreens provide fresh greenery throughout the year and reliably screen off anything unsightly. Apart from that, they spare the gardener the onerous task of sweeping up autumnen leaves. The growing habits of trees and shrubs must be considered when planning a garden. Planting should generally take place during the dormant period between autumn and mid-spring. The weather determines when the time is right. Frozen or very wet soil means that planting should be postponed. Trees and shrubs can undergo vegetative propagation with layering or cuttings or they can be grown from seed.

  50–100 cm   Late spring to early summer

Abies concolour 'Archer's Dwarf'
White fir

Abies concolour is not only an extremely handsome, but also a very elegant fir tree, although at heights of 20 to 25 metres, it is clearly too tall for most gardens. In fact, it is barely conceivable that such a pretty, practical, pocket-sized dwarf could be grown from a tree the height of a house, fitting effortlessly into any rockery. 'Archer's Dwarf' is a variety that grows round or cone-shaped with short, close-growing, slightly-hooked needles in a powdery bluish-green colour. Very slow growing, it prefers sunny but not hot sites (it will also tolerate partial shade) and fertile, moist, well-drained, mildly acid soils. The dwarf variety works best in rockeries or heather gardens, but also does well in containers.

10–15 cm | 8–12 cm | Late spring | Late summer

Acer campestre Hedge maple

In late summer the hedge maple's green flowers turn into pretty reddish-tinged keys, which remain attached to the branches for some time. The medium-sized tree with its oval crown is excellent for medium-height hedges, being tolerant of trimming, and can be planted to provide wind protection. It also offers a valuable nesting site for birds. *A. campestre* is very easy-going and happy in any soil. Trim two to three times annually when used as a formal hedge.

Acer negundo **'Kelly's Gold'** Golden box elder

This small maple is a truly shining jewel with its attractive golden-yellow spring foliage, which turns yellowish green in summer and recovers its delicate yellow hue in autumn just before the leaves autumn. The leaves are so thin that they can easily be composted in winter. The greenish-yellow flowers appear in pendent racemes and the tree bears bright yellow keys from early autumn. 'Kelly's Gold' changes in no time into a pretty shade tree. It is happy in any fertile, moist but well-drained soil. Water well in summer during the early years; it will tolerate some dryness later.

5–7 m | Early to mid-spring | Early autumn

Acer palmatum Japanese maple

The many varieties of *A. palmatum* offer a full range of wonderful autumnal colours, from bright yellow to crimson. The general rule is the sunnier the site, the more dazzling the colour of the foliage. This plant is also popular on account of its fine, lobate leaves. The delicate beauty needs a deep, loamy-sandy, mildly acid soil and should preferably be sheltered from winds. Winter protection is recommended in cold climates by spreading mulch over the roots and around the planting site. Because Japanese maples are very slow growing, they do well in containers during the early years.

Up to 8 m | Up to 10 m | Late spring | Late summer

| 2–4 m | Up to 2 m | Late spring to early summer |

Aloe arborescens Octopus plant, candelabra plant

In its native South Africa, *A. arborescens* is used, among other things, as a living fence. With its branched, tree-like growth and long, arched, fleshy, greyish-green leaves with their sharp, toothed margins, this evergreen succulent creates an impenetrable wall. The striking red flowers appear on stems up to 1 metre long. *A. arborescens* has health-promoting properties and the jam-like liquid from its leaves helps heal small cuts and abrasions. This beautiful plant with its medicinal properties is very frugal, preferring fertile, well-drained soil and easily tolerating dry spells. However, the accepted minimum temperature is around 50°F (10°C), which means it has to be grown in containers in areas at risk from frost.

| Up to 10 m | Up to 12 m | Mid-spring | Late summer |

Amelanchier lamarckii Snowy mespilus

Snowy mespilus is said to have a special treat in store for every season. In spring, bronze-coloured leaves unfold. As soon as they are in danger of turning a commonplace green, a whole host of glorious, white racemes appears, raising the plant's profile once again. The bluish-black fruit of late summer are not only decorative, but can also be eaten and are ideal for making jams and juices. The final crowning glory of this all-rounder is its magnificent blaze of yellowish-red autumnal colours. Even in winter, its fine, ornamental shoots will impress the onlooker. *A. lamarckii* is also a good bee pasture. The fruit are very popular with birdlife.

| Up to 2 m | Late spring | Late summer |

cer palmatum var. *dissectum*
panese maple

e dwarf tree has truly earned a rticularly outstanding position as a ecimen plant. The leaves of this variety e especially deep-cut, giving them an even er appearance.

| | Up to 5 m | | Up to 5 m | | Late summer to early autumn | | Autumn | | | | |

Aralia elata 'Variegata'
Japanese angelica tree

The mildly exotic, sweeping *A. elata* is certainly a tree for the larger garden, growing almost as wide as it is tall. The less vigorous 'Variegata' is characterised by the pretty, irregular, creamy-white margin of its leaves, which turn an orangey purple in autumn. The small, white flowers hang in long umbels from late summer, before ripening into round, black fruit. The plant needs a fertile, well-drained site sheltered from winds. Shoots with single-coloured foliage should be removed.

Berberis julianae Wintergreen barberry

The bushy *B. julianae* is characterised by two major performances a year. From late spring it produces clusters of soft, yellow flowers, which are succeeded by pretty, bluish-black glaucous berries in the autumn. Its large-leafed, shiny dark green, almost leathery foliage is evergreen, except for the odd area of yellowish red in the autumn. However attractive it may look, though, the plant has very definite defense mechanisms. Armed with up to 4 centimetre long thorns, it creates an impenetrable barrier, which is why barberries are, as a rule, particularly popular and suitable for use as hedges. But keeping one thing out protects another, which is why barberries are traditional bird sanctuaries. The flowers produce pollen and nectar for bees and other insects. For its part, *B. julianae* has modest needs – shelter from winds, partial shade, little frost, and a simple, well-drained soil suffice. If it is not growing freely, the plant can quite happily undergo radical renewal pruning. **Take care:** contact with the thorns may lead to skin irritations. Do not ingest any plant parts from ornamental varieties. Barberry jam is only made using berries from the *B. vulgaris*.

| | 3–4 m | | Late spring to early summer | | Autumn | | | |

| | Up to 3 m | | Spring | | Autumn | | | | | |

Berberis × stenophylla 'Crawley Gem'
Narrow-leafed barberry

The clustered racemes of deep yellow flowers of the evergreen 'Crawley Gem' give way in autumn to a whole sea of spherical, blue, glaucous fruit. This is also a good, reliable hedge plant, as well as being a magnificent addition to the shrubbery. Same conditions as for *B. julianae*.

Brugmansia suaveolens Scented angels' trumpets

To make absolutely sure that all eyes are on them, scented angels' trumpets have a tendency to overstate. Apart from the plant's noble stature, large leaves, and enormous white, sometimes yellow or pink, trumpet-shaped flowers with neatly reflexed lobes, it also comes with an intense evening scent. So much tropical elegance undoubtedly needs a worthy position where it can be appreciated to full effect, as well as a sheltered, cool, bright spot, to survive cold winters. It loves sun and moist, fertile soil. **Take care:** all parts of this beguiling beauty are extremely poisonous.

Up to 5 m | 2.5–3 m | Early summer to autumn

Up to 1.5 m | Mid-spring | Autumn

Berberis thunbergii 'Rose Glow'
Thunberg's barberry

The deciduous shrub 'Rose Glow' is a delightful sight with its crimson foliage decoratively marbled with white. It bears yellow flowers in spring and red berries in autumn. It is easy-going and a good choice for hedging. It tolerates sun and partial shade.

⚘ Up to 4 m	⅄ Up to 4 m	✿✿ Early summer	❄❄❄ ✦ ☕ ◗

Buddleja alternifolia Weeping butterfly bush

This pretty, deciduous shrub or, depending on its stature, small tree produces clusters of fragrant, lilac flowers that cascade down from the branches of the previous year's growth in early summer. It should only be lightly pruned, to keep its shape. If cut back hard, it will only flower again in the second year. The tree makes an ideal specimen plant. Location requirements as for *B. davidii* hybrids.

Buddleja davidii 'Fascinating'
Butterfly bush

This plant owes its name to the magnetic attraction it presents to butterflies. Its wide, fragrant, purple panicles attract them by the dozen. 'Fascinating' panicles grow to a magnificent length of 30 to 60 centimetres. Butterfly bushes are always eye-catchers, irrespective of whether they are planted individually or in groups. Being such a magnet to butterflies naturally makes the plant particularly nice to have close to terraces or sitting areas. The sweeping, deciduous shrub prefers to stand resplendent in a warm, sunny, protected position. On the other hand, it will be content with normal, well-drained soil, which may be dry and infertile. The shoots die back slightly in winter and should be cut back hard to a third or quarter in early spring. Cutting back also promotes flower growth, since *B. davidii* flowers on annual growth.

⚘ 2–3 m	✿✿ High summer to autumn	❄❄❄ ✦ ◗

⚘ Up to 1.5 m	✿✿ High summer to autumn	❄❄❄ ✦ ☕ ◗

Buddleja davidii 'White Ball'
Butterfly bush

The broadly compact, wide-branched but low-growing stature with hairy, silvery leaves is the special feature of 'White Ball', which produces an abundant display of panicles of white flowers from high summer. This beautiful dwarf plant is also a good choice for cultivating in pots on balconies or roof gardens.

Buxus sempervirens

European box, common box

The *Buxus sempervirens* takes its time and needs many years to grow into a handsome shrub. It is worth the wait, though, because the evergreen European box is one of the most versatile, well-loved garden plants around. One of its most popular features is its small, egg-shaped, leathery leaves and its adaptability, because it can easily be clipped into any artificial shape or size desired. Although its yellowish, sometimes greenish, clusters of small fragrant flowers are fairly inconspicuous, they still attract swarms of insects. Thanks to its tolerance of clipping, it can be used multifariously in both formal and natural planting – either as a hedge or to edge a bed, as evergreen background planting for roses and shrubs or as a figurative artistic shape standing alone for striking effect. Also worth mentioning is its tremendous adaptability to different positions, provided the soil is rich in humus and well drained. **Take care:** all plant parts, particularly the bark and leaves, are extremely poisonous.

Up to 5 m	Up to 5 m	Mid- to late spring	!

Callistemon citrinus Crimson bottlebrush

This shrub takes its name from its profusion of spectacular, blazing, crimson-red flowers. Apart from its blossom – the second blossom in late summer is not quite as lavish – the tough, evergreen leaves add to its beauty. It is happy in full sun and moist, well-drained, moderately fertile soil. It is only suitable for gardens in frost-free regions and can be cultivated to some extent as a container plant.

1.5–8 m	1.5–8 m	Late spring and late summer

| 15–25 cm | Up to 55 cm | Late autumn |

Calluna vulgaris 'Peter Sparkes'
Heather, ling

A tall, upright plant with long racemes of double, rose-pink flowers, 'Peter Sparkes' enhances any heather garden. It is a good idea to combine it with varieties of *C. Vulgaris* in different colours, such as white, lilac, or red. The low-growing species of evergreen shrub loves sites in full sun to partial shade with well-drained, acid, fresh to dry soil. 'Peter Sparkes' is an ideal choice as a cut flower. Remove the previous year's flower panicles and cut back any excessively long shoots.

Camellia 'Barbara Clark' Camellia, tea shrub

Camellias – enchanting exotics. These evergreen shrubs from East Asia are truly adorable with their stunningly unique flowers. Yet behind all the beauty is hidden a somewhat sensitive soul, because the enjoyment of its magnificent blooms requires a degree of finesse. What is certain is that the position and temperature must be right. Partial shade is ideal. It should be sufficiently moist and, where possible, sheltered from cold winds and burning morning sun, particularly after a frosty night, as both these things will damage buds. The optimum conditions are warm, bright summers, alternating with cool, but frost-free winters. If these basic requirements are not met, there will be fewer flowers or even none at all. The plant likes moderately acid, well-drained soil rich in humus. One of these captivating plant divas is 'Barbara Clark', a semi-double camellia with an exquisite pale pink flower forming a wide pyramid shape.

| Up to 2 m | Early to mid-spring |

Camellia japonica 'Mark Alan'
Common camellia

The claret-red, semi-double to anemone-form variety with its upright growth produces large flowers with narrow petals. A long flowerer. During periods of frost, cover the root area with a thick layer of leaf mold and if possible construct a thatch of conifer branches around the plant. This camellia should not be planted out in the garden until it is at least four years old. The best planting time is spring. Do not plant too deep; the root ball should only have a light covering of soil.

| Up to 2.5 m | Early spring |

Up to 4 m | Mid- to late spring

Camellia × williamsii 'Joan Trehane'

The fairy-tale beauty 'Joan Trehane' looks almost like a rose, with its rose-pink, rose-form flowers. The vigorous, upright-growing camellia has the same needs as other plants of its genus. Cut back slightly in early summer after flowering, prune and fertilise.

10–25 cm | Up to 20 m | Early spring | Early autumn

Carpinus betulus Common hornbeam

C. betulus is often used as a classic hedging plant, producing fresh, green foliage in spring and summer and bright, golden-yellow foliage from autumn on, providing a good screen. Some of the leaves shrivel up and remain on the branches throughout the winter until the new growth comes in spring, thereby showing a constantly changing face during the course of the year. The greenish-yellow catkins are fairly inconspicuous, but the yellowish-brown, nut-like seedheads are more striking. Hedges grown from *C. betulus* are extremely popular nesting sites with birds. The plant will tolerate very hard pruning, if necessary, in mid- to late summer. Easy-going and robust, the plant will be happy with almost any type of soils, although sites with deep, humus soils are best.

1.8–2 m | Mid- to late spring

mellia japonica 'Takanini'
mmon camellia

wonderful long flowerer. Another claret-
, anemone-form species whose flowers
n a bluish colour in time. Ideal for hedges
border planting.

Caryopteris × clandonensis 'Heavenly Blue' Verbenaceae

You can't fail to be attracted to this delicate, deciduous shrub with its mass of tiny, feathery, blue flowers that appear in late summer. In cool contrast to these are the grey-green, silver-haired leaves. 'Heavenly Blue' prefers light, moderately fertile, well-drained soils, including chalk, in full sun. In cold regions with cool summers, it is best to choose a site close to a sheltered wall. Otherwise, this elegant, upright-growing little shrub can also be an excellent addition to a shrubbery. Cut back the previous year's shoots in early spring to encourage flowering.

| | Up to 1 m | | Up to 1.5 m | | Late summer to autumn | | | |

Catalpa bignonioides Indian bean tree

The exotic, wide-spreading bean tree, which only produces its broad, heart-shaped leaves in late spring, is anything but commonplace. Its display of up to 20 centimetres long panicles of full, bell-shaped, white flowers is nothing short of lavish. Scarcely has flowering come to an end than the next highlight follows on its heels – the long, eye-catching, bean-like seedpods. A tree that offers so many interesting displays has truly earned its place as a specimen plant. Best suited to a sunny site, sheltered from winds, with moist, fertile, well-drained soil. In young plants, the trunk should be protected from hard frosts with a thick layer of mulch.

| | Up to 15 m | | Up to 15 m | | High to late summer | | | |

Ceanothus 'Pin Cushion' Californian lilac

Anyone with a penchant for blue flowers will find it impossible to pass by this 'Pin Cushion'. The rounded, evergreen shrub with its dark green, elliptical leaves is immersed in a sea of soft, mid- to light blue flower panicles in late spring. All it requires is a position in full sun within the shrubbery or a sheltered site against a wall, coupled with fertile, well-drained soil. Trim back lightly in spring to retain its shape. Protect against frost with an extra-thick layer of dry leaf mould.

| | Up to 2 m | | Up to 2 m | | Late spring | | | |

Up to 1.5 m | Up to 1.5 m

Cedrus deodara 'Golden Horizon' Deodar cedar

C. deodara normally grows into a handsome, impressive tree measuring up to 40 metres tall, but is then only really suitable for large gardens. Lucky, then, that there are also compact, slow-growing dwarf varieties, which are suitable for small gardens, rockeries, or troughs. 'Golden Horizon' is one of these attractive miniatures, which produces yellow or yellowish-green needles on the sunny side, while it is more bluish green in the shade. Its growth is wide spreading, reaching around 1.5 metres in both height and width. It likes sandy, humus, well-drained soils in a sunny position, but should be protected from the winter sun, as extremely sunny sites can lead to scorching. The plant should also be protected against harsh, exposed locations.

Up to 10 m | Up to 10 m | Mid- to late spring

Cercis siliquastrum Judas tree

The most beautiful feature of the wide-spreading *C. siliquastrum* is its clusters of vibrant, magenta to pink flowers, which grow on the trunk and older branches. Shortly after or during flowering, the pretty, heart-shaped, yellow-green leaves emerge, which turn golden yellow in the autumn. *C. siliquastrum* will thrive in a sunny, sheltered site in well-drained, chalky soil. Its growth is most impressive if left untrimmed. The young plant is tender, so plant in a sheltered spot.

Up to 1.5 m | High summer to autumn

...eanothus × *pallidus* 'Marie Simon'
...alifornian lilac hybrid

...he bushy, deciduous shrub 'Marie Simon' ...th its oval, toothed leaves produces pale ...owers in panicles. Cut back right up to the ...ain branches in spring. Provide light frost ...otection in the first year.

Chaenomeles japonica 'Cido'
Japanese quince

'Cido' is also referred to as Nordic lemon, not just because of the colour and shape of its fruit, but above all their exceptionally high vitamin C content and culinary value. The fruit can be used to make jam and juice, although they are unpalatable raw. The special feature of the deciduous 'Cido' is that it is a non-spiny cultivar. Single, orange flowers appear in spring – a real bee meadow – followed by yellow fruit the size of apples in autumn. The plant is also extremely robust. It needs fertile, moderately limy soils in sun or partial shade.

| Up to 1.5 m | Up to 2 m | Late spring to early summer | Autumn | | | |

Chaenomeles × superba 'Pink Lady' Ornamental quince

This upright, spiny, deciduous shrub produces its beautiful, dark pink flowers early in the year which are followed by large, yellow fruit in the autumn. The popular front garden plant is most noteworthy and is also a good addition to shrubberies or in front of dry-stone walls. Thanks to its spines, it can also be used as a natural hedge. When it comes to cultivation, this plant is rarely easy-going; it only needs pruning now and again when necessary after flowering. 'Pink Lady' is sufficiently hardy to endure a winter without any sudden severe frosts.

| Up to 1.5 m | Mid-spring | | | |

Chamaecyparis lawsoniana 'Lutea' Lawson cypress

Due to its tremendous height, 'Lutea' is certainly best suited to large, park-like gardens. The narrow, conical column with its clustered, golden yellow-tinged leaves has clearly earned its place as a specimen plant, but it will adapt to conditions. Sun and a simple soil, which is not too dry but not excessively moisture-retentive, are all it requires. 'Lutea' may not be too happy in strong winds. Cones appear twice a year, the male cones emerging in spring and the female ones in summer. **Take care:** contact with the foliage may cause skin irritations.

| 15–20 m | 2–5 m | Spring and autumn | | | | ! |

| | Up to 10 m | | Late spring to summer | | Early autumn | | | |

Citrus aurantium Seville orange

The *C. aurantium* will tolerate temperatures of around 37 to 41°F (3 to 5°C) and the beautiful Seville orange will overwinter in moist, well-drained soil and full sun. At lower temperatures, cultivation as a container plant is recommended. The fruit can be used to make marmalade and juice. Fragrant flowers.

| | 3–10 m | | 1–4 m | | Summer | | Early autumn | | | | |

| | Up to 1 m | | Up to 1 m | | Summer | | | |

...tus × *purpureus* 'Alan Fradd'

...ple rock rose

...if created by the artist's hand, this plant ...es the impression of having been made ...m the finest white tissue paper, with a ...v dabs of colour having been painted on ...the finishing touch. The delicate, white ...wer appears in summer on the rounded, ...rgreen shrub, which prefers a sheltered ...e in full sun with moderately fertile, ...l-drained soil. Shoots should be nipped ...young plants to promote bushy growth. ...m lightly after flowering to retain the ...nt's shape. Winter protection is needed ...cold regions.

Cordyline australis 'Atropurpurea' Cabbage tree

The palm-like cabbage tree brings a hint of the exotic to a garden. In frost-free locations it makes a beautiful structural plant that develops a tree-like shape in time. It prefers a site protected from rain with fertile soil in sun or partial shade. The beautiful, red-leafed variety 'Atropurpurea' also makes an excellent container plant, especially since it has very moderate growth and can be cut back when needed.

Cornus alba 'Elegantissima'
Red-barked dogwood

The defining characteristic of 'Elegantissima' is its beautiful foliage. The grey-green leaves with their irregular, creamy-white margins are very striking. Quite apart from the white flowers and blue-tinged fruit, the decorative shrub still has an added bonus for winter, when the leaves fall giving an uninterrupted view of the stunning, red bark. The plant is best cut back hard in spring to promote the growth of young, colourful shoots.

Up to 3 m | Up to 3 m | Late spring to early summer

Cornus controversa 'Variegata' Giant dogwood

Like a delicate *étagère*, the rounded, deciduous *C. controversa* 'Variegata' is actually able to grow as wide as it is tall. To avoid losing this effect, the tree should always be assured a free-standing position. The dark green leaves are characterised by their thick, creamy-white margins and also turn a fabulous, rich purple red in autumn. White flowers and spherical, blue-black fruit ably round off the extremely positive overall impression. If this were not enough, 'Variegata' is also an easy-going, robust variety. Simple, well-drained, fresh soil, which may contain chalk, is all it requires.

Up to 8 m | Early summer

Cornus florida f. rubra
Flowering dogwood

A hairsplitting detail to start with — what may appear to be a pink flower is in actual fact a collection of strikingly coloured bracts surrounding a small, unimpressive flower. Nevertheless, it is an enchanting sight and anything of such beauty can afford to be demanding too. The deciduous flowering dogwood loves sun, but prefers a degree of shade at noon. A fertile, very well-drained, neutral to acid, definitely chalk-free soil sees to the rest. No pruning is necessary. Young plants grow very slowly into shrubs or trees.

Up to 6 m | Up to 8 m | Late spring

Corylopsis sinensis Chinese witch hazel, winter hazel

Before a single green leaf can appear on the thin branches of *C. sinensis*, it produces an abundance of small, lemon-yellow, bell-shaped flowers in pendent racemes. The leaves emerge after the stunning blossom, obovate and dark green. The delicate, spreading shrub is happiest in any normal soil in partial shade. Old branches or unwanted shoots can be removed straight after flowering. For best effect, plant with other early-flowering trees such as magnolia, *Salix*, or *Corylus*.

Cornus kousa
Japanese flowering dogwood

the fruit of *C. kousa* hang from the tree like fleshy, ripe strawberries. They are another highpoint in the life of the sensational flowering dogwood, their appearance filling the interval between flowering and autumnal colours.

Corylus avellana 'Contorta' Common filbert, corkscrew filbert

The strikingly twisted branches of the corkscrew filbert can be seen to best effect in early spring, when numerous yellow catkins hang from the tree-like shrub. This robust plant thrives in any humus soil, which is neither too moist nor too dry. It may be pruned if necessary in winter or spring. **Tip:** the beautiful branches can be used for flower arranging.

| 20–25 cm | Up to 50 cm | | Late spring to early summer | | |

Erica carnea syn. *E. herbacea* 'March Seedling' Alpine heath

The robust Alpine heath flowers from early winter to late spring, depending on the variety. The vigorous, spreading, mid-green 'March Seedling' is one of the late flowerers. With its moderate racemes of bell-shaped, purple-pink flowers, the evergreen shrub is an ideal addition to the heather garden. Apart from sun, it also tolerates open, partially shaded sites with well-drained, acid soil. After flowering, cut back the flower shoots by a few centimetres into the old wood. Tolerates sun and partial shade.

| Up to 3 m | | Late summer to autumn | | |

Euonymus planipes Spindle tree

If you come across *E. planipes* in summer, there is every chance that you will completely overlook what appears to be a green backdrop. The upright, deciduous shrub with its matt green leaves and inconspicuous yellow-green flowers is so totally unremarkable during this season. Its true potential only really emerges in late summer. When its dainty, crimson fruit capsules with their orange seeds appear on the scene and envelop the entire shrub in a bright, orange-red autumn mantle, its lack of expression suddenly disappears. This sleight of hand has certainly earned it its own place in the sun, where the autumn foliage and fruit are presented to best effect. When it comes to soil, the shrub is fairly easy-going, being happy with simple soil and occasional compost.

| Up to 1.2 m | Up to 1.3 m | Early spring to early summer |

Euphorbia characias subsp. *wulfenii* Spurge, lambrook gold

This living work of art, which produces a highly visible green focus in the garden, is anything but unremarkable. The unbelievably bizarre, giant heads of full, yellow-green flowers stand erect on vertical, purple-tinged stems bearing attractive, narrow, linear, green-grey leaves all around. It is quite simply unique. The evergreen shrub is perfect as a structural element in mixed beds or shrubberies, where it becomes a focal point in spring and winter. It goes well with green foliage and structural plants and likes light, well-drained soils. It is recommended that plants be protected with brushwood in winter. **Take care:** spurge exudes a milky sap that can lead to skin irritations. It is advisable to wear gloves when handling the plant.

| Up to 1 m | Up to 1 m | Mid-spring to high summer |

Euphorbia × *martinii* Spurge

E. × martinii is a striking plant in spring with its pale green cymes, from which a dark red 'eye' blinks. Yet its reddish shoots and pretty, initially purple-tinged, later mid-green, narrow leaves also add to the charisma of this evergreen sub-shrub. The compact variety grows in sunny sites in well-drained soil and makes a perfect addition to small, sunny beds. It is also ideally suited to coastal gardens.

Exochorda racemosa Common pearlbush

The pearlbush presents itself in late spring with an impressive array of fine, pure white flowers, which are shown to particular advantage against the narrow, obovate, pale green foliage. The deciduous flowering shrub has a distinctive, slightly overhanging shape and can be used as an impressive specimen or group plant. *E. racemosa* grows in sun or partial shade in moist, well-drained soil rich in humus. The long, twig-like shoots can be supported in young plants, so that the shrub branches out. However, no further pruning is necessary.

| | 3–4 m | | 3–4 m | | Late spring | | | | |

Fagus sylvatica 'Atropunicea'

Common beech, European beech

In view of the size achieved by the 'Atropunicea', the question of where it can be grown almost answers itself. For those who do not have parkland or a rambling garden, the common beech makes an elegant hedge plant, which creates an excellent visual screen and offers exceptional wind protection. It is fast growing and has the enormous advantage of keeping its dry spring foliage over winter, thereby fulfilling its screening function. It likes fertile, well-drained soils that retain moisture.

| | 20–30 m | | Up to 15 m | | Late spring | | Early autumn | | | |

Fatsia japonica Japanese aralia

With its strikingly palmate, shiny, lobed leaves – they reach diameters of between 15 and 40 centimetres – *F. japonica* is an ideal structural plant for lightly shaded areas of gardens with a hint of the exotic. In the autumn, rounded, creamy-white flowers appear in branching umbels, followed by small, spherical, black fruit. The spreading, evergreen shrub offers an attractive contrast to plants with feathery foliage, such as ferns. Planting close to a building protects *F. japonica* from cold winds and permafrost. In cold regions, it is also kept as a container plant. The variegated varieties of this genus are not very hardy.

| | 1.5–4 m | | Autumn | | | |

| | Up to 3 m | | Up to 3 m | | Early to mid-spring | | | | | |

Forsythia × intermedia Border forsythia

The bright, golden-yellow, closely compact flowers are one of the most beautiful heralds of spring. They grow reliably along branches of old wood before the leaves are borne. The bushy, deciduous shrub makes an attractive focus in groups of shrubs and trees and against walls or fences and can also be used for informal hedging. Forsythias should undergo regular renewal pruning after flowering, so that there are still sufficient shoots on the shrub. Never cut back radically, otherwise there will be few, if any, flowers the following year. This tree is tolerant when it comes to location. It likes sun or partial shade and thrives in any fertile, well-drained soil. The sprays of flowers also look nice in a vase.

| | Up to 2.5 m | | Up to 2 m | | Late spring to early summer | | | | | |

Fothergilla major Large fothergilla

The upright, deciduous shrub is popular mainly due to its peculiar, fragrant, white, pink-tinged cymes that sit on the branches like bottle brushes, appearing even before the leaves. The attractive, toothed, dark green leaves change colour in autumn into a gorgeous red, orange, and golden yellow. The plant likes moist, well-drained, acid soil. Both the flowers and the autumnal colours are at their best in the sun.

| | Up to 3 m | | Up to 4 m | | Late autumn | | | | |

ﬁcus carica Common fig

part from the mouth-watering figs borne by is species, the decorative, slightly leathery, eciduous fig leaves are undoubtedly the main traction of *F. carica*. Unlike other species of g, this plant is fully hardy. In areas with mild inters, it can be planted as a specimen, while cooler climates it grows well against a wall, here it is sheltered from cold winds. The oung shoots should be trained and unwanted hoots removed in late winter or spring. The ant likes moist, well-drained soil.

▶ *Fuchsia* **'Lady in Grey'** Fuchsia

The double flowers of the 'Lady in Grey' are truly elegant. They have a grey-blue petal merging into pink and a green-white sepal. A tall variety.

75–120 cm	Early to late summer

Fuchsia Fuchsia

80–100 cm	Early to late summer

30–40 cm	Early summer to early autumn

◀ *Fuchsia* **'Margaret Roe'**

'Margaret Roe' is a bushy shrub. The single flowers are turned outward. Pink-red stamen with pale purple-violet petal.

Summer

▲ *Fuchsia* **'Rieksken Boland'**

Somewhat demure with its pale and dark shades of aubergine, the semi-trailing 'Rieksken Boland' has double flowers.

◀ *Fuchsia* **'Saturnus'**

The small, striking 'Saturnus' has red sepals standing like wings over the single, purple-red petal.

Its flowers resemble cheerful, pendent bells and are simply unbeatable eye-catchers. With its vast array of species, the fuchsia's flower shape and colour variations are a delight. There are double, semi-double, single, and long-tubed flowers in white, pink, red, violet, orange, or even two colours. Fuchsias prefer sites with partial shade sheltered from the wind, where they emerge as truly long-flowerers. One thing is certain, though, fuchsias do not like frost. Thanks to a small number of hardy varieties, they are able to overwinter outdoors in milder regions, provided they have the appropriate winter protection. Choose a moist, fertile, well-drained soil and ensure planting depths are sufficient. There should be a minimum of 5 centimetres between the base of the plant and the soil surface. Tender varieties should be removed from the soil in autumn and overwintered at 41 to 51°F (5 to 10°C) or cultivated in a container. Regularly removing wilted flowers promotes flower growth. Fuchsias flower on young wood, which means that cutting them back in spring promotes new flower shoots.

▶ *Fuchsia* **'Taudens Heil'**

The characteristic feature of the *Triphylla* hybrid is its long-tubed, single flower. The shrub-like, medium-sized 'Taudens Heil' has a salmon-pink sepal and an orange-red petal.

1–2 m   High summer to early autumn

▲ *Fuchsia magellanica* **'Georg'**

The impressive hedge fuchsia is an upright shrub that reaches a height of 1 to 2 metres and is ideal for frost-free regions. In a partially shaded site with a protective canopy of foliage, it will grow into a tireless flowerer. Bears a single flower with a deep red sepal and purple-red petal. *F. magellanica* is a robust, wild species from Chile.

Fuchsia **'Waveney Sunrise'**

The delicate pink sepal curves upwards to reveal the bright red petal. Bears a single flower, medium-sized variety.

40–60 cm

Ginkgo biloba 'Horizontalis'
Maidenhair tree

The *G. biloba* is known for its typical, fan-shaped, sometimes deeply-divided, yellow to mid-green leaves, which are highly decorative. The deciduous tree, basically a living fossil, is neither a broad-leaf nor a conifer, but instead belongs to the *Ginkgoaceae* family. It can grow up to 3 metres high. 'Horizontalis' is a low-growing variety, which, as the name suggests, forms a wide-spreading, shady canopy with its horizontal-growing crown. The bark is striking due to its deep furrows. The foliage becomes a pretty, yellow colour in autumn. Ideal for smaller gardens. The female flowers produce fruit, which can have a very unpleasant aroma. The plant is very easy-going, but prefers well-drained soil.

| | 2–3 m | | 4–6 m | | Mid- to late spring | | Autumn | | | |

Gleditsia triacanthos Honeylocust

This wide-spreading tree will not be a favourite with tree-climbers, because *G. triacanthos* is armed with a very spiny trunk and branches. *G. triacanthos* is prized for its pinnate leaves, which turn yellow in autumn, and the extraordinary, sickle-shaped, long seedpods. These easy-going trees like well-drained, fertile soil in full sun. Due to its decorative value, this tree has earned its place as a specimen. A popular site with nesting birds.

| | Up to 30 m | | Autumn | | | |

Hamamelis × intermedia 'Jelena' Witch hazel hybrid

The irresistible charm of the witch hazel is that it comes into blossom at a time when most plants have finished flowering. Right in the middle of winter it produces the most brilliant summer colours. 'Jelena' bears its copper- to orange-coloured, spidery flowers on the bare branches of this vase-shaped shrub. This fabulous spectacle is preceded by glorious, orange-red autumnal colours. A sunny to partially-shaded site with moist, fertile, slightly acid soil is needed. The shrub requires no pruning, although misplaced shoots can be removed. Preferably used as a specimen plant.

| | Up to 4 m | | Up to 4 m | | Early to mid-winter | | | | |

| Up to 2 m | Up to 1.5 m | High summer to autumn | | | | |

Hebe 'Midsummer Beauty' Hebe

With its narrow, bright green leaves, up to 10 centimetres long, which are flushed crimson when young, 'Midsummer Beauty' offers fresh, lively style. Because this upright-growing, evergreen, rounded hebe – unlike other plants of this variety – can reach heights of up to 2 metres, it has earned a say in the composition of the garden. From high summer to autumn, full, lavender-coloured flowers, fading to white, are borne on racemes producing a wealth of nectar for worker bees and bumblebees. Hebe tolerates most soils, including those rich in lime, and prefers a sheltered, sunny site. The shrub will have no objections to being cut back after flowering, although its special charm develops better without pruning. Overwinter in a frost-protected environment in cold regions.

| Up to 1 m | Up to 1.5 m | Early to high summer | | | |

| Up to 1 m | Up to 1.2 m | Early to high summer | | | |

be odora syn. H. anomala, buxifolia Hebe

s spreading, evergreen shrub with its
ight, skyward-pointing shoots brings
nty of structure to rockeries and heather
dens or shrub borders. The small, glossy
ves have delicate, yellow margins. White
wers appear in early summer.

Hebe rakaiensis Hebe

Racemes full of large, white flowers emerge from early summer beyond the plant's fresh, glossy, green leaves, which are slightly reminiscent of *Buxus* in shape. The dense, evergreen shrub with its slightly rounded shape is excellent as a structural plant in sunny locations. As with all hebes, this variety will also tolerate a degree of air pollution and salty air.

Heliotropium arborescens 'Marine'
Heliotrope

The bushy *H. arborescens* is a classic cottage garden plant, which is loved for its copious, sweetly scented flowers. The short-lived sub-shrub is often cultivated as an annual. In summer, 'Marine' displays lasting, deep violet-blue flowerheads, which can measure up to 15 centimetres across. The plant prefers a bright spot with uniformly moist, fertile soil. Suitable as summer bedding plants or for pots in frost-prone regions. Remove wilted flowers regularly.

| Up to 45 cm | 30–45 cm | Summer | | | | |

Hibiscus syriacus 'Oiseau Bleu' Hibiscus

With its large, exotic-looking flowers, 'Oiseau Bleu' brightens up the dying remnants of summer for the onlooker. Its magnificent flowers are large, bright violet blue with a dark red centre and appear en masse. This is the best of the blue varieties. It is important, above all, for the deciduous shrub to have sun if it is to flower well and a sheltered site in cold climates. Cool, fertile soil that is not too moist in winter is ideal. Due to its hardiness, the hibiscus is most frequently cultivated in cool areas. Cut back the shoots slightly after winter.

| Up to 2.5 m | Late summer to mid-autumn | | |

Hippophae rhamnoides
Sea buckthorn

Only those with a male and a female plant close to one another will be able to enjoy these spherical, blazing orange-red fruit. Female plants produce the exceptionally decorative berries, rich in vitamin C, after flowering, which comes before the leaves appear. However, the densely branched, deciduous shrub with its spiny shoots is also popular on account of its narrow, silvery leaves. Easy-going and robust, it will tolerate virtually any well-drained soil. *H. rhamnoides* is a good choice as a specimen plant, for shrubberies and mixed beds, and particularly for sandy, coastal gardens.

| Up to 6 m | Up to 6 m | Mid-spring | High summer | | | | |

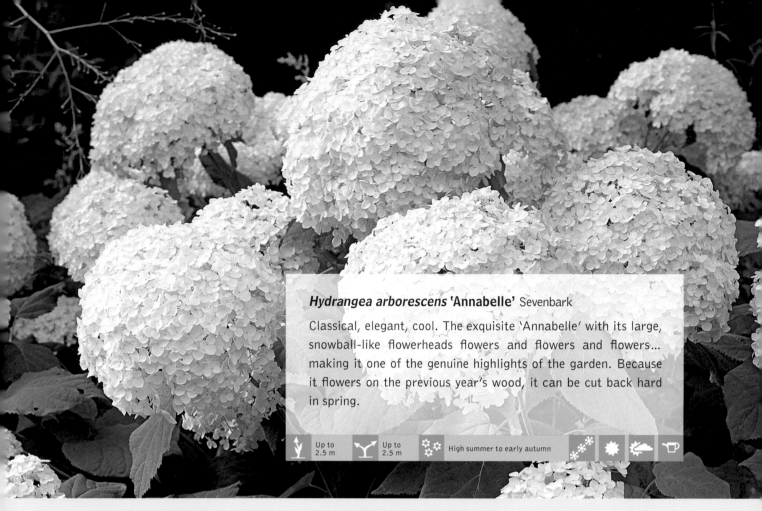

Hydrangea arborescens 'Annabelle' Sevenbark

Classical, elegant, cool. The exquisite 'Annabelle' with its large, snowball-like flowerheads flowers and flowers and flowers... making it one of the genuine highlights of the garden. Because it flowers on the previous year's wood, it can be cut back hard in spring.

Up to 2.5 m   Up to 2.5 m   High summer to early autumn

Hydrangea Hydrangea

Large, showy flowers in a whole host of wonderful colours and shapes, accompanied by an endlessly long flowering season – these are, in short, the essential characteristics of the hydrangea. No wonder, then, that they number among the absolute favourites when it comes to garden shrubs.

Hydrangeas are classic garden plants, which were originally grown in typical cottage gardens or romantic country houses. With their enchanting flowerheads, they are deserving specimens, but also offer a fascinating play of colours when used in group plantings; they break up shrubberies, bring colour to green trees and shrubs, create whole hedges or adorn the terrace from containers. As the season draws to an end, the flowers are slowly immersed in the most beautiful, warm autumnal colours, showing a completely new, surprising side and remaining decorative

until the first night frost. Many varieties also impress with their unusually shaped and coloured foliage, more so even than with their flowers.

The array of flower shapes varies from the simple to the spectacular. They flower as long panicles, flat, plate-shaped umbrellas, or gigantic balls. Hydrangeas are hard to pin down when it comes to the colour of the flowers too. This is because the colour of hydrangea flowers depends less on the variety than on the acidity of the soil. They will flower blue in acid soil and pink in alkaline soils. In neutral soils, the colours merge into a bluish rose-coloured blend. Here, by adding a blue-coloured hydrangea, a beautiful blue flower can be achieved. White-flowering varieties remain unimpressed by such manipulation – they are colour-fast.

Hydrangea aspera 'Macrophylla'
Common hydrangea

Very large, downy leaves and beautiful, flat-topped, lilac-pink corymbs with white, sterile marginal flowers give 'Macrophylla' its unmistakable flair.

Up to 2 m | High to late summer

Hydrangea Hydrangea

The Hydrangea is — *nomen est omen* — an extremely thirsty plant, which needs a particularly large amount of water, especially in summer. This is particularly true when it is in a sunny location. The deciduous shrub is happiest in loose, fertile, moist but well-drained soil, in partial shade sheltered from the wind — the perfect place is in the light shade of a tree.

Most varieties of hydrangea can be cut back after flowering. The shoots should be pruned just beneath the flower bud, as many varieties flower on two-year-old wood and the following year's flowers are already developing in the leaf axis below.

Up to 1.5 m | High to late summer

▲ **Hydrangea macrophylla 'Ayesha'** Common hydrangea

Its flowers resemble lilac in appearance, with small, waxy, cupped sepals that appear pale pink to light blue. Rather romantic.

▼ **Hydrangea macrophylla 'Kardinal'** Common hydrangea

An awesome play of colours is offered by the umbrella-shaped flower of 'Kardinal'. A vivid pink violet on the outside with a lavender blue inside. A magnificent contrast to the green foliage.

Up to 1.5 m | High to late summer

▶ *Hydrangea macrophylla* 'Lilacina'
Common hydrangea

Numerous small, cupped heads with pale pink to pale blue, sterile marginal flowers characterise the plate-type hydrangea 'Lilacina'. A genuinely persistent flowerer.

| | Up to 1.5 m | | High summer to autumn | | |

◀ *Hydrangea macrophylla* 'Mousmee'
Common hydrangea

The fast-growing, large-flowered hydrangea displays a rare colour combination: a magenta outside and a pale blue inside.

| | Up to 1.5 m | | Early to high summer | | |

▶ *Hydrangea paniculata* Hydrangea

The delicate conical panicles of *H. paniculata* remain extremely decorative right into the autumn, long after the white flower colour has yielded. The autumn inflorescences make a beautiful display as cut flowers too. Like 'Annabelle', this variety flowers on the previous year's wood and can be cut back in spring.

| | 3–7 m | | High to late summer | | |

Hydrangea quercifolia
Oak-leafed hydrangea

It is not so much the long, pretty panicles of white, sterile flowers that make *H. quercifolia* so spectacular, but rather its leaves, which are deeply lobed like oak leaves and turn a blazing bronze red in autumn.

| | Up to 2 m | | High summer to autumn | | |

Hypericum androsaemum Tutsan

Being both easy-going and robust, the bushy, deciduous *H. androsaemum* is perfect as a filler shrub for group plantings of shrubs and trees. Here it will produce a discreet summer display of abundant yellow flowers, which develop into spherical red-brown and later black berries. As long as the soil is sufficiently well drained, sites in either sun or partial shade are wholly acceptable. Pruning is not necessary. Propagation is through seeds or cuttings.

	Up to 75 cm		High summer				

Ilex aquifolium 'Golden van Tol' Common holly

Evergreen hollies are distinctive at the start of winter, due not only to their striking red berries, which are an important source of food for birds, but also their interestingly coloured leaves. Those of the *Ilex* 'Golden van Tol' have bright golden-yellow margins and, happily, only a few spiny teeth. The variety is so decorative that it looks lovely in the house in winter too. 'Golden van Tol' tolerates almost any position, provided the soil is well drained and not too dry. The variegated variety prefers full sun, but should not be allowed to dry out. It livens up group plantings of trees and shrubs or can also be used as informal hedging. *I. aquifolium* can be freely pruned and clipped into almost any shape. The poisonous berries only develop if male and female plants are grown together.

	Up to 4 m		Autumn				!

Juglans regia Common walnut

This tree will quite definitely bring pleasure to many generations, having been known to reach the grand old age of 600. The slow-growing, deciduous all-rounder not only produces delicious walnuts, but also wood for fine furniture. Its shiny, green leaves with their aromatic scent make this tree an excellent provider of shade and its green-brown, male catkins are also decorative. It loves warm, sunny, open sites with deep, fresh, fertile soil.

	Up to 30 m		Up to 15 m		Mid- to late spring		Early to late autumn			

| Up to 80 cm | Mid- to late spring | From early autumn | | ! |

niperus communis 'Compressa'
mmon juniper

e ideal place for the columnar, dwarf
ompressa' is the heather or rock garden,
ere it is a natural choice as a structural
ment, due to its shortness. Its branches
ar small, blue-green needles, which
main green even in winter. In autumn blue
iper berries appear on female shrubs,
ovided there is a male plant close by.
e berries are fairly slow to ripen and are
ly ready for picking after about three
ars. Their special flavour has a variety
culinary uses. Junipers like sandy, well-
ained, completely dry soil. They do not
cessarily need to be in full sun and will
erate partial shade. This robust, easy-
ing plant does not require special care or
d to be pruned. **Take care:** contact with
e needles can lead to skin irritation.

| Up to 60 cm | Up to 1.5 m | Early summer | |

Kalmia angustifolia Sheep laurel

One of the most beautiful evergreen, flowering shrubs, it produces an abundance of wide, bell-shaped, purple-red flowers. Partial shade with moist, acid soil or sun if the soil is sufficiently moist. The plant is at its most beautiful when grown informally, so no pruning is required.

| Up to 3 m | Up to 3 m | Mid- to late spring | |

Kerria japonica 'Pleniflora'
Japanese rose

In spring, the pompon-like, golden-yellow, double flowers of 'Peniflora' hang in abundance from the rod-like, light green branches. The deciduous foliage is a shiny pale green. The vigorous plant needs space and works best when planted between other shrubs; it loses its charisma when planted alone. It produces creeping roots and can therefore be propagated by division. Cut back after flowering and remove older branches every three to four years.

Kolkwitzia amabilis Beautybush

In late spring, a thick cloud of pale pink-coloured, bell-shaped flowers hangs in corymbs from this charmingly overhanging shrub, creating a picturesque sight. The well-known deciduous shrub with its dark green foliage is impressive when used alone or also in mixed hedges or in a group planting of trees and shrubs. It has no particular requirements in relation to soil type or location. The elegant shape should preferably be left undisturbed; carefully trim older plants if necessary. Propagate using cuttings.

Up to 3 m · Up to 4 m · Late spring to early summer

Laburnum × *watereri* Hybrid golden rain

This is one of the garden's golden-yellow seductresses and is simply unbelievably stunning, with its innumerable racemes that hang down loosely from its branches from late spring. It has become an almost essential component of garden design – whether as a specimen plant or along with other flowering trees and shrubs. Wherever it is, the deciduous tree captivates with its brilliant abundance of flowers. It is important for it to receive sufficient sun and a well-drained soil. It can also be used to create charming treillages, pergolas, or pretty arches, by training the supple, young branches around a suitable framework. Combining this hybrid with violet or blue plants produces a beautiful contrast. The natural growing shape is a large part of its special aesthetic charm, which is why the tree is prettiest left unpruned. **Take care:** all plant parts, particularly the seeds, are highly toxic.

Up to 8 m · Late spring to early summer

Lantana camara Shrub verbena

The flowers of the shrub verbena vary their colour during the flowering period, changing from white to yellow, orange to red, and pink to rose. In frost-prone regions, the plant is grown in containers, as it is tender. Overwinter in a bright, cool location. Whether it is grown in containers or in the open garden, the shrub verbena only needs a moderate amount of water. Waterlogging is not tolerated, but the soil should not dry out either.

1–2 m | Late spring to late autumn

Up to 12 m | Up to 10 m | Spring

Laurus nobilis Bay laurel, sweet bay

The classical, evergreen, Mediterranean culinary and decorative plant is a delight with its excellent tolerance of clipping and its elegant appearance, particularly alongside other formally trimmed plants, such as *Buxus*. Because it is only moderately hardy, *L. nobilis* should preferably be kept as a container plant in cold regions. It likes cool, dry winter quarters in the semi-dark. It can only be planted out in the garden in mild climates, where it prefers a moist, water-bearing soil and shelter from winds. The aromatic essential oils contained in the shiny, dark green leaves are also widely used in cooking. Clip into shape, branch by branch, after flowering.

Lavandula angustifolia English lavender

Robust, low-maintenance with a naturally wonderful fragrance. The evergreen shrub with its fragrant, dark purple flowers, rich in nectar, and its aromatic, grey-green foliage is irresistible not only to bees; lavender is also an ideal accompaniment to roses, keeping greenflies away and also acting as a windbreaker in winter. Yet it also works its Mediterranean charm as a low-edging plant, in herb gardens or simply in a pot. In terms of location, a sandy, chalky, well-drained soil is perfect. Lavender is adapted to dry environments and therefore needs little water. Only the flowered shoots should be cut back in the autumn after flowering. Cutting back hard in spring promotes nice, bushy growth and prevents the plant from becoming too woody. **Tip:** sachets filled with the dried flowerheads keep wardrobes free from clothes moths. To dry the flowerheads, cut the flowering shoots at the start of the flowering season and hang them upside down.

Up to 1 m | High to late summer

Lavandula angustifolia 'Hidcote'
English lavender

The dense flower spikes and strong, deep purple flowers of 'Hidcote' create a beautiful contrast with the silvery-grey foliage. Typical for this popular variety is its compact, slightly short habit.

Up to 60 cm | Up to 75 cm | High to late summer

2–3 m | Early to high summer

Ligustrum ovalifolium 'Aureum' Golden privet

The striking thing about this plant is its golden yellow-margined or single-coloured, slightly oval leaves, some of which may be lost in a sharp frost. Granted, the plant is not particularly spectacular at first sight, but it has acquired a good reputation as a reliable hedging plant, which is tolerant of clipping and produces a first-class screen. Coupled with the fact that it is completely undemanding, this plant is entirely deserving of the attention it has received. Propagate using cuttings.

Up to 2 m | Early summer to early autumn

Lavatera olbia 'Barnsley'
Tree lavatera, bush mallow

Thanks to its abundance of flowers, the bush mallow is not only one of the most popular flowering shrubs, but also one of the most beautiful. The delicate persistent, mass flowerer combines a number of advantages. It is easy to cultivate and extremely undemanding. The main requirement is for a sunny site with loose, well-drained soil. The semi-evergreen 'Barnsley' with its romantic, funnel-shaped, delicate pink flowers and pink-red centres is also fully frost-hardy. It makes an ideal background planting for summer beds and complements plants such as delphinium, marguerite, or wolfsbane. If 'Barnsley' is cut back hard in spring right down to the soil, the reward will be a magnificent display of flowers. Winter protection is recommended in bleak locations.

15–20 cm | 60 cm | Late spring and summer

Lithodora diffusa 'Heavenly Blue' Lithodora

The extent of its spread betrays the fact that 'Heavenly Blue' is a contemporary that tends to offer ground cover and is used to best effect in rock gardens, raised beds, or troughs. Being fast growing, it quickly conceals unattractive areas of ground. But this evergreen, many-branched sub-shrub is not only practical. It is also fascinating, due in particular to its persistent, funnel-shaped, azure-blue flowers, to which it rightly owes its name. The dark green leaves, hairy above and beneath, help it to store moisture in dry locations. The pretty dwarf needs acid soil, preferably enriched with organic matter, and full sun.

Magnolia × *soulangeana* 'Rustica Rubra' Tulip magnolia

The dark purplish-red flowers of 'Rustica Rubra', with their alabaster-white insides, are shaped like tulips and look as if they were made of fine porcelain. Apart from the elegant, sepal-shaped flowers, which adorn the bare branches in hundreds in mid-spring, 'Rustica Rubra' impresses with its handsome, wide-spreading stature. This majestic eye-catcher is therefore quite justified in laying claim to an exposed, sunny to partially shaded spot in the garden sheltered from winds. In addition, the deciduous tree, with its decorative, leathery leaves, needs fertile, acid soil. Its care routine is relatively modest: no pruning, but plenty of water in summer.

 Up to 6 m Mid- to late spring

Magnolia stellata 'Rosea' Star magnolia

'Rosea' is an exceptionally sophisticated variety. While its buds, which appear in early spring, are still purple in colour, the star-shaped, fragrant flower is white flushed with a delicate pink. The uniformly spreading habit of this slow-growing deciduous shrub is also picturesque. Late frosts can damage the flowers, but will not affect the plant itself.

Up to 3 m   Up to 4 m   Early to mid-spring

| | 4–6 m | | Spring | | Autumn | | | |

Malus 'Evereste' Crab apple

'Evereste' looks good all year round. In spring, it produces red buds and white flowers; in the autumn it turns golden yellow with orange-red fruit that attract birds and still hang from the branches well into winter. Fresh, fertile soil.

| | Up to 3 m | | Up to 3 m | | Early summer to autumn | | | |

Myrtus communis Common myrtle

The evergreen *M. communis* spreads classical Mediterranean flair with its ornamental, shiny, dark green, aromatic foliage. The persistent flowerer bears white, sweetly-scented flowers, which develop into purple-black berries. The branches of the bushy shrub arch elegantly with age. The common myrtle needs a warm, sheltered site with moist, well-drained, moderately fertile soil. Suitable for use as a hedging plant, for beds, walls, or pots. Sensitive to frost.

| | Up to 1 m | | Up to 1.5 m | | Mid-spring | | Late summer to winter | | | |

Mahonia aquifolium Oregon grape

Whenever a bushy, evergreen, ornamental shrub is needed for difficult sites, *M. aquifolium* fits the bill. It is happy in any situation, from sun to shade, in any normal soil, provided it is well drained. Pruning? Any way, any time. Yet despite its indiscriminate nature, it has plenty to offer. The glossy, spiny-toothed leaves remain attractive throughout the year. Fresh shoots are bronze red, while leaves emerge after a hard frost in a superb, purple winter colour. In spring, the Oregon grape has a surprise in store in the shape of a rich, long-lasting, luscious yellow flower, which is rich in nectar and pollen. The flowers later ripen into black, glaucous blue berries, which can be used to make wine, compote, and jam. It is ideal for town gardens or as a container plant.

| Up to 1.2 m | Up to 1 m | Late summer to early autumn | | | | |

Perovskia atriplicifolia 'Blue Spire'
Russian sage

The violet-blue flower spikes, up to 30 centimetres long, silver-grey, aromatic foliage, the long, stick-like branches, and the casual, upright habit of 'Blue Spire' are vaguely reminiscent of lavender. The plant needs a dry, sheltered site in order to develop properly. It makes an ideal partner for roses, in rock gardens and also in sandy or chalky soil and coastal conditions. Cut back to within a hand's width of the soil in spring to create a woody structure. The branches may be frozen off in winter, but are replaced after cutting back. Quick growing.

Philadelphus 'Belle Etoile' Mock orange

The incredible number of sweet, jasmine-like, star-shaped fragrant flowers is the highlight of this arching, finely-branched, deciduous shrub. The flowers of 'Belle Etoile' are cup-shaped and waxen-white with a pale purple centre. Mock orange has no particular location needs. It will thrive even where there is little light, although it bears more flowers in sunny locations. In terms of soil, a good food supply is sufficient. The fulsome supply of flowers creates a striking focus in hedges or group plantings of trees and shrubs, and is particularly attractive when combined with roses or lilac. It is also easy to imagine it as a specimen. The mock orange flowers on short branches on the previous year's wood. Cutting back hard will reduce the abundance of flowers.

| Up to 1.2 m | Up to 2.5 m | Late spring to early summer | |

| Up to 5 m | Up to 5 m | Mid- to late spring | | | |

Photinia × fraseri 'Red Robin'
Christmas berry

The compact, evergreen shrub or tree is popular mainly due to its unbelievably attractive foliage and full, small, white flowers produced in panicles. Its leaves are bright red when young, turning a glossy dark green later. Ideal for informal hedging or as a specimen plant. In frost-prone areas, plant against a south-facing wall for protection.

| Up to 4 m | Up to 2 m | Mid- to late spring |

Pieris 'Forest Flame' Lily of the valley bush

Wonderfully colourful foliage, changing once in spring. *Pieris* is a bushy, evergreen shrub popular for its shiny, leathery leaves and dense flower panicles. As it likes acid soil, it is an ideal partner for evergreen shrubs and trees such as rhododendrons and does well in heather gardens or even tubs. The varieties are distinguished not only by the colour of the flowers and foliage, but also by their winter hardiness. 'Forest Flame' is one of those varieties that undergoes an extraordinary metamorphosis in the colour of its foliage, changing from a blazing red in young foliage, through pink, followed by a creamy white, after which the desired dark green emerges as the plant becomes more mature. The shrub is laden with panicles of small, white flowers in spring. 'Forest Flame' should definitely be protected from heavy frosts in the garden.

| Up to 1.5 m |

| 1.5–3 m | 1.5–2 m |

cea glauca 'Conica' White spruce

ow growing, dense, cone-shaped, ergreen dwarf variety with fine, bluish- een needles. Likes deep, moist, acid soil. nsitive to dryness and heat. For rockeries heather gardens.

Pinus mugo 'Mops'
Dwarf mountain pine

The low, evergreen variety is almost spherical and very slow growing. This makes it perfect for small gardens, heather or rock gardens, as an accompaniment for rhododendrons, informal hedges, or troughs. It likes well-drained, humus, moderately dry soil.

Pittosporum tenuifolium Kohuhu, tawhiwhi

Its glossy, leathery, mid-green leaves and bell-shaped, black-red, pleasantly-scented flowers make it an exceptionally attractive plant. It should be grown in containers in frost-prone areas because of its sensitivity to frost. In mild climates it can be grown as a specimen or also as a hedging plant, as it is good for shaping. It prefers morning and evening sun, with partial shade for the rest of the day and fresh, fertile soil.

4–10 m | 2–5 m | Late spring to early summer

Potentilla fruticosa 'Princess'

Bush cinquefoil

A tirelessly persistent flowerer whose pale pink blooms have an air of fine, wild rose flowers, this small, bushy shrub with its pinnate, elongated leaves will adorn a shrub border or group planting of shrubs for weeks on end. Because it tends to be more spreading than upright growing, the deciduous shrub is also perfect for ground cover or low-hedge planting. All it needs is a poor to moderately fertile soil, preferably in full sun, although partial shade is tolerated. The shrub should be pruned roughly every two to three years to encourage flowering and retain its shape. It will continue producing shoots even after it has been cut back hard.

Up to 60 cm | Late spring to mid-autumn

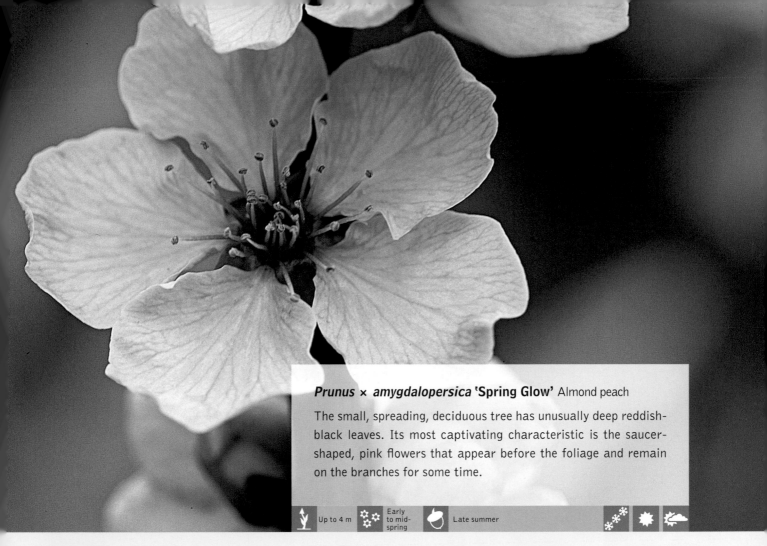

Prunus × _amygdalopersica_ 'Spring Glow' Almond peach

The small, spreading, deciduous tree has unusually deep reddish-black leaves. Its most captivating characteristic is the saucer-shaped, pink flowers that appear before the foliage and remain on the branches for some time.

Up to 4 m | Early to mid-spring | Late summer

Prunus Apricot, cherry, cherry laurel, almond, peach, plum, blackthorn, black cherry, sour cherry, damson

The genus *Prunus* includes not only a wide variety of fruit trees, such as cherry, plum, and almond, but also numerous ornamental trees and shrubs. These can be divided into evergreen and deciduous varieties. The deciduous varieties number among the most beautiful, ornate garden trees and shrubs and are particularly striking due to their white or pink clusters of flowers, which appear in spring or even in mild winters, depending on the variety. Other varieties are grown for their decorative bark or pretty autumnal colours. The evergreen varieties are popular less for their flowers, which are usually completely unremarkable, than for their dense, glossy foliage.

The deciduous varieties love sun, while the evergreens will also tolerate shadier locations. Both prosper in almost any moist, but well-drained, deep, moderately fertile soil.

They are used individually, in group plantings of flowering trees and shrubs or also as formal or informal hedging. The majority of deciduous varieties are most attractive when left unpruned. The evergreen *P. laurocerasus* will tolerate being cut back hard.

◀ *Prunus* × *cistena* Purple leaf sandcherry

This decorative, deciduous ornamental shrub with its deep red foliage bears hundreds of delicate, white flowers, which appear with the foliage. They are then followed by purple-black fruit in late summer.

Up to 1.5 m | Late spring

Prunus Apricot, cherry, cherry laurel, almond, peach, plum, blackthorn, black cherry, sour cherry, damson

Up to 5 m | Mid- to late spring

▲ *Prunus laurocerasus* 'Marbled White'
Cherry laurel

The surprising feature of this dense, evergreen shrub is its attractively glossy, marbled-white foliage. Also grows in shady sites.

Up to 2 m | Mid- to late spring

◀ *Prunus laurocerasus* 'Schipkaensis'
Cherry laurel

Special feature: the evergreen 'Schipkaensis' is a spreading shrub that flowers profusely.

▶ *Prunus serrula*
Tibetan cherry

This gracious, rounded tree develops a beautiful, glossy, smooth, mahogany-coloured bark on its older branches. It bears white flowers.

Up to 10 m | Late spring

▶ *Prunus serrulata* **'Kiku-shidare-zakura'**
Cheal's weeping cherry

This beautiful ornamental plant grows into a weeping, deciduous tree and bears countless double, pink flowers. It produces bronze-coloured leaves. Beautiful autumnal colours.

Up to 5 m | Up to 8 m | Late spring

▲ *Prunus serrulata* **'Shôgetsu'** Shôgetsu cherry

The rounded, spring-flowerer is also called 'Shimidsu-zakura'. It is captivating in spring with its masses of pink buds from which frilly-margined, white flowers emerge. Its mid-green, initially bronze foliage changes to an orange red in autumn.

Up to 5 m | Mid- to late spring

Prunus spinosa 'Rosea'

The foliage of this very dense and bushy blackthorn is reddish brown when the first shoots appear, turning greenish later. In spring, delicate, single, pink flowers emerge before the foliage appears. It produces glaucous, edible, black fruit later. Deciduous.

Up to 4 m | Early to mid-spring

▶ *Prunus subhirtella* 'Autumnalis' Higan cherry

The spreading 'Autumnalis' is a very pretty, winter-flowering, small tree that displays a wealth of semi-double, pink-tinged, white flowers during mild periods. A true winter highlight.

Up to 5 m · Winter to mid-spring

Prunus Apricot, cherry, cherry laurel, almond, peach, plum, blackthorn, black cherry, sour cherry, damson

Up to 3 m · Early to mid-spring

◀ *Prunus triloba* Flowering almond

The bushy, free-flowering shrub is densely branched. The small, pink flowers appear even before the foliage shoots. Ideal for small and front gardens.

Up to 2.5 m · Early spring

Up to 10 m · Early spring

▶ *Prunus tomentosa*
Japanese almond cherry

The small shrub blooms in spring with pretty, white flowers. The red fruit are very popular with birds.

◀ *Prunus × yedoensis* Yoshino cherry

Since this variety is quite tall and spreading, it is probably better suited to the larger garden. The pink buds open into white flowers in early spring before the foliage appears.

Pyracantha 'Orange Glow'
Firethorn

There are three striking features that make 'Orange Glow' particularly noteworthy: its glossy dark, evergreen leaves, the dense corymbs of small, white flowers, and its crowning glory, trusses of persistent, shiny orange-red, autumn berries. The firethorn is a particularly robust plant, growing in fertile, well-drained, and also dry soil, provided it is not too acidic. It is happy in partial shade or full sun. It may lose its foliage in very hard winters. Protect from cold winds in winter. It has a versatile range of uses. It may be free-standing, planted in shrubberies, as hedging or wall cover, along fences or trellises. It can be pruned according to its use. In free-standing plants, stray branches should be removed in early spring and hedges trimmed in high summer. **Take care:** the firethorn is very thorny and it is a good idea to wear gloves when planting or trimming. The berries are not edible.

Up to 3 m	Up to 3 m	Late spring	Late summer		!

Rhododendron 'Blue Tit Magor'

The free-flowering, evergreen, lavender-blue 'Blue Tit Magor' is the Tom Thumb of the rhododendron world and is absolutely perfect for the small garden. The small-leafed plant also tolerates clipping as a hedge. An *Impeditum* hybrid.

Up to 50 cm	Mid- to late spring				

Rhododendron Azalea, rhododendron

The rhododendron is one of the best-established garden plants: resilient, unbelievably free-flowering, and a safe bet for shady parts of the garden. In all cases, the rhododendron flower is one of the highlights of the garden year, guaranteeing the range and intensity of colour usually only found in summer beds – even in less favourable locations.

The range of varieties available is in no way inferior to the array of colours on offer, extending from dwarf shrubs to majestic trees. From a botanical viewpoint, evergreen rhododendrons – mainly hybrids in the garden – can be differentiated from azaleas, although azaleas belong to the Rhododendron genus.

Rhododendron 'Comte de Gomer'

Mollis hybrid azalea. The deciduous 'Comte de Gomer' has beautiful, funnel-shaped, long-lasting, salmon-pink flowers. The flowers appear after the foliage.

Up to 2.5 m | Mid- to late spring

Rhododendron Azalea, rhododendron

Up to 2 m | Late spring to early summer

Most deciduous azaleas – the exception here being the Japanese azalea – enrich the already wide range of designs with their deep shades of orange and striking autumn foliage.

However, certain requirements must be met if good growth with dark green, glossy leaves and rich flowers is to be achieved. The basis for this is choosing the right location and preparing the soil carefully.

Rhododendrons will thrive in partial shade, sheltered from winds, against a hedge or house wall. The best place, though, is a woodland-type setting under tall, well-established trees. However, only deep-rooted trees such as pines, oaks, acacias, or laburnums are potential shade-providers, as they will not enter into competition with the shallow-rooted trees. In addition, the foliage of these trees produces quick-rotting, acid mulch, because rhododendrons need loose, acid, humus soil.

If these conditions are not available, the soil should be prepared accordingly with special compost, for instance.

Up to 3 m | Late spring to early summer

▲ *Rhododendron* 'Dairymaid'

Large, cream-coloured flowerheads with delicate pink lines characterise this large-flowered, evergreen hybrid.

◄ *Rhododendron* 'Furnivall's Daughter'

'Furnivall's Daughter' tends to produce blazing pink, funnel-shaped flowers with a striking, strawberry-red flare. The evergreen, broad bushy shrub has particularly large, wide-oval leaves. A *Caucasicum* hybrid. It tolerates exposed locations and can also be used as a hedge or screen.

▶ *Rhododendron* 'Goldkrone'

Rhododendron Goldilocks

'Goldkrone' is a captivating sight with its funnel-shaped, golden-yellow flowers with delicate ruby-red speckles. A very robust, evergreen shrub.

Up to 1.5 m | Mid-spring

◀ *Rhododendron* 'Hollandia'

Pontica azalea. Densely branched, deciduous shrub with blazing yellow flowers. 'Hollandia' blooms as the leaves unfold.

Up to 1.5 m | Late spring

▶ *Rhododendron* 'Homebush' Azalea

Knap Hill-Exbury azalea. The compact, deciduous shrub overflows in spring with trumpet-shaped, semi-double, pink flowers. Otherwise, it displays pale green, medium-sized leaves.

Up to 1.5 m | Late spring

R. 'Jolie Madame'

Azalea

Viscosum azalea. The deep pink, wide-opening flowers have a delicate, golden-orange flare. The thing that sets 'Jolie Madame' apart is its wonderful scent. The deciduous, free-growing shrub is easy to grow.

Up to 1.5 m | Mid-to late spring

▶ *Rhododendron* 'Lilac Time'

The name says it all: 'Lilac Time' flowers are a delicate lilac. Its habitat is the same as that of a dwarf shrub. The Japanese azalea, the group to which it belongs, is evergreen. Ideal for small gardens. Shelter is recommended in windy locations.

Up to 1.5 m | Late spring to early summer

Rhododendron Azalea, rhododendron

Up to 1.3 m | Late spring

Up to 1.5 m | Late spring

◀ *Rhododendron* 'Lilofee'

Large-flowered, evergreen hybrid in blazing purple lilac. The reddish-brown flair in the throat of the flower and the long, white stamens ensure a lively contrast with the flower colour. Broad, compact, medium growth.

Up to 1.5 m | Late winter to early spring

▲ *Rhododendron* 'Praecox' syn.
R. × praecox Early spring rhododendron

Beautiful flowering plant of spring. The low, evergreen shrub with its small leaves also tolerates sunny sites. Can be cultivated for hedging.

◀ *Rhododendron* 'Silvester'

Evergreen Japanese azalea. In late spring, 'Silvester' produces an unbelievably dense sea of pale pink and pinkish-red flowers.

Regular fertilising or mulching also improves growth. Rhododendrons need plenty of water. If they are in dry soil, they should be watered thoroughly. The basic rule is: the more suitable the site they are planted in, the less watering is needed.

They will also tolerate being cut back hard. Rhododendrons – except for hedges – are usually left unpruned, so that they can develop their natural shape. Only dead heads should occasionally be nipped off.

Because rhododendrons are slow growing, they are also suitable for the small garden. Planted individually or in groups, they delightfully display their full blooms and dark green foliage the whole year round.

Up to 2.5 m — Late spring

▲ *Rhododendron* 'The Hon. Jean Marie Montague' syn. *R.* 'Jean Marie Montague'

The dense trusses of funnel-shaped, scarlet-crimson flowers allow the evergreen shrub to make a real impression. The honourable 'Jean Marie Montague' will be happy in any conditions. Whether in sun, heat, or an exposed site, it will stay in good shape. *Arboreum* group.

Rhododendron 'Viscy'

For lovers of the more discreet, delicate shades, the beautiful 'Viscy' is the right one. The large-flowered, evergreen plant bears wonderful, cream then light orange-coloured flowers with a delicate, reddish flare.

Up to 1.5 m — Mid-spring

Syringa meyeri 'Palibin' Meyer lilac

'Palibin' is the name given to the ornamental dwarf variety of scented lilac. The leaves are significantly smaller than those of the common lilac. The sweetly-scented, lavender-pink flowers are arranged in loose panicles. They appear in late spring and provide a rich bee meadow. 'Palibin' is well suited to scented gardens; its compact, slow-growing habit also makes it an excellent container or decorative plant. As with all lilacs, it will be quite happy in a sunny site with a simple, fertile soil. Resistant to dry weather.

| | 1.5–2 m | | Up to 1.5 m | | Late spring to early summer | | | | |

Syringa vulgaris 'Andenken an Ludwig Späth' Ludwig Späth lilac

There is no suggestion of this being yesterday's plant. With its panicles to almost 30 centimetres long of fragrant, dark purple flowers, a 'Ludwig Späth lilac' is still one of the unsurpassed garden classics. A few cultivation tips: it is important to remove the dead panicles. If they are left on the branches, too much energy goes into seed formation and the plant does not flower as well the following year. Because the common lilac can grow into a strong shrub, it should be thinned out occasionally. The best time for this is straight after flowering, because the buds are already formed in spring.

| | Up to 7 m | | Late spring to early summer | | | |

Tamarix tetrandra Salt cedar, tamarisk

T. tetrandra belongs to the group of ornamental shrubs offering the best resistance to dryness. It grows easily in dry, sandy soil in full sun. Because it has its origins in coastal regions, it is also unaffected by a salty climate. Thus far for the practical side. The other thing that _T. tetrandra_ has going for it is that the deciduous, feathery shrub with its rod-like branches emerges in spring as an unbelievably impressive cloud of light pink flowers. Predestined to be a specimen.

| | Up to 5 m | | Up to 5 m | | Mid- to late spring | | | |

| | Up to 2 m | Autumn | ❄❄❄ | ☀ | ☁ | ! |

xus baccata 'Lutea'

glish yew

e evergreen, densely-branched tree is ning in popularity, with its beautiful edles, which appear in different shades green and yellow, and its great variety shapes. Growing to around 2 metres, utea' is a somewhat low-growing variety at bears pretty, spherical, yellow fruit in tumn. The yellow, or in other varieties en red, berries are a popular food for ds, but only appear on female plants, ws being dioecious; in other words, male d female flowers are produced on different nts. 'Lutea' is an ideal choice as a single rub, for cultivating a dense, formal hedge as a background for shrub beds. It has tually no location requirements and will erate sun or shade and any fresh soil. ke care: all plant parts, except for the ls, are highly toxic.

| | 10–20 cm | Y | 3–5 m | | Early autumn | ❄❄❄ | ☀ | 🫖 | ! |

Thuja occidentalis White cedar

This tree has a variety of uses, but as an evergreen screen it is virtually unbeatable. The rounded, conical conifer can be clipped however you please and it is suited to any soil type, provided there is sufficient moisture present. Light-loving. **Take care:** the cones are poisonous.

| | Up to 4 m | Y | Up to 8 m | | Autumn | ❄❄❄ | ☀ | 🌿 |

Tsuga canadensis 'Pendula' Eastern hemlock

The delicate 'Pendula', with its cascading branches, is almost predestined to be a specimen and ably makes its impression hanging over walls and banks. Its beautiful weeping shape and fine, natural-looking needles make it an outstandingly elegant, evergreen conifer. It likes fresh, humus, acid to neutral soil. Protection from cold winds and the hot midday sun is recommended.

◀ *Viburnum × bodnantense*
Bodnant viburnum

A spring-flowering shrub with delicate, scented, pink-white flowers, which start emerging from their buds as early as late autumn in mild conditions. However, flowering reaches its peak in spring. Before the leaves are shed, the dark green foliage turns a brownish purple again. Produces purple fruit.

Up to 3 m | Up to 2 m | Late autumn to spring

Viburnum Viburnum

◀ *Viburnum × burkwoodii* 'Anne Russell'
Burkwood's viburnum

The initially pink, later white, flowers of 'Anne Russell' seem to create a large, scented dome of flowers. The compact shrub sheds its shiny, dark green leaves in autumn, unlike other varieties of this species. Its growing habit makes it suitable for small gardens too. The fruit start off red, turning black later. So that the beautifully fragrant flowers can be enjoyed, a sunny or partially shaded site close to a patio is ideal.

Up to 2 m | Mid- to late spring

Up to 1.5 m | Late spring

◀ *Viburnum davidii* David's viburnum

The evergreen *V. davidii* with its veined, slightly wrinkly, hairy foliage grows into a somewhat flat shrub. On female plants, the light pink tubular flowers grow into glaucous, dark blue, poisonous berries. Unlike the deciduous varieties, this shrub requires quite a sheltered site in partial shade. It also makes a good container plant.

Viburnum is valued as a decorative garden plant, particularly for its unbelievably profuse white to pink flowers, decorative red, blue, or black berries, and its foliage, which takes on many different shapes and structures.

The many varieties differ markedly. There are summer, winter, and evergreen viburnums, scented and unscented, varieties with bright autumnal foliage, and those that slip off inconspicuously into the next season. But there is a practical side too. Some varieties, such as *V. opulus*, are an important source of food for birds and insects or provide a nesting ground. For the gardener, on the other hand, viburnum is a flowering addition to trees and shrubs, mixed beds, as a specimen or hedge. As far as soil is concerned, viburnum will tolerate most types of moderately fertile, moist, or well-drained soils. The evergreen varieties do not need pruning, although any unwanted branches should be removed in early spring, while the deciduous varieties and *V. tinus* will usually tolerate hard cutting back.

▶ *Viburnum opulus* 'Roseum'

European snowball bush,
European cranberrybush, rose cranberrybush

A true favourite. The double flowers of the relaxed, bushy 'Roseum' actually look just like big, white snowballs. The flowers change colour from a greenish white to a hint of pink. Its foliage is also captivating, with its light green leaves that turn a beautiful wine to dark red colour in autumn. The red, poisonous fruit remain on the branches for some time. Sun to partial shade.

| Up to 3 m | | Late spring to early summer | | | |

▲ *Viburnum plicatum* 'Mariesii' Japanese snowball bush

The astonishing thing about the 'Mariesii' is the tiered growth of its branches and flowers. The deciduous plant grows layer by layer, thereby achieving a wonderfully uniform shape. The umbel-like flowers blossom from the outside in, which makes the flowering period particularly long. The veined foliage turns a vivid, purple red in autumn. A classical specimen plant that prefers sunny to partially shaded sites.

| Up to 4 m | | Late spring to early summer | |

Viburnum tinus 'Eve Price'
Laurustinus

The evergreen shrub with the dark, shiny foliage is rounded and compact. Depending on the weather, 'Eve Price' can start flowering in late winter, the flowers being followed by bluish-black fruit. It likes shelter from winds and needs winter protection, although it will tolerate temperatures of between 23 and 14°F (−5 and −10°C) for short periods.

| Up to 3 m | | Late winter to early spring | | |

Weigela florida 'Variegata'
Weigela

In early summer, the deciduous weigela is adorned with a sea of pinkish-white, bell-shaped flowers. 'Variegata' has the added appeal of beautiful, grey-green leaves with creamy-white margins. Another advantage is its spreading, softly pendulous habit. All in all, a reliable, distinctive flowerer, which is happy in any well-drained soil. Each year after flowering, the oldest branches should be removed from the base to maintain the plant's shape and encourage flowering. Very effective when planted alongside flowering shrubs such as lilac or mock orange.

| | Up to 2.5 m | | Up to 2.5 m | | Late spring to early summer | | | |

Yucca filamentosa 'Bright Edge' Adam's needle

The elegant, lance-shaped leaves with their wide, golden-yellow margins point impressively skywards. Its strong constitution – unlike other varieties, it is stemless – makes the evergreen 'Bright Edge' a striking architectural plant for succulent beds or other exotic trees and shrubs. In summer, an impressive flower panicle up to 2 metres high emerges from the middle of the plant, bearing numerous nodding, bell-shaped white flowers. This should be removed after flowering. The plant has no soil requirements, preferring dry soil but accepting any good, well-drained soil in full sun. Although it is anything but demure, it prefers a somewhat mild climate. In areas with severe frosts, it should therefore be overwintered in a frost-free environment.

| | Up to 75 cm | | High to late summer | | | |

CLIMBERS

Green Walls and Sumptuous Curtains of Flowers

They creep, twine and climb along walls, trellises, pergolas and fences. They provide colour and greenery; they flower and bear fruit. They beautify, cover and conceal; they lend shade. Blessed with boundless energy, these plants strive to climb higher or just stretch sideways, at a very slow pace or with incredible speed. They live for one or two summers – but sometimes for many years.

Vines can provide an abundance of greenery and colour even in the smallest of areas, because they love to grow upward. They create an illusion of space and provide a focus for the eye. There are a few basics if you plan to use them as a design feature. Annuals or biennials provide short-term interest, but choose perennials for long-term cover. Sometimes they need a little help from a climbing support. Otherwise they are not really particularly demanding, provided that you pay attention to their location and soil requirements. Vines also provide a perfect habitat for insects and birds.

 6–10 m Early summer

Actinidia chinensis syn. *A. deliciosa*
Chinese gooseberry, kiwi fruit

Suddenly it was the name on everyone's lips: the kiwi. This delicious, healthy fruit grows on the perennial, deciduous vine *A. deliciosa*. Its attraction is in its large, rich green leaves. In early summer, the creamy-white to yellow flowers appear. In warm, sunny climates the fruit follow in late summer – on the female plants. With good care, these plants can grow to be older than their owners. They have been known to live for up to 80 years, but to do so, they do have several requirements: they love warm, sunny, and sheltered sites and fertile, well-drained soil. Light winter protection is recommended, with a trellis or wires for support. Cold frame required from autumn onward. **Tip:** vigorous growth. Cut back in late winter to limit growth.

5–10 m | Late summer to autumn

Campsis radicans 'Flava'
Yellow trumpet vine, trumpet creeper

A plant for conjuring up a tropical atmosphere. With its trumpet-shaped flowers, the yellow-flowering variety brings an exotic blaze of colour into the garden. It has deciduous toothed leaflets. It takes several years for the flowers to appear. Loves full sun, sheltered site. However, the roots should be in the shade. Cut back faded flowers in the spring or late summer, as the flowers grow on one-year-old growth. Vigorous, fast-growing, twining vine with aerial rootlets. Needs additional support. Garden soil adequate. Layering or semi-ripe cuttings.

Up to 10 m | Late summer to autumn

Campsis × tagliabuana 'Madame Galen'
Trumpet vine

Although related to *C. radicans*, *C × tagliabuana* is less vigorous and not quite as frost-hardy. Its flowers grow up to 8 centimetres long and are orange on the outside and scarlet on the inside. Because of its sensitivity to frost it is particularly suitable for south-facing façades or walls. *C. tagliabuana* grows in moderately fertile, well-drained soil.

Celastrus orbiculatus 'Diana'
Oriental bittersweet, staff vine

The vigorous growing *C. orbiculatus* can develop true strength. Guttering and water pipes are not safe from its clutches. Before you've had time to notice, it will have entwined and strangled them. Not a nice way to behave. So right from the start it's best to let it climb where it can't destroy anything: on walls, arbours, pergolas, or old trees. It definitely needs a support. But at the same time it is particularly attractive when the leaves turn yellow in the autumn and the pea-sized scarlet fruit appear – provided that you have male and female plants. It can run riot in a sunny to partially shaded site with quite normal soil.

6–10 m | Summer | Autumn

Clematis alpina 'Pink Flamingo'
Alpine clematis (Group 1)

Pretty, medium-sized early-flowerer; the semi-double flower can reach a diameter of 6 to 7 centimetres. Vibrant pink on the outside, much lighter inside. The flowers are complemented by delicate, light green foliage.

2–4 m | Early spring and high summer

Clematis Clematis

The queen of the vines, clematis covers trellises and pergolas, trees and bushes with an extravagant show of colour. But she is also rather vain and demands attention from her admirers. Or in other words: the lady wants to be pampered. As a woody plant, she loves a sunny to partially shaded site for her flowers, but prefers shade and a fresh chill for her feet, as well as a fertile and well-drained soil. Dryness during the growth stage makes her susceptible to 'clematis wilt', causing the plant to die above ground level and dulling her energetic compulsion to spread. An imprudent snip will be punished with a refusal to flower.

▶ *Clematis* × *jackmanii* 'Jackmanii Superba'
Jackman clematis (Group 3)

The classic among the large-flowered, late-flowering clematises. The deep violet-coloured, almost velvety, flat flowers which can measure up to 12 centimetres are guaranteed to provide a wonderful sight. Can also be used as ground cover.

2–4 m   Late summer to autumn

Clematis Clematis

2–3 m   Late spring and late summer

◀ *Clematis* 'Josephine'
Clematis (Group 2)

The double-flowered 'Josephine' blooms not once but twice, in the spring and summer. You simply don't get any more flowers than this. It likes full sun to partial shade.

▼ *Clematis macropetala* 'Maidwell Hall' syn. *C.* 'Maidwell Hall'
Large-flowered clematis (Group 1)

Masses of lilac-blue flowers stand proudly, as if drawn out magically by an invisible force. The early flowerer bears semi-double flowers up to 5 centimetres across. Sunny to partial shade.

2–4 m   Late spring to early summer

This is the reason why the various types of Clematis are divided into three groups with different pruning requirements.

Group 1
Early-flowering, generally small-flowered varieties. They include many wild types such as *C. alpina*, *C. macropetala*, *C. montana*. Don't need any pruning; after flowering cut out dry or weak shoots.

Group 2
Early- to mid-season flowering, large-flowered hybrids. Prune in late autumn or early spring before there is new growth.

Group 3
Late-flowering, large-flowered species. Prune to 20 to 40 centimetres above the ground in late autumn or early spring before there is new growth.

The wild varieties and their cultivars are generally deemed more robust and less sensitive to clematis wilt. The spring-flowering hybrids tend to be most vulnerable.

▶ *Clematis montana* 'New Dawn'
Clematis Montana (Group 1)

Delightful cultivar with masses of flowers imbued with a hint of pink.

◀ *Clematis montana* 'Freda'
Clematis Montana (Group 1)

The delicate bright cherry-pink flowers form a lovely contrast to the dark green foliage.

4–7 m · Early summer

4–7 m · Early summer

▶ *Clematis* 'Pixie' Clematis (Group 1)

A real dwarf, but the wintergreen 'Pixie' appears with a profusion of sweetly-scented, lime-yellow flowers. Winter protection required in cold climates.

1–1.5 m · Late spring

Clematis orientalis
Chinese clematis
(Group 3)

The small, lantern-shaped, greenish-yellow flowers with lightly recurved petal tips appear in the summer. Their dark green foliage and their striking, feathery seedheads make them appear bushy and delicate. Vigorous climber. Wild species not susceptible to clematis wilt.

3–6 m · High summer to autumn

Clematis tangutica 'Lambton Park'
Clematis tangutica (Group 3)

Easy to grow, hardy variety with small, long, golden-yellow flowers and silvery seedheads.

3–4 m | High summer to late autumn

▼ **Clematis texensis 'Etoile Rose'** Clematis texensis (Group 3)

An extremely attractive species with small, bell-shaped, nodding flowers in a bright cherry red with silver-pink-coloured edges. Semi-herbaceous. Sunny to partially shaded sites.

2–3 m | High summer to autumn

The best time to plant clematis is from August to October. Ideally the base of the plant should be shaded with leaves or a mulch or underplanted with shallow-rooted plants. Keep the root area moist, but do not allow to stand in water. Basic care includes regular watering and application of fertiliser from the second growing year.

The clematis is a fast climber, and requires no encouragement to use canes, trellises, twine, or fences as a climbing support. Apart from house walls, pergolas, or fences, the climber looks beautiful growing naturally through shrubs, trees, or hedges. However, the prettiest effect – the absolute classic – is achieved by combining clematis with colour-coordinated climbing roses. It is recommended that the rose is given a couple of years' advantage and the clematis planted later.

Clematis also makes a wonderful cut flower. Place the fully opened flowers into a vase immediately after cutting.

▶ *Clematis viticella* 'Etoile Violette'

Italian clematis (Group 3)

With its deep violet-purple flowers, 'Etoile Violette' looks particularly attractive against a light background. A robust and hardy plant.

3–4 m   High summer to late autumn

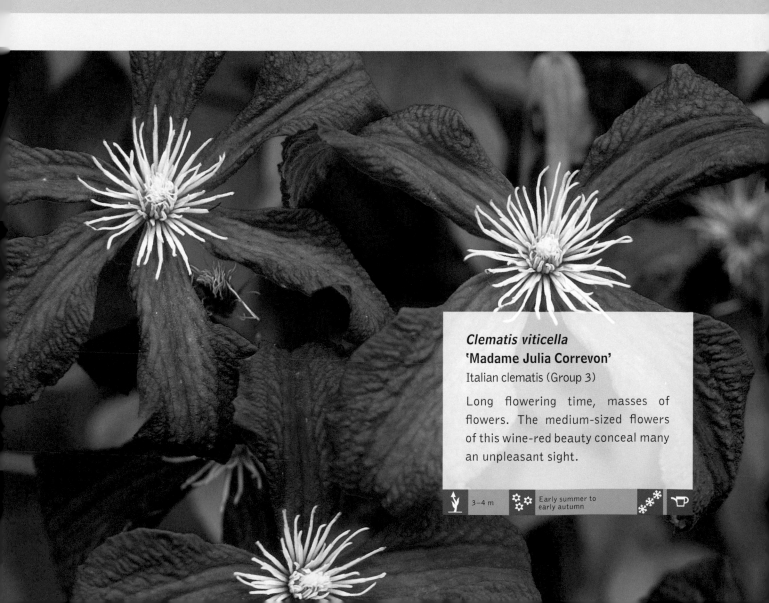

Clematis viticella 'Madame Julia Correvon'

Italian clematis (Group 3)

Long flowering time, masses of flowers. The medium-sized flowers of this wine-red beauty conceal many an unpleasant sight.

3–4 m   Early summer to early autumn

10–20 m | High summer to autumn

Cobaea scandens
Cathedral bells, cup-and-saucer vine

For anyone in a hurry... It covers a great distance within a very short space of time. In cool regions, the frost-sensitive, evergreen climbers are treated as annuals and during this extremely short growth period they achieve a height of several metres. The fragrant, bell-shaped flowers – yellowish green then violet – develop from mid-summer to autumn. Luxurious oval leaflets lend them an air of the exotic. Climbing support necessary. It prefers sunny or partially shaded sites with fresh soil. It survives the winter in warm climates, and should be cut back severely in the spring.

Euonymus fortunei Winter creeper

With its compact shape, the slow-growing *E. fortunei* creeps and crawls along making somewhat arduous progress. Now, this may not sound particularly exciting. But its advantages speak for themselves: the creeper is evergreen, fully frost-hardy, tolerates sunny as well as shaded sites and doesn't need to be pruned. As it climbs by aerial roots, it doesn't need any support to creep up walls and tree trunks, so provides an alternative to *Hedera*. The small oval leaves often have contrasting colours or are variegated with white. Later in the year they become tinged with pink. Inconspicuous flowers appear early to late summer on older plants only. In the winter it bears white fruit. Requires moist, sandy, humus-rich soil. Also suitable as ground cover. **Tip:** securing the long shoots with modelling wax assists their steady climb.

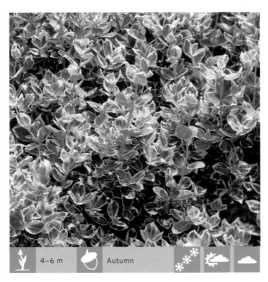

4–6 m | Autumn

Autumnopia baldschuanica
Russian vine, mile-a-minute vine

Sworn enemies condemn it like the plague, but others are effusive in their praise of it. One thing is for sure: it must be one of the most hard-working biomass producers ever. It manages to grow more than 4 metres per year, so covers anything within sight at an incredible rate. Initially it needs light support. It is not choosy as regards soil, and shoots up in sun or partial shade. Needs heavy pruning in spring. Can damage gutters and roof tiles. Deciduous.

10–15 m | Late summer to autumn

Hedera colchica 'Dentata Variegata'
Colchis ivy, Persian ivy

Useful for brightening shady corners. This cultivar has large leaves with wide, creamy-white edges and is suitable for covering walls or as ground cover. If it gets too rampant it can be cut back at any time. The stems turn reddish brown in winter.

Up to 5 m   Autumn

Hedera Ivy

Hedera Ivy

The strong, evergreen vine is invaluable not just for creating a romantic ivy-covered look, but also for covering walls and fences. The leaves come in an unbelievable variety of different shapes and shades of green, from dark to light, from silver variegated to golden. In its youth, *Hedera* grows slowly, but once established it climbs vigorously upward thanks to strong aerial roots. After approximately seven to ten years, the juvenile form gives way to what is known as the adult form. It suddenly begins to flower in the autumn and to bear fruit.

▶ *Hedera colchica* 'Sulphur heart'

Colchis ivy

Sulphur-yellow leaves. Looks almost like the negative of 'Dentata Variegata'. However, this cultivar grows more quickly and the leaves are longer. Particularly good for wall cover.

Up to 5 m · Autumn

Up to 10 m · Autumn

Hedera Ivy

◀ *Hedera helix*

Common ivy, English ivy

A fast-growing and reliable vine with lobed leaves, *H. helix* is the mother plant of numerous variants and cultivars. Doesn't need any support. Can be cut back at any time.

The decorative, pea-sized fruit that appear in the winter are a valuable source of food for birds, but are mildly poisonous to people. Another peculiarity: older forms of ivy grow vertical shoots – without aerial roots – with unlobed, egg-shaped leaves.

Hedera prefers fertile, slightly chalky, moist, but well-drained soil. Green-leafed ivies tolerate shade. However, those with variegated or coloured foliage prefer more sunlight to allow the shades of colour to develop better. Protect from cold winds. Cutting back to prevent upward growth can be done at any time. Take cuttings of young shoots with aerial roots in the summer.

As ivy grows away from the light, damage to masonry can occur as it invades crevices and fissures. Stable masonry is generally not subject to damage. Torn-off shoots leave traces on walls. Smooth walls aren't suitable for climbing ivies.

Take care: all parts of this plant are poisonous.

Up to 8 m · Autumn

▲ *Hedera helix* 'Cavendishii' syn. 'Marginata Minor'

Common ivy, English ivy

A slow-growing variety with medium-sized leaves with fine, creamy-yellow edges. Suitable for wall cover.

▶ *Hedera helix* 'Glacier'

Grey-green, almost triangular, lobed leaves with silver variegation and narrow, cream-coloured edges. Looks cold, but introduces brightness into shady corners.

Up to 2 m | Autumn

◀ *Hedera helix* 'Goldheart'

Is slow to establish, but then it can't grow fast enough. Dark green, medium-sized, three-lobed leaf with golden heart.

Up to 8 m | Autumn

▶ *Hedera helix* 'Midas Touch' syn. 'Golden Kolibri'

Small, compact climber with bright yellow, egg-shaped leaves and restricted growth height, making it ideal for screening low walls or fences.

Up to 1 m | Autumn

Hedera helix 'Thorndale'

Leathery, dark green, shiny leaves with bright veins. Very hardy and vigorous. 'Thorndale' is keen to grow high and is perfect for wall cover. Tolerates partial shade to shady sites. Grows approximately 0.5 to 1 metre every year.

Up to 20 m | Autumn

Up to 6 m | Summer

Hydrangea anomala subsp. Petiolaris Climbing hydrangea

Good things come to those who wait. A truism that applies particularly to the climbing hydrangea. Because for the first four to five years it is very slow growing, and is equally sparing with its flowers. But patience is rewarded. Once its aerial rootlets have become fully established, it is one of the prettiest climbers there is. In the summer, large, flat umbels appear with striking, sweetly-scented flowers that look like little white stars. The heart-shaped, deciduous, shiny leaves turn yellow in the autumn. Shoots early with decorative buds. Tolerates moist, cool sites in shade or partial shade on loose, well-drained soil. Avoids chalk. Perfect for dark, wet, cold walls or growing up trees.

Humulus lupulus 'Aureus'
Common hop, golden hop vine

The rambling hop vine grows best on a post or tree. It prefers very moist, humus-rich soil and a partially shaded site. The 'Aureus' cultivar is not a prolific bloomer, producing only a few female flower spikes in the summer, which are green at first, turning straw coloured later. The yellow-green, sycamore-shaped leaves provide its decoration. Care should be taken as they may burn in strong sunshine. In the winter it dies back completely, and produces shoots again in the early spring. Remove dead shoots in the spring.

Up to 15 m | High summer

Ipomoea tricolour 'Heavenly Blue' syn. I. violacea, Pharbitis rubrocaerulea
Heavenly blue morning glory

It doesn't hang around for long. The showy, sky-blue, trumpet-shaped flowers with their yellow-white throats open in the morning and shortly after midday are already past. However, I. tricolour flowers throughout the whole summer. In a sunny and sheltered site on fertile soil it reaches a height of 3 metres. A few wires provide adequate climbing support. Planting time depends upon the temperature, but this should be above 50°F (10°C). As an annual or short-lived herbaceous perennial it prefers a minimum temperature of 45°F (7°C). **Take care:** contains highly toxic seeds.

3–4 m | Summer

| 2–3 m | | Late winter to mid-spring |

Jasminum nudiflorum Winter jasmine

The remarkable thing about the deciduous *J. nudiflorum* is its flowering time. In mild weather, the bright yellow flowers can appear before the leaves in December, and there can be subsequent flowering until mid-spring. With its lacy leaves and slow growth it may appear somewhat inconspicuous in the summer, but is unsurpassed in the winter. The twining vine doesn't just scramble over trees, walls, or trellises, but can also be used to screen buildings or as ground cover. It prefers nutrient-rich, deep, light soils in sun or partial shade. Spring pruning approximately every two years, flowers on young wood.

| 2.5–3 m | | Early spring |

Jasminum mesnyi Primrose jasmine

...mon-yellow, semi-double, but unscented ...wers. *J. mesnyi* likes warm, sunny, ...ght site. Also tolerates partial shade. ...ere temperatures sink to as low as 14°F ...0°C), it is recommended that *J. mesnyi* ...moved indoors for the winter. Climbing ...pport necessary, grows wide.

| Up to 12 m | | High summer to early autumn |

Jasminum officinale True jasmine, common white jasmine, jessamine

Scent is in the air at last. Because with its profusion of small white flowers from summer to autumn, *J. officinale* gives off a heady fragrance. The feathery-leafed shoots can grow up to 2 metres long in one year and need a good support structure. Full sun, fertile, well-drained soil. Winter protection necessary if there is danger of frost. Thin out older plants after flowering.

Climbers   307

Up to 2 m   Early summer to early autumn

Lathyrus latifolius

Perennial pea, everlasting peavine

The perennial *L. latifolius* is a really persistent flowerer. The red, pink, and white papilionaceous flowers appear in clusters from late spring through to autumn. It is best suited to scrambling over fences, trellises, or unattractive walls, which are soon covered by the shoots which grow up to 2 metres long. Prefers humus-rich, fertile soil in a sunny site. Dies back in winter.

Lathyrus odoratus 'New Dawn' Sweet pea

There really is no good reason not to have a sweet pea in the garden: it is an incredibly fast-growing vine that twines itself quickly around any support. It makes a wonderful cut flower, and doesn't need any sophisticated flower arrangements. It has masses of flowers that smell of the summer, simply seductive. It thrives in humus-rich, well-drained soil, and a little chalk won't go amiss. To grow prolifically it needs sun or partial shade. *L. odoratus* can be grown from seed. Soften the seeds in warm water for one day before planting. Annual. Remove dead flowers regularly, provide sufficient nutrients.

2–2.5 m   Early summer to early autumn

Lathyrus odoratus 'Warrior'

Sweet pea

'Warrior' conducts its campaign in the garden with sheer determination to win. Its red-white flowers visibly mark its conquests: pergolas, arbours, fences. Climbs valiantly and eagerly anywhere it is trained to go. It flowers persistently – and in incredible profusion – pushing itself energetically into the foreground – making its mark: look how far I have come already! There's absolutely no hint of pulling back, because next year there will be others campaigning for their right to conquer a piece of the garden.

2–3 m   Early summer to early autumn

Lonicera × _americana_ Pam's pink honeysuckle

Extremely pretty, deciduous cultivar with cream-coloured flowers tinged with soft pink. Strongly scented. Multiple flowerer with masses of blooms.

| | Up to 7 m | | High summer to early autumn | | | | | | |

Lonicera Honeysuckle

This classic cottage garden plant was a common sight even back in our grandparents' time. The rambling varieties are extremely popular, because they are very adaptable, twining happily round climbing supports, bushes, trees, or growing with enthusiasm over the ground.

A characteristic feature are the tubular flowers that appear to hang around in small clusters looking rather tousled. Because of their fragrance many _Lonicera_ varieties are particularly popular in the vicinity of seating areas. **Take care:** eating the berries can cause food poisoning.

Up to 4 m | Early to late summer | *** | !

◀ *Lonicera* × *brownii* **'Dropmore Scarlet'**
Scarlet trumpet honeysuckle

The deciduous 'Dropmore Scarlet' is a prolific flowerer. Unfortunately, its orangy-red flowers don't smell, but the young shoots are tinged with pink. In the autumn it gets orange-red berries. Semi-evergreen. Loves sunny to partially shaded sites.

Lonicera Honeysuckle

4–6 m | Early to high summer | *** | !

Lonicera is not particularly choosy as regards location. In actual fact, the various cultivars grow and thrive on any fertile, well-drained, fresh to moist soil. Being a plant that is typically found on the edges of forests, most varieties tolerate partial shade, but also thrive in more shaded sites. However, plants in a shady location will produce fewer flowers. To prevent the roots from drying out and fluctuations in temperature it is recommended that they are underplanted with a mulch.

▲ *Lonicera henryi* **'Cooper Beauty'** Henry's honeysuckle

It is less the flowers than the small, round, blue-black berries that catch the eye. Evergreen. Winter protection required.

Lonicera are medium-growing woody-stemmed twining climbers. They can form a very dense curtain of leaves, so are ideal for screening purposes. Well suited to scrambling over free-standing climbing supports such as pergolas, fences, and stranded wire.

Up to 7 m | High to late summer | *** |

◀ *Lonicera periclymenum*
Woodbine, European honeysuckle, common honeysuckle

The shining berries of *L. periclymenum* look so tempting, but they are not edible. Fragrant flowers.

The leaves of the deciduous cultivars remain on the plant from about mid-spring to autumn, with the leaves of the semi-evergreen varieties remaining through to the winter. Shoots appear early in the season. Thinning out is recommended after flowering, with more aggressive cutting back if necessary. Otherwise *Lonicera* is a vigorous and relatively undemanding vine.

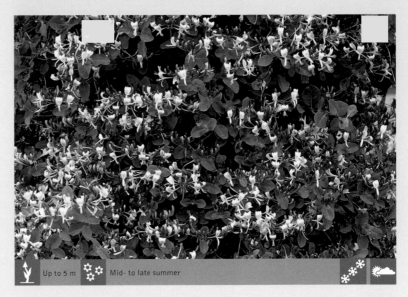

▶ *Lonicera periclymenum* **'Belgica Select'**

Common honeysuckle, woodbine

Quick-growing, deciduous, scented species which boasts an impressive display of flowers. In the summer, masses of yellow-white flowers appear which turn purple. Attracts insects and birds which feast on its berries.

Up to 5 m   Mid- to late summer

Lonicera × *tellmanniana*

Redgold honeysuckle

The coppery-yellow trumpet-shaped flowers are followed in the autumn by bright red fruit. This undemanding deciduous plant twines vigorously.

Up to 5 m   Late spring to high summer

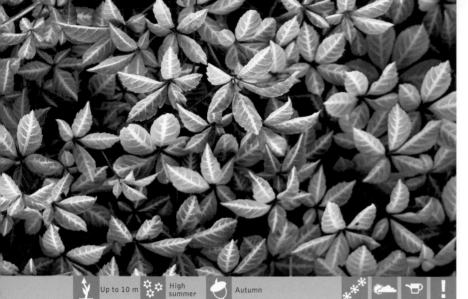

Up to 10 m | High summer | Autumn

Parthenocissus henryana
Chinese Virginia creeper, silvervein creeper

P. henryana puts on not just one, but two spectacular shows. The bronze-green leaves with striking, silver-yellow veins are highly decorative. But as if that weren't enough, in the autumn they turn a wonderful red colour, which is complemented by small, dark blue berries. **Take care:** berries are poisonous, except to birds. To survive the winter, it needs a well-protected wall. Deciduous.

Parthenocissus quinquefolia Five-leafed ivy, Virginia creeper

P. quinquefolia is only a little less reserved when it produces its dull green, toothed leaflets from late spring to early autumn. In late autumn, it crowns its appearance by turning a spectacular crimson-red colour. Blue-black berries follow the insignificant flowers which appear in the early summer on red stalks. Very decorative as well as being a popular source of food for birds. It is not choosy as regards its site: it tolerates full sun or shade – although the autumn colouring is more pronounced in sunny sites – and fertile, well-drained soil. *P. quinquefolia* is ideal for growing up trees, arbours, and pergolas. Horizontal support in the form of wire or twine should be provided if the Virginia creeper is to be grown to cover the façades of buildings. Young plants should be supported until they can cling on by themselves with their adhesive pads. Deciduous. **Take care:** the berries are poisonous.

Up to 15 m | Autumn

Parthenocissus tricuspidata
Japanese creeper, Boston ivy

P. tricuspidata is a showy climbing vine guaranteed to provide a colourful autumnal backdrop at the same time as being one of the most popular plants for covering façades. Thanks to powerful sticky disks it covers large areas in a very short space of time. And it doesn't need any support to do so. Inconspicuous, green-yellow flowers in early summer, followed by blue-black berries that provide a food source for birds. Leaves stay from late spring to autumn. Spectacular autumn colouring. Deciduous. Prune in summer and winter.

Up to 20 m | Autumn

Up to 10 m   Early summer to late autumn

Passiflora caerulea Blue passion flower, common passion flower

P. caerulea is one of the most well-known and popular *Passiflora*. It owes this distinction to several important qualities: it is regarded as an undemanding, strong-growing, extremely prolific flowerer, and being the hardiest of all the *Passiflora* species, it also tolerates low winter temperatures. *P. caerulea* should be the choice of anyone looking for a passion flower for planting out all year round or growing in a pot on the terrace over the winter. In cold regions during the winter the roots should be protected under a thick leaf mulch in ground that is not too moist. Plants can tolerate a minimum winter temperature of 5°F (−15°C), but the ideal temperature is over 41°F (5°C). Bears orange-coloured fruit the size of hens' eggs in late summer, provided that pollination has occurred. Sunny site. Moist, well-drained soil. Protection from wind.

Passiflora edulis Passion fruit, maracuja, yellow granadilla

Sensational, fantastic display of flowers, paired with delicious, maracuja fruit rich in vitamins. Unfortunately not frost-hardy. Needs 60°F (16°C) minimum. In cold regions it is a real eye-catcher as a pot plant.

Up to 5 m   Summer

6–9 m   High summer to early autumn

assiflora × *belotii* 'Imperatrice ugenie' Passion flower

evokes memories of hot summer days. he fragrant long-flowering climber with e pink-violet and white petal ring literally ives you a feeling of warmth and sunshine.

4–7 m | High summer to early autumn

Phaseolus coccineus

Scarlet runner bean, fire bean

It is not suited to extremes, tolerating neither hard frosts nor great heat. However, it is a reliable provider of short-term, annual enjoyment: vigorous and quick growing, it forms thick green walls of foliage with fire-red flowers. The young beans are edible when cooked. Perfect summer cover for arbours, seating areas, or fences in warm sunny positions and humus-rich soft soils. Water during dry periods. Sow in late spring, allow seeds to swell for 24 hours before planting.

Plumbago auriculata Cape leadwort

A fast-growing, evergreen, but frost-sensitive summer flowerer with vibrant matt green leaves that attracts attention because of its sky-blue flowers which it carries in thick clusters. In a mild climate and with adequate support it scrambles up walls, pergolas, and arches and can reach heights of 3 to 6 metres. In cooler regions, it should be kept in a pot or container when temperatures reach 44°F (7°C) and moved into a light greenhouse when it gets colder. Shoots should be rigorously cut back. *P. auriculata* is suitable for fertile, well-drained soils in full sun and protected from the wind. If planted in a pot use nutrient-rich compost. Keep sufficiently moist in the summer. Regular pruning encourages a longer flowering time. The 'Alba' cultivar develops glowing white flowers.

3–6 m | Summer to late autumn

Up to 3 m | Summer to autumn

Rhodochiton atrosanguineus

Purple bell vine

Dangling red-purple calyces with a velvety purple tubular flower. Simply delightful. The frost-tender, evergreen, perennial climber requires temperatures of at least 37 to 41°F (3 to 5°C). In temperate climates it is therefore cultivated as an annual or kept as a pot plant. Prefers full sun and fertile, moist, well-drained soils. Requires a lattice support structure. Perfect for patios or conservatories, also for arches. Prolific flowerer.

| Up to 12 m | High summer | | | | |

chizophragma hydrangeoides
apanese hydrangea vine

he deciduous, slow-growing Japanese ydrangea vine becomes a real heavyweight nce it finally reaches maturity. It should herefore be grown on a sturdy climbing upport that will not buckle under its eight. A wall or tree to climb up are lso perfect. Its dark green, egg-shaped, oarsely-toothed leaves turn light yellow in ne autumn. In mid-summer, small, lightly-ragranced, creamy-white flowers with eye-atching, diamond-shaped, creamy-white epals appear over several weeks. To show he flowers at their best, it needs some sun to artial shade and moist, humus-rich, well-rained soil. The young shoots should be ied until the aerial rootlets have sufficient old. Cut back excessive growth in spring.

| Up to 6 m | Early summer to early autumn | Autumn | | | |

Solanum crispum Chilean potato vine

Creates an exotic effect by cloaking a warm, sunny wall with its opulent, bell-shaped, violet flowers. *S. crispum* prefers to climb along wires or trellises. Loves full sun and well-drained alkaline, fertile soils. Mulch young plants in the winter. In cold regions overwinter as a pot plant in frost-free conditions. Looks pretty combined with jasmine or roses.

Up to 3 m | Early to high summer

Thladiantha dubia

Goldencreeper, manchu tuber-gourd, wild potato

T. dubia shoots up quickly, covering walls and fences with a lush light green and an ocean of delicate yellow, bell-shaped flowers. It requires a climbing support in a sheltered location, sun or partial shade, and a fertile, well-drained soil. The vine is an annual.

Thunbergia alata Black-eyed-Susan vine

The delicate little plant with a slender growth habit is particularly popular because of its small, bright orange-yellow flowers. The dark brown 'eye' at the centre of each flower looks as if it is peering at its observer inquisitively. With its twining shoots, *T. alata* easily scrambles over bushes and arches or climbs up trellises mounted on walls and fences. The young shoots should be tied to the structure at the start to give them a helping hand. A child of the tropics, *T. alata* loves a site in full sun protected from the rain and thrives best in moist, fertile soil. Because it is frost-sensitive it can only be grown as an annual or pot plant in moderate climates. It can be cut back after flowering.

Up to 2.5 m | Early summer to autumn

Up to 4 m | Early summer to autumn

Thunbergia gregorii

Orange clock vine

The cheerful, glowing orange flowerheads of *T. gregorii* reach out in pleasure toward the sun. *T. gregorii* thrives in similar conditions to those enjoyed by *T. alata*, but is even more sensitive to the cold. Combined with other annual climbers such as *Lathyrus*, it provides summer blossoms in abundance. As an annual, it reaches a height of up to 2.5 metres, and as a perennial it can grow to a height of 4 metres or more. *Thunbergia* are perennial flowerers.

5–9 m | High to late summer

rachelospermum jasminoides
tar jasmine, confederate jasmine

ositioned by the sunny, warm wall of a house
d protected from the wind, *T. jasminoides*
an develop its white, scented flowers to
erfection. Requires support and nutrient-
ch soil. In very cold regions overwinter in
bright frost-free environment.

2.5–4 m | Summer to autumn

Tropaeolum peregrinum Canary creeper, canary bird flower

The annual, vigorous canary creeper is a pretty climber with its small,
fringed, bright yellow flowers that are reminiscent of wings. The
delicate, lobed, grey-green leaves are also particularly attractive. The
canary creeper grows even more rampantly than the related *Tropaeolum
majus* (nasturtium) and doesn't take long to cover trellises and fences,
even in partial shade.

Vitis coignetiae Crimson glory vine

A climbing beauty with particularly large, heart-shaped, weakly-lobed leaves. The thick, dark green foliage transforms arbours and pergolas into secluded refuges and provides welcome shade for seating areas. *V. coignetiae* is a vigorous grower and thrives best in a warm, sunny site on well-drained, weakly alkaline, humus-rich soil. Splendid autumn colouring. The oblong blue-black grapes are not edible. Cut back excessive growth in winter and again in summer.

Up to 15 m | Autumn

Up to 7 m | Autumn

Vitis vinifera 'Purpurea' Purple-leafed vine

'Purpurea' is a treat for the eyes when its ravishing autumn leaf colours cloak walls, pergolas, fences, trees, and bushes in a violet-red sea of colours. Perfectly matching, round, purple-coloured grapes appear in the autumn, and these are best left to hang on the plants for decoration, because they really have no particular taste at all. Location and care are the same as for *V. coignetiae*. Propagation by hardwood cuttings in the winter or layering in the autumn. Leaf colour in the summer grey-green.

| 9 m and over | Spring to early summer | Late summer to early autumn | | | | |

Wisteria sinensis Chinese wisteria

The light green leafy growth of the Chinese wisteria is not just effective in lending new character to façades, pergolas, and arches. It is particularly popular because of its elegant, scented, blue-violet racemes, which decorate every bough in a spectacular fashion. But there is also a downside: wisteria is extremely demanding and vigorous; like an octopus it embraces everything that it meets. Regular cutting back, preferably twice a year, is required to control it. The flowers are followed by bean-shaped, grey-green, velvety seedpods. *W. sinensis* blooms before or at the same time as the leaves emerge, and in its youth can sometimes be rather reluctant to flower. Loves a warm and sunny site, sheltered from the wind with deep, fresh, humus-rich soil. Needs a vertical and very stable climbing support against a wall. **Tip:** goes beautifully with golden rain (*Laburnum*).

| 9 m and over | Spring to early summer | Late summer to early autumn | | | | |

Wisteria sinensis 'Alba' Chinese wisteria

The 'Alba' cultivar bears masses of sprays of white flowers 20 to 30 centimetres in size, and is the undisputed equal of the blue *W. sinensis*. Point of interest: *W. sinensis* twines anti-clockwise around a support and can grow to be several hundred years old. The scent of the flowers attracts bees and bumblebees.

| 9 m and over | From early summer | | | | |

isteria floribunda 'Alba'
anese wisteria

ows profusely, unusually long trusses of wers up to 60 centimetres and blooms er than *W. sinensis*, after the leaves have med. Twines to the right.

HERBS AND SPICES

Fresh from the Herb Garden

Fresh herbs and sophisticated spices are the latest trend, both in the garden and in the kitchen. Herbs you have grown yourself simply taste better; they are available fresh and they turn your garden into an aromatic, fragrant oasis. Whether you grow them in a flowerbed, window-box, or pot, you can find a suitable spot for herbs, even in the smallest space, and many herbs look wonderful in a well-designed garden. What's more, most are relatively easy and uncomplicated to care for. Most herbs will winter out of doors, with a cut back in the autumn and, if necessary, some winter mulch of leaves and brushwood. Herbs that are not frost-hardy can overwinter indoors with no problems. Nearly all herbs can be preserved. To dry, tie the ends together to form bunches and hang them up with the tips downward. Freezing, too, will help herbs keep their scent and taste, active ingredients, and colour. Wash the herbs, dab them dry, then freeze them whole or chopped. You can also conserve them in oil or vinegar, preserving the taste and flavour of fresh herbs.

 Up to 90 cm   Up to 1.5 m   High summer to early autumn

Agastache foeniculum Blue giant hyssop

This leafy, erect plant with its broad habit of growth has elegant, violet to blue flower spikes and would find its place in either a herb or a flower garden. The pale green leaves have a fine scent of anise. If picked before flowering, they can be used for desserts, salads, or teas. The dried leaves and flowers are suitable for fragrant herb cushions or herb pillows to aid sleep. The slender flowerheads have an intense fragrance that also attracts bees, bumblebees, and butterflies.

As *A. foeniculum* is not fully frost-hardy, a protective winter mulch is recommended. The plant likes a well-drained, sandy to loamy soil in full sunlight. This pretty perennial is also well-suited for growing in containers.

Allium schoenoprasum Wild chives

Who isn't familiar with the slightly sharp taste of *A. schoenoprasum*, better known as chives? This onion-like plant is generally used in salads or added to cream cheese. The dense, usually purple but more rarely white flowerheads are very pretty. They make a pleasing decoration. You can harvest chives all the year round. This member of the onion family likes well-drained, fertile soil, preferably in semi-shade. Planted in the garden, it is said to keep away greenfly. **Tip:** dried chive stems can be freshened with salad dressing or lemon juice.

30–60 cm | Summer

Allium ursinum Bear's garlic, wild garlic

The large leaves of *A. ursinum* are easily confused with those of the poisonous lily of the valley, but have a marked garlic-like scent. The good thing is that you can enjoy the fine, peppery flavour without any unfortunate side effects, as the garlic smell will disperse after a few moments. The aromatic leaves can be used to make tasty soups, pesto or cream cheese, and salad dishes. Eating the fresh leaves is supposed to have a cleansing, detoxifying effect. The delicate, white, scented flowers can be chopped and used in salad dressings. Harvesting of this bulb plant's leaves ends in early summer, as the plant dies back after flowering. It needs loose, humus, moist soil.

20–30 cm | Mid-spring to early summer

Up to 60 cm | High summer

Anethum graveolens Dill

The tall stems of dill, bizarrely branched and bearing delicate leaves, mean that dill is not only an ornamental plant for herb and cottage gardens, but also looks good in flower arrangements. The tall stems of this herb, which originates in India, are used particularly for salads, marinades, and fish dishes. It can be used, with its flowers, to make herb vinegars, for pickled dill cucumbers, for example. A tea of the seeds will ease stomach and digestive problems. Dill needs a moist, loose, humus soil and shelter from wind. The plant is annual, but will self-seed.

| | Up to 1 m | | Up to 1 m | | Late summer | | | | |

Artemisia abrotanum Southernwood

This erect, semi-evergreen shrub has grey-green, feathery leaves. Their strong, lemony scent is so intense that they should be used quite sparingly. It goes well with sauces, meat dishes, and salads. Stitched into fragrance cushions, southernwood also helps keep moths out of wardrobes. As a tea, the leaves are supposed to strengthen the stomach and stimulate the appetite. In late summer, little yellowish flowerheads appear. The plant loves humus soils with a lime content, and the ground should be dry rather than too moist. Southernwood can be trimmed into shape.

| | Up to 50 cm | | High summer | | | | |

| | Up to 1.2 m | | Late summer | | | | |

nthriscus cerefolium Garden chervil

he parsley-like leaves of garden chervil are ainly used for soups, vegetables, or salads. s aromatic flavour is slightly reminiscent f anise. Its flowers form smallish white mbels. This erect annual is for the most art self-seeding and likes loose, fairly oist soils. **Tip:** it is best to use chervil hen fresh, otherwise it will lose scent nd flavour.

Artemisia dracunculus Tarragon

Tarragon has two very different varieties. Russian tarragon (*A. dracunculus*) is a robust plant, fully frost-hardy, of dense growth and bearing plenty of leaves, but the fine touch that defines tarragon is completely missing. French tarragon (*Artemisia dracunculus* var. *sativa*), on the other hand, is as a whole rather more delicate in cultivation, but has that typical incomparable aroma that makes international cuisine esteem it so highly. It goes well with fine sauces, dips, marinades, and salad dressings. This semi-shrub likes well-drained, fertile soils. Harvest before flowering. **Tip:** when dried, the aroma of French tarragon leaves is even more intense. To survive the winter, it will need protection from frost.

| Up to 1.2 m | High summer to autumn | | | |

Artemisia ludoviciana White sagebrush

The ornamental value of the tall-growing white sagebrush is greater than its culinary usefulness. The silver-grey leaves, sharply incised at the edges, make a wonderful contrast to crimson and pink shades in beds of tall plants and herbs. The wormwood-like aroma of the leaves can be used in teas. The plant forms wooly white panicles with brownish-yellow flowerheads, and prefers a well-drained soil in a warm position.

Artemisia vulgaris 'Variegata' Common wormwood

'Variegata' has white spotted leaves, especially the new growth. This gives the common wormwood an ornamental value and the right to a place in any flowerbed, not just in the herb garden. Its leaves can be used for decoration in salads. The bitter principles contained in the leaves help to digest rich food. It is particularly fond of a warm sunny spot in nutrient-rich soil, which may be slightly on the moist side.

| Up to 1 m | Summer | | | |

| Up to 60 cm | Summer | | | | |

Borago officinalis

Common borage, annual borage

Making annual *B. officinalis* a firm fixture in your herb bed is worthwhile, if only because of the delicate blue star-shaped flowers that it keeps on producing throughout the summer. This branching, bristly-haired plant has a splendid, airy, wild look about it. The flowers are edible and look pretty decorating in a salad. The fresh leaves taste like cucumber and are well-suited to sauces, salads, and dips. *B. officinalis* needs a humus soil with a good supply of water, but in other respects it is undemanding. **Tip:** in summer, freeze the flowers in ice cubes. They will enrich any refreshing drink.

Up to 50 cm · High summer to autumn

Coriandrum sativum Coriander, cilantro

Coriander seeds, in particular, are most often used in Asian cuisine and give its dishes the typical bergamot-like flavour. But the freshly chopped leaves also have the same flavour and can be sprinkled over Asian dishes, fresh salads, and soups or used in herb dips and yogurt drinks. Its effect is said to aid the digestion. *C. sativum* is annual and has glossy, bright green leaves. From high summer onward, delicate white flowers appear, which then develop into the golden-brown seeds. When deciding on a site, consider the harvest you require: a sunny location will encourage seeds; semi-shade will ensure a plentiful growth of leaves.

Up to 1.8 m · High to late summer

Foeniculum vulgare 'Giant Bronze' syn. *Ferula* 'Giant Bronze'
Sweet fennel

Fennel is a very ancient culinary and medicinal herb. The seed, with its anise-like scent and flavour, has long been used for bread and cakes, fish, soups, salads, and teas. Apart from the flavour, sweet fennel has a marked anti-spasmodic and appetite-stimulating effect. Aside from all these useful aspects, though, sweet fennel is a striking tall plant, and looks very decorative in a herb or flowerbed. Sweet fennel likes warm, sunny sites with loose, moist, well-drained soil. **Tip:** individual shoots of fennel look striking and unusual in a vase.

Up to 45 cm · Summer

Calamintha nepeta subsp. *nepeta*
Lesser calamint

In the summer, airy, feathery flowerheads appear, with little white to pale blue flowers. This bushy, low-growing shrub has an intense scent of mint, well-suited to herb teas. The plant likes well-drained soils.

Origanum majorana Sweet marjoram

This evergreen semi-shrub is often cultivated as an annual or biennial. Its ovate, downy leaves have a slightly bitter, aromatic, very savoury flavour, and can be used fresh or dried in oven-baked dishes, minced meat and tomato dishes, with poultry, or in stews. You can cook the herb with the other ingredients. Marjoram needs a sunny flowerbed with nutrient-rich, well-drained, loose soil. In summer, it bears white or pink flowers. Harvest before flowering.

Up to 80 cm | Early to late summer

Origanum vulgare 'Rosenkuppel' Oregano

'Rosenkuppel' has more than fragrant leaves to offer – beautiful, deep rose-red flowers. This erect perennial attracts bees to herb gardens or rockeries and is also suited to growing in pots. Fresh or dried, this herb, commonly known as oregano, enriches pizzas and pasta dishes, sauces, and oven-baked dishes with a bitter to dry, slightly hot, and peppery flavour. It can be cooked with the other ingredients. A suitable site for oregano would be warm, sunny, dry, and well drained. Harvest before flowering. **Tip:** the flowering stems can be made into pretty herb posies.

Up to 40 cm | High summer to early autumn

10–25 cm | Summer

Petroselinum crispum Parsley

Fresh, savoury and slightly bitter. The flat-leafed variety is famed as being the more aromatic, but curly parsley is simply unmistakable, the absolute classic. Parsley has many different uses in the kitchen. It gives a last refining touch to salads, spicy dishes, and even potatoes – used fresh, of course, and sprinkled over the food. Soups and stews can be made with the root. This biennial herb can even be part of the design of a garden: as a decorative structural element or to border a herb bed. It loves humus, moist soils. Harvest before flowering.

| Up to 1.5 m | Up to 1.5 m | Mid-spring to early summer |

Rosmarinus officinalis Rosemary

This shrub with its penetrating scent is a classic in Mediterranean cuisine and is a must-have for every herb garden. The leathery, dark green, needle-like leaves have a powerful, almost perfumed taste, thanks to their high essential oil content. The flavour gives a special touch to meat and potato dishes, marinades, and vegetables. The herb also stimulates the appetite and the digestion. Rosemary is not fully frost-hardy and needs a lot of warmth, so in gardens where there is a danger of frost it should be grown in a container. In locations less at risk from frost, it likes a well-drained, moderately fertile soil; best of all is a site in front of a south-facing wall. This magnificent plant flowers from mid-spring onward, with purplish-blue to white flowers appearing in the little axils between leaf and stem. Rosemary is also evergreen and can be harvested at any time. It can be used fresh or dried, although its flavour when dried is far more intense than when fresh.

| Up to 1 m | Summer |

Ruta graveolens Common rue

Rue is not all that popular as a culinary herb due to its almost bitter, hot flavour, and is used only in small quantities, mainly for alcoholic drinks. But this is a roundish shrub; the leaves are delicately pinnate with ovate leaflets, and the plant has a decorative value that means it belongs in any herb or cottage garden as a background planting. In the summer, too, it bears many little yellow flowers. It likes a sunny, poor soil. Summer dryness is not a problem. **Take care:** contact with the leaves can lead to over-sensitivity to light. Do not consume too much of the herb.

| 40–60 cm | Early to high summer |

impinella anisum Anise burnet saxifrage

he typical aroma of anise is in the seeds of nis delicate plant. This means that it must e allowed to flower so that the seeds can be arvested. Anise imparts an unmistakable avour to sweet and savoury dishes. The ull aroma of the seeds is at its best if they re crushed by a pestle and mortar shortly efore use. This annual plant loves a well-rained, sunny spot.

ROSES

MAGICAL BLOOMS

Charisma, intoxicating scent, perfect, magnificent flowers. The eternal symbol of love and beauty, but also of pain and transience. The rose is one of the oldest cultivated plants, and also richest in mythology. It is right at the top of the scale of plant popularity, whether as a garden plant or as a cut flower. Its elegant and also nostalgically shaped blooms have an almost magical attraction. Roses display their colourful charm either all through the summer or once only, but with great profusion. Over time, an almost incomprehensible wealth of habits, of growth, magnificent colours, and intoxicating fragrances has come about. There is hardly a garden that can manage without roses, and thanks to their vast variety there is a suitable rose to be found for every garden. Roses earn respect, and not just because of their perfectly beautiful appearance. They display a certain amount of aggression, indeed a rather scratchy irritability, which makes itself felt if you come too close without taking any precautions. But once you have autumnen under the rose's spell, you will forgive even that.

Rosa Rose

 Up to 1.1 m   Up to 75 cm   Summer to autumn

Rosa 'Blessings' Hybrid Tea

Elegant and shapely, strong in growth and sturdy; noble 'Blessings' combines all these dream attributes. In lavish, extravagant profusion, it displays its large-flowered, double, urn-shaped blooms in salmon pink – and what's more, it does so several times a year. The dark green, slightly glossy foliage provides the effective, fitting background. Sweet-scented 'Blessings' is perfectly suited to a sunny rose bed with a fertile, moist, well-drained soil. Like all fine roses, it makes a wonderful cut flower.

▶ *Rosa* **'Blue River' ('Korsicht')**
Hybrid Tea

'Blue River' is one of the most intensely scented varieties. The wonderful, pink to purple, large-flowered, double blooms of this hybrid Tea appear several times a year; it is a good remontant or repeat bloomer. It has dark, glossy foliage.

60–80 cm | Summer to autumn

Rosa Rose

50–70 cm | Summer to autumn

◀ *Rosa* **'Duftwolke' ('Tanellis') syn.**
R. **'Fragrant Cloud', *R.* 'Nuage Parfumé'**
Hybrid Tea

'Fragrant Cloud' lives up to its name with its overwhelming, fruity scent. Also, the fine coral-red, well-filled double flowers bloom in lavish profusion — and they will even tolerate semi-shade. A good repeat flowerer. Erect, bushy habit of growth.

Up to 1.1 m | Summer to autumn

◀ *Rosa* **'Eden Rose'** Hybrid Tea

Scented, double, dark pink 'Eden Rose' brings a touch of romantic charm. Its petals are pale pink on the underside. The elegant flowers make a lovely contrast with the olive green leaves. Repeat bloomer. Will tolerate a sunny site.

70–80 cm | Summer to autumn

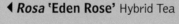

◀ *Rosa* **'Lolita' ('Korlita')** Hybrid Tea

'Lolita', richly scented, delights you with its gold to bronze-coloured, double flowers. A sturdy, robust rose. Good repeat bloomer.

Garden roses are classified according to their habit of growth or their descent. These classes do not always have clear boundaries, but in some cases overlap. The main differentiation is between old garden roses and modern roses.

Old garden roses were the first roses to be cultivated. They include all the rose varieties introduced before 1867. The cultivation of the first hybrid Tea rose, 'La France', in 1867 was the foundation of the class of modern roses.

Species roses, also known as wild roses or botanical roses, are outside this division. They are the ancestors of the garden roses, and all cultivated varieties are descended from them.

Modern Garden Roses
Aristocratic beauties – hybrid Tea roses
The hybrid Tea roses are considered the noblest class of roses. The elegant, often fragrant, double flowers have long stems, on which they grow singly or in groups of three to five.

▶ *Rosa* 'Mainzer Fastnacht' ('Tannacht') syn. *R.* 'Blue Moon' syn. *R.* 'Sissi'
Hybrid Tea

The large double flowers of this 'blue' rose are lilac coloured. It is sweet-scented, and has matt, dark green leaves. Repeat bloomer.

◀ *Rosa* 'Mildred Scheel' syn. *R.* 'Deep Secret' Hybrid Tea

'Deep Secret's' deep scarlet, double, spherical bloom is mysterious, almost magical. Strongly scented, robustly growing variety with glossy, dark green foliage. Good repeat bloomer.

Up to 1 m | Summer and autumn

Up to 1 m | Summer to autumn

▶ *Rosa* 'Mme. Caroline Testout' Hybrid Tea

Well filled, very large, long lasting, and intensely scented – such are the large, beautifully-rounded, pink flowers of 'Mme. Caroline Testout', which are also faintly flushed with carmine red. This vigorous, bushy hybrid Tea has large, mid-green leaves and big red thorns. A good repeat bloomer.

Up to 1 m | Summer to autumn

Rosa 'Peer Gynt'
Hybrid Tea

A light scent wafts around the round, double, yellow flowers with the reddish-pink coloured edges. The large-flowered 'Peer Gynt' has quite a vigorous growth habit and rich green leaves. Flowers several times.

Up to 80 cm | Summer to autumn

◀ *Rosa* **'Prima Ballerina'** Hybrid Tea

The bright pink, double, urn-shaped flowers appear from summer to autumn. Such scented tenacity has earned 'Prima Ballerina' a lot of applause. This hybrid Tea has mid-green, leathery leaves. A good repeat bloomer.

Up to 1 m | Summer to autumn

Rosa Rose

Up to 80 cm | Summer to autumn

◀ *Rosa* **'Rosemary Harkness'** **('Harrowbond')** Hybrid Tea

The intoxicating scent of the orange to salmon-pink double flower of 'Rosemary Harkness' is reminiscent of passion fruit. This bushy variety has glossy, dark green leaves. Flowers several times.

Up to 50 cm | Summer to autumn

◀ *Rosa* **'Amber Queen' ('Harroony') syn.** ***R.* 'Prince Eugen von Savoyen'** Floribunda rose

This pretty floribunda rose, which forms a wide bush, bears beautiful, amber, spicy, scented, double flowers. It has leathery, dark green foliage, with reddish new shoots. Repeat bloomer.

Up to 75 cm | Summer to autumn

◀ *Rosa* **'Escapade' ('Harpade')** Floribunda rose

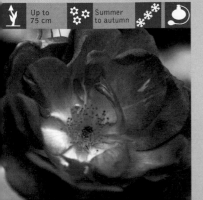

Long-lasting flowers for sunny sites. The semi-double flowers are a glowing pink to violet colour with a modest white centre. The rose has a slight scent of musk and dense growth.

Hybrid Tea roses have mid- to dark green, matt, or glossy foliage and are usually distinguished by a sturdy, erect, and upright habit of growth. The broad range of colours includes almost every shade except blue. Hybrid Tea roses can be planted as individual roses, in hedges, or in flowerbeds, and make a classic cut flower. Repeat blooming.

Clusters of floral splendour – floribunda roses, polyantha roses

These two classes of rose ensure fresh flowers through the summer. Typical features are the branching flower stems with their multiple blooms, which means that they are often planted in flowerbeds as bushes with clusters of flowers. The flowers are rather small, single or double, and sometimes scented. They appear in groups of up to 25 flowerheads. Their growth tends to be bushy, and on average they range in height from about 50 to 100 centimetres. Because they keep on flowering, they are popular plants to make groups in flowerbeds or hedges. They flower on the new growth and in short shoots on

▶ *Rosa* 'Eye Paint' ('Maceye')
Floribunda rose

The bright scarlet flowers with the white centres open in large groups, from the summer onward. These are cup-shaped to flat, single flowers. The foliage is dense and dark green, the growth bushy. A good repeat bloomer.

◀ *Rosa* 'Friesia' ('Korresia') syn.
R. 'Sunsprite' Floribunda rose

The pale yellow petals of 'Korresia' are slightly wavy at the margins. The double, scented, urn- to cup-shaped flowers open from summer to autumn. The growth is compact, with pale green foliage. An early and repeat bloomer.

Up to 75 cm · Summer to autumn

Up to 1.1 m · Summer to autumn

▶ *Rosa* 'Gruß an Aachen' Floribunda rose

As beautiful as a dream, the pale pink, almost creamy-white, lavishly-filled, spherical flowers contrast with the dark green, leathery foliage of this small erect floribunda rose. It is sweet scented and a repeat bloomer.

Up to 45 cm · Summer to autumn

Up to 80 cm · Summer to autumn

◀ *Rosa* 'Margaret Merril' ('Harkuly')
Floribunda rose

This rose is pearly white with a delicate blush of pink and has brown stamens. The fine, double, cup-shaped flowers of profusely flowering 'Margaret Merril' appear individually or in umbels. It has a bushy growth with firm leaves and a very strong scent. Repeat bloomer.

▶ *Rosa* 'Marlena'

Floribunda rose, miniature rose

Somehow classic: crimson, slightly-scented flowers and dark green leaves. From summer to autumn, low-growing, compact 'Marlena' displays numerous clusters of these beautiful, double, cup-shaped flowers. A very good repeat bloomer.

| ↕ Up to 45 cm | ✿✿ Summer to autumn | ❋❋❋ ❋ 🌢 |

Rosa Rose

| ↕ Up to 80 cm | ✿✿ Summer to autumn | ❋❋❋ 🌢 |

two-year-old growth. The varieties are mostly robust and healthy.

Small and dainty – miniature and miniflora roses

Miniature roses are the smallest roses of all. These dainty, branching, compact tiny roses are usually covered with a profusion of small-flowered, single or double, only infrequently scented clusters of flowers on very short stems. They flower in several shifts from summer to autumn. Miniflora roses are somewhat taller than miniature roses but like the latter have very many small flowers, usually unscented, in umbels. Both are suitable for edging paths, as low hedges, for flowerbeds, as ground cover, or in pots.

▲ *Rosa* 'Schneewittchen' ('Korbin') syn. *R.* 'Iceberg', *R.* 'Fée de Neige'

Polyantha rose

The enchanting pure white 'Iceberg' is one of the best known floribunda roses. The cup-shaped double flowers appear in large groups, blooming reliably throughout the season. The rose has a strong scent of musk.

◀ *Rosa* 'The Fairy' Polyantha rose

'The Fairy' is as wide as it is tall in its growth, making it a pretty ground cover plant. The small, well-filled double flowers appear from late summer onward, in luxuriant clusters. This is a late-flowering rose and repeat flowering is irregular.

| ↕ 60–90 cm | ✿✿ Late summer to autumn | ❋❋❋ ❋ |

Carpets of blooms, easy to care for – groundcover roses

With their strongly spreading or creeping, sometimes also overhanging growth, groundcover roses are ideally suited to flowerbeds and plant enclosures, as they leave no opportunity for weeds. They border paths and steps, or grow over low walls or

▶ *Rosa* 'Angela Rippon' ('Ocaru') syn. *R.* 'Ocarina' Miniature rose

From summer to autumn, the rose to salmon-pink, urn-shaped, double flowers appear against the dark green foliage. This rose is erect in growth and a repeat bloomer.

Up to 45 cm | Summer to autumn

◀ *Rosa* 'Baby Faurax' Miniature rose

'Baby Faurax' displays little rosette-shaped double flowers in dense clusters, flowering throughout the season. Low, bushy growth with dense, matt green foliage. Repeat bloomer.

Up to 45 cm | Summer to autumn

▶ *Rosa* 'Bluenette' Miniature rose

Pretty 'Bluenette' displays lilac to violet shades. Its low, compact growth makes it ideal for pots and window-boxes. It flowers several times a season and has a very faint scent.

30–40 cm | Summer to autumn

Rosa 'Mandarin' ('Korcelin') Miniature rose

The densely-growing, compact 'Mandarin' is one of the most attractive of the low-growing roses. Its very unusual colour mixture of salmon pink, carmine, and orange does indeed give it something of the colour of a mandarin orange. It has a light, sweet scent and flowers almost continuously.

Up to 60 cm | Summer to autumn

Rosa 'Zwergkönig 78' Miniature rose

This tried and tested, compact miniature rose brings out its pretty, double, glowing blood-red flowers in loose clusters throughout the summer. The flowers are quite weather-resistant and will survive even longer showers of rain. Blooms several times.

Up to 50 cm | Summer to autumn

Rosa 'Blühwunder' ('Koredan') syn. R. 'Flower Power' Miniflora rose

There is a touch of wild romanticism about the cup-shaped, double, peach to salmon-pink flowers of the compact 'Flower Power'. This is a beautiful, delicately-scented miniflora rose, and a repeat bloomer.

Up to 35 cm | Summer to autumn

Rosa Rose

◀ Rosa 'Heidesommer' ('Korlirus') syn. R. 'Cévennes' Groundcover rose

This bushy, profusely-flowering groundcover rose has radiant white blooms with creamy inner petals and yellow stamens. It has a charming sweet scent. Repeat bloomer.

Up to 60 cm | Summer to autumn

◀ Rosa 'Mainaufeuer' ('Kortemma') syn. R. 'Chilterns', R. 'Red Ribbons', R. 'Canterbury', R. 'Fiery Sensation' Groundcover rose

Up to over 2.2 metres in width, the sturdy growth of 'Chilterns' will cover quite large areas. The flowers are deep red and scented. It flowers early and for a long time, several times a season. A valuable garden plant.

Up to 75 cm | Summer to autumn

Up to 75 cm | Summer to autumn

◀ Rosa 'Mirato' ('Tanotax') syn. R. 'Chatsworth', R. 'Footloose' Groundcover rose, shrub rose

'Chatsworth' has semi-double, scented, pink flowers, contrasting magnificently with the glossy green foliage. It flowers almost continuously.

the slopes of terraces. The flowers, single or double, sometimes also fragrant, grow in dense clusters.

Some varieties only flower in the summer on the two-year-old growth some are repeat bloomers and flower even on the new growth. All varieties have two things in common: dense foliage and good branching.

Majestic in size – shrub roses

Almost man-high, shrub roses open their splendid flowers, providing height and structure in the garden. Strictly speaking, all roses are shrubs. The very varied group of shrub roses includes primarily large, sturdy roses that cannot easily be classified in other groups, including the English roses or old roses. They have some features in common. They are generally 1.2 metres in height. The flowers can be single or double or well filled, growing singly or in clusters. They are usually fragrant and flower more than once. The growth habit is for the most part tall and bushy, but can be overhanging. Some varieties have stems that are long enough to train them as climbers. They are just as suited to planting

◀ *Rosa* 'Nozomi' syn. *R.* 'Heideröslein Nozomi' Groundcover rose

The mother-of-pearl coloured flowers have a slight scent of musk. The effect is of delicate porcelain bowls that, in summer, cover the plant entirely. Up to almost 1.5 metres wide. Flowers once per season.

| 🌱 Up to 50 cm | ✿ Summer | ❋❋❋ | 🌿 |

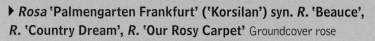

▶ *Rosa* 'Palmengarten Frankfurt' ('Korsilan') syn. *R.* 'Beauce', *R.* 'Country Dream', *R.* 'Our Rosy Carpet' Groundcover rose

Seen as a whole, 'Palmengarten Frankfurt' makes a picturesque pattern. The slightly-filled, saucer-shaped flowers appear in great profusion from the summer onward. This is definitely a robust plant, forming easy-to-care-for ground cover, and it will also tolerate semi-shade and heat. Repeat bloomer.

| 🌱 Up to 80 cm | ✿ Summer to autumn | ❋❋❋ | 🌿 |

Rosa 'Pink Spray' ('Lenspra')
Groundcover rose

Probably the most important quality of this prostrate little rose is the profusion of its flowers. The enchanting dark pink blooms with the pale centres and golden stamens completely cover the plant when it flowers. The flowers are followed by cinnabar-red rosehips. Flowers once per season.

| 🌱 Up to 50 cm | ✿ Summer | ❋❋❋ | 🌟 |

Rosa 'Royal Bassino' ('Korfungo')
syn. R. 'Country Prince' Groundcover rose

The brilliant red 'Royal Bassino' flowers right until the late autumn, with dense clusters of up to 25 semi-double flowers. A robust variety, with sturdy growth, for the smaller garden. It is slightly and delicately scented, and a good repeat bloomer.

Up to 50 cm | Summer to autumn

Rosa Rose

Up to 60 cm | Summer to autumn

◀ Rosa 'Schneeflocke' ('Noaschnee')
syn. R. 'White Flower Carpet'
Groundcover rose

'White Flower Carpet' has impressive flowers: beautiful, large, radiant white, and semi-double, with slightly crimped petals and a wreath of yellow stamens. It flowers several times a season and will tolerate sun.

Up to 80 cm | Summer to autumn

◀ Rosa 'Sommerwind' ('Korlanum') syn.
R. 'Surrey', R. 'Vent d'Été'
Groundcover rose, shrub rose

Its qualities are obvious: a luxuriant covering of magical pink double flowers and the fact that it blooms to the end of the season. It has a slight musk fragrance.

Up to 1.5 m | Summer to autumn

◀ Rosa 'Angela' ('Korday') syn.
R. 'Angelica' Shrub rose

Incredibly lovely saucer-shaped, pale pink flowers with carmine red on the back of the petals appear in dense clusters in summer. This is a sturdy shrub rose with a profusion of flowers.

as individual specimens as to planting in a mixed border. The more robust and sturdy varieties can be grown as hedges or borders, since thanks to their prickly branches they are almost impenetrable.

High-risers to enchant you – climbing and rambler roses

They want to get to the top, they need little space at ground level and are ideal for small gardens. Whether you grow them to decorate pergolas, espaliers, façades, or arches, their marvellous flowers ensure a fairy-tale, romantic atmosphere. These are not climbing plants in the classical sense, as the stems have to be tied to an appropriate climbing aid. These roses are classified into two groups according to habit of growth. Climbers grow like shrub roses, with stiff, longish stems that have to be guided with the appropriate supports. The ramblers class has been disbanded and its members have been reclassed as either large-flowered climber or hybrid Wichurana.

▶ *Rosa* 'Dirigent' syn. *R.* 'The Conductor'
Shrub rose, floribunda rose

'Dirigent' develops into a large, broad bush and is therefore also classed as a shrub rose. The blood-red clusters of flowers are resistant to rain, which means that 'Dirigent' is much esteemed in regions with a rainy climate. A good repeat bloomer.

Up to 1.2 m | Summer to autumn

◀ *Rosa* 'Fimbriata' syn. *R.* 'Phoebe's Frilled Pink'
Hybrid Rugosa, shrub rose

The special thing about the overhanging, attractive 'Fimbriata' is the crimped and frilled margin, giving almost the effect of a carnation. The shallow double flowers appear in loose clusters and start out pale pink, becoming white later. This rose is robust, with a vigorous growth. It flowers in mid-season and irregularly thereafter.

Up to 1.5 m | Summer to autumn

▶ *Rosa* 'Golden Wings' Shrub rose

Although it looks so fragile, 'Golden Wings' is very resistant to weather. The lemon-yellow, saucer-shaped flowers later turn to creamy-white and then to orange rosehips. This rose has a fruity scent and is a good repeat bloomer.

Up to 2 m | Summer to autumn

Rosa 'Lavender Dream' ('Interlav')
Shrub rose

The very prickly stems of the weather-hardy and profuse-flowering 'Lavender Dream' can, in warm regions, quickly reach a length of up to 2 metres, though in colder regions they might only be just about half as long. The flowers are small, deep pink to a pale pinkish-violet, semi-double. A good repeat bloomer.

Up to 1.5 m | Summer to autumn

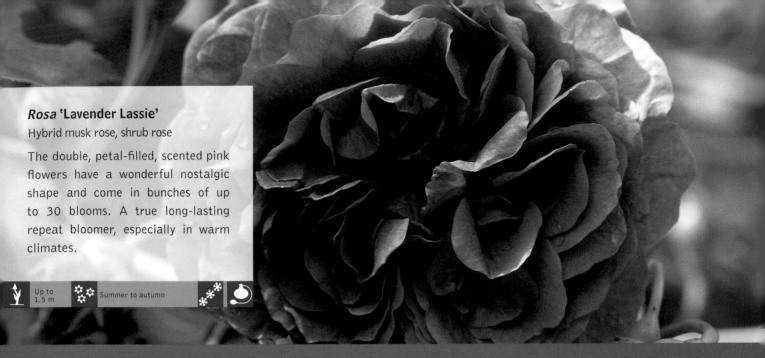

Rosa 'Lavender Lassie'
Hybrid musk rose, shrub rose

The double, petal-filled, scented pink flowers have a wonderful nostalgic shape and come in bunches of up to 30 blooms. A true long-lasting repeat bloomer, especially in warm climates.

Up to 1.5 m | Summer to autumn

Rosa Rose

Up to 2.2 m | Early summer

Nostalgic flower magic – English roses
The English roses, with their Baroque style of splendour, go back to the English rose breeder David Austin, who began in the 1960s to cross old roses with modern roses and thereby created a whole new category in rose breeding. English roses have the dense-petaled double flower, the intoxicating scent, and the robust strength of old roses and also the size and the repeat flowering ability of the modern varieties. They actually belong to the class of shrub roses, but they differ from other varieties so distinctly because of their characteristic romantic flair that they can quite justifiably be given a place in a group of their own. Thanks to their wonderful qualities, they are excellent planted close to sitting places in the garden, and they also harmonise well with other decorative shrubs and plants.

Up to 1 m | Summer to autumn

▲ *Rosa* 'Nevada' Shrub rose

Its long stems curve elegantly outward and are covered with giant, shallow white flowers. This is a true early-flowering rose.

◀ *Rosa* 'Pearl Drift' ('Leggab') Shrub rose

The mother-of-pearl, saucer-shaped flowers with their tinge of pink contrast beautifully with the very dark foliage. This rose has a light scent of musk and is a repeat bloomer.

▶ *Rosa* 'Rhapsody in Blue' ('Frantasia')
Shrub rose

The cup-shaped, semi-double flowers are a red-toned, bluish-violet colour. They grow in clusters and have a pleasant scent.

Up to 1.6 m | Summer to autumn

◀ *Rosa* 'Rosika' ('Harmusky') Shrub rose

The petal-filled double flowers are pure pink inside when they first bloom and pale pink toward the edge. This is a profusely flowering variety with vigorous growth, and flowers several times a season.

Up to 1.2 m | Summer to autumn

▶ *Rosa* 'Westerland' ('Korwest') Shrub rose, climbing rose

Sturdy 'Westerland' is a true all-rounder, with semi-double, apricot-orange, fruit-scented flowers. In warm climates, it is considered a low-growing climber, but it nevertheless can reach over 2.5 metres. 'Westerland' will tolerate semi-shade and its flowers are rain-resistant. It flowers several times a season.

Up to 2 m | Summer to autumn

Rosa 'Albertine'
Wichurana rose

The intensely-scented, salmon-pink, double flowers form a charming contrast with the darker buds. The profuse flowers of this variety appear only once a season, but they are incomparable.

Up to 5 m | High summer

◄ *Rosa* 'Alchymist' Climbing rose, shrub rose

Once every summer, 'Alchymist' brings out its yellow to orange, densely petal-filled double blooms with their tinge of pink. They radiate nostalgic charm, and also give off a strong, fruity scent. This is one of the most beautiful once-blooming climbing roses. It is resistant to heat and to very cold winters.

| 🌱 Up to 3.5 m | ✿✿ | Summer | ❄❄❄ | 🌸 |

Rosa Rose

| 🌱 Up to 5 m | ✿✿ | High summer | ❄❄❄ | 🌸 |

◄ *Rosa* 'American Pillar'
Wichurana rose

'American Pillar', with its numerous slender stems, covered with large thorns, forms an almost impenetrable thicket. Once a year, it bears slightly fragrant, single, carmine-red flowers with brilliant white centres.

◄ *Rosa* 'Bantry Bay' Climbing rose

The semi-double, slightly fragrant, large flowers bloom throughout the summer in a modest dark pink. The rose has a light, sweet scent and will tolerate a sunny location.

| 🌱 Up to 4 m | ✿✿ | Summer to autumn | ❄❄❄ | 🌸 |

| 🌱 Up to 3.5 m | ✿✿ | Summer | ❄❄❄ | 🌸 |

◄ *Rosa* 'Bleu Magenta'
Multiflora rose

This is one of the bluest among the violet climbing roses. The individual flowers grow in dense clusters and change colour from carmine to violet. Lightly scented, this rose flowers once a season.

Old roses

Old roses, cultivated before 1867, were the first garden roses. The main divisions are:

Alba roses

The colour spectrum of the Alba roses, which flower once a season, is limited to white, pale pink, and pink. Most varieties have a pleasant fragrance. Their growth habit is vigorously bushy, often overhanging, and they can reach heights of 1.8 metres or more. They will thrive in the most difficult conditions and in semi-shady spots. For locations that require a particularly frost-hardy, very resistant rose, an Alba rose is bound to be the right choice.

Bourbon rose

The repeat-blooming Bourbon roses mark the transition from the old roses to modern hybrid Tea roses. Their range of colours extends from white through pink to scarlet. From summer to autumn, they display wonderfully fragrant double flowers. They have a vigorous growth and can be trained as climbing roses.

▶ *Rosa* 'Blush Rambler' Multiflora rose

Neat and smart, the pale pink, only slightly semi-double, strongly-scented flowers grow in large, loose clusters. It looks best in dry regions, as spots appear on the flowers when it rains. It flowers once a season.

Up to 4 m		Late summer		

◀ *Rosa* 'Bobbie James' Multiflora rose

Robust 'Bobbie James' flowers twice a season, with large clusters of creamy-white, slightly semi-double, gloriously fragrant blooms, which later turn into innumerable tiny, orange-red rosehips. This is one of the best small-flowered rambler roses, and will tolerate semi-shade and north-facing façades.

Up to 8 m		Summer		

▶ *Rosa* 'Ghislaine de Félingonde' Multiflora rose

This little rambler rose is almost without thorns, and also makes an excellent shrub rose. In early summer, it bears large clusters of apricot-yellow, double, musk-scented flowers, which appear again for a second, later, but less profuse flowering. A lighter, later bloom in the autumn.

Up to 3 m		Summer to autumn		

Rosa 'May Queen'
Wichurana rose

'May Queen' has extremely vigorous growth and displays splendid, shirred, deep pink flowers with fourfold petals. The weight of the pretty clusters of flowers makes them slightly overhanging. The flowers are apple scented, the buds red. Blooms once, early in the season.

Up to 4 m		Summer		

Rosa 'New Dawn' syn. R. 'The New Dawn'
Climbing rose

One of the most resilient and popular climbing roses, this is ideal for walls, pergolas, and arches. It will tolerate semi-shade, heat, and hard frosts. The flowers are a delicate mother-of-pearl pink. Repeat bloomer.

Up to 3 m | Summer to autumn

Rosa Rose

Up to 10 m | Summer

Up to 2.5 m | Summer

Up to 3 m | Summer to autumn

◀ *Rosa* 'Paul's Himalayan Musk' syn. *R.* 'Paul's Himalayan Rambler'
Musk rose

This rambler rose flowers once a season, has remarkably vigorous growth and can reach dizzying heights. The small, double, violet-pink flowers fade to creamy white within a few days. The lush clusters of flowers are very effective when the rose climbs into trees.

◀ *Rosa* 'Paul's Scarlet Climber'
Climbing rose

The brilliant carmine clusters of flowers with their touch of scarlet grow on long stems and make good cut flowers. This is a robust, very winter-hardy variety with a light scent. It flowers profusely once a season, and will tolerate full sun.

◀ *Rosa* 'Pink Perpétue' Climbing rose

The pink flowers of 'Perpétue' appear all through the summer. This low-growing climber is well-suited to cooler regions. A good repeat bloomer.

Centifolia roses

The profuse double flowers of the 'hundred-leaf rose' range from white through pink to dark red. The growth is high and loose. These roses are still very popular today due to their intense fragrance. Flowers once in a season.

China roses

Small- to medium-sized shrub roses, which flower several times in the course of the summer and autumn. The flowers are slightly scented or unscented.

Damask roses

The colours of damask roses range from pure white to brilliant crimson. Almost all varieties have a heavy scent. They grow up to 2 metres and their habit of growth is mostly vigorous, with long, overhanging stems. Some varieties flower on the new growth in the autumn. They are very winter-hardy and thorny, and are used to obtain oil of roses.

▶ *Rosa* 'Sander's White Rambler'
Wichurana rose

It blooms once, late in the season, when it is loaded down with clusters of strongly scented white flowers. Its sprawling form will quickly fill trees or unused garden corners.

Up to 4 m | Late summer

◀ *Rosa* 'Santana' ('Tanklesant')
Climbing rose

The blood-red flowers, contrasting with the glossy foliage, are semi-filled, long-lasting, and resistant to bad weather. Profuse repeat bloomer. Will flower up to the first frost. Winter-hardy.

Up to 3 m | Summer to autumn

▶ *Rosa* 'Sympathie' Climbing rose, hybrid Kordesii

The double, dark red, elegant flowers of 'Sympathie' have a velvety appearance. The weather-resistant clusters of flowers will reappear after the lavish first bloom, though somewhat more restrained, and will continue to bloom until late autumn. The leaves are a strong, glossy green.

Up to 3 m | Summer to autumn

Rosa 'Venusta Pendula' Climbing rose

'Venusta Pendula' makes quite an entrance, with vigorous growth and profuse flowers once in a season. The double, white flowers with a pink blush come in little clusters on long, slender stems. This rose has a strong fragrance of musk and myrrh, many thorns, and red rosehips. The leaves are small and dark green with bright red shoots.

Up to 4 m | Summer

▶ *Rosa* 'Abraham Darby' ('Auscot')

English rose, shrub rose, climbing rose

'Abraham Darby' trumps them all with one of the most desirable shades in a rose: a shining coppery apricot, with a pale pink shimmer on the outside of the bloom. The densely-packed, large double flowers have a scent of fruit. This vigorously bushy beauty is one of the most successful English roses. A good repeat bloomer.

Up to 2 m | Summer to autumn

Rosa Rose

Up to 75 cm | Summer to autumn

Up to 1.5 m | Summer

◀ *Rosa* 'Ambridge Rose' ('Auswonder')

English rose, shrub rose

The very attractive 'Ambridge Rose' is a reliable bloomer. It bears pale pink to apricot-coloured rosette-shaped flowers, singly or in little clusters, rapidly one after another. The flowers have a strong fragrance.

Up to 2 m | Summer to autumn

▲ *Rosa* 'Charles Austin' ('Ausles')

English rose, shrub rose

The bushy, erect 'Charles Austin' is distinguished by its large, fully double, apricot-coloured flowers. A repeat bloomer.

◀ *Rosa* 'Chianti' English rose, shrub rose

These violet to carmine-red flowers, which develop into pompons when they open fully, are very impressive. This rose flowers once in a season and makes a good cut flower.

Gallica roses

The loosely-packed, double, generally fragrant flowers of this group of roses were already being used in the Middle Ages to make oil of roses. Gallica roses are among the oldest roses of all and are distinguished by their excellent winter hardiness. The colour spectrum ranges from a porcelain pink to carmine red and crimson. Many varieties are streaked, spotted, or patched in colour. In the autumn, the shrubs bear spherical, erect rosehips. Flowers once in a season.

Moss roses

The flowers of moss roses are generally double and pleasantly scented. Their particular charm comes from the feature that gives them their name, the mossy growth on the calices and stems, with its resinous fragrance. The stems usually bear very strong thorns. Flowers once in a season.

Portland roses

Delicate pink to carmine red and crimson, these flowers have an intense, sweet fragrance. Many varieties of the compact Portland roses flower again in late summer.

▶ *Rosa* 'Constance Spry' ('Austance')

English rose, shrub rose, climbing rose

The archetype of the English roses. Its large round double flowers, lovely as a dream, open in the summer. Overhanging in growth, it flowers once in a season, and has a scent of myrrh.

Up to 2.5 m | Summer

◀ *Rosa* 'Corvedale' English rose, shrub rose

This compact shrub bears cup-shaped flowers in a clear dark pink, with a lovely fragrance of myrrh. It makes a good cut flower.

Up to 1.5 m | Summer to autumn

▶ *R.* 'Cressida' ('Auscress') English rose, shrub rose, climbing rose

In warm regions 'Cressida' can reach heights of up to 3 metres, and can therefore be cultivated as a bushy climber. Its large, bowl-shaped, conspicuously lovely flowers are apricot coloured at first, then more of a blush shade. In the autumn, they form clusters of up to 20 blooms. The scent is intense and fruity.

Up to 1.5 m | Summer to autumn

◀ *Rosa* 'Eglantyne' ('Ausmak')

English rose, shrub rose

The pale pink rosette-shaped blooms of 'Eglantyne' are full of nostalgic charm. It is one of the most profuse bloomers among the English roses, and one of the most beautiful. It has a strong fragrance and is almost a perpetual bloomer.

Rosa 'Falstaff' ('Ausverse')

English rose, shrub rose, climbing rose

In warm regions, glowing carmine-red 'Falstaff' can be cultivated as a climbing rose, and will then grow up to almost 3 metres. Its lovely double flowers later turn a matt violet. A strong, sweet fragrance.

Up to 1.5 m | Summer to autumn

Up to 1.25 m | Summer to autumn

Up to 80 cm | Summer to autumn

Up to 1.75 m | Summer to autumn

◀ *Rosa* 'Gertrude Jekyll' ('Ausbord')

English rose, shrub rose

From summer onward, this vigorous shrub covers itself with densely-packed, double, deep pink rosette-shaped flowers. It has a strong fragrance and grows quickly in warm regions. A good repeat bloomer, this rose will also tolerate semi-shade.

◀ *Rosa* 'Glamis Castle' ('Auslevel')

English rose, shrub rose

'Glamis Castle' is low growing and bushy, with numerous slender branches. The white, saucer-shaped, rain-resistant flowers are of unusual fullness and flower continuously. This rose will tolerate sun.

◀ *Rosa* 'Graham Thomas' ('Ausmas')

English rose, shrub rose

This is a classic to be grateful for. In warm regions, loosely overhanging 'Graham Thomas' can easily reach heights of 3 to 4 metres or more. Its glowing yellow-gold, densely-packed double flowers contrast prettily with the large, glossy pale green leaves. A very good repeat bloomer, with a strong, fruity scent.

Hybrid Perpetual

Pure white, pink, scarlet, crimson, or even two-coloured, and usually fragrant, the hybrid Perpetual roses reach heights of close to 1.8 metres. All of them bloom more than once, although the second flowering is often rather sparse.

Species roses

Species roses usually have single, fragrant flowers with five petals and numerous stamens in the centre. They are generally distinguished by a single flowering period early in the season and attractive rosehips in the autumn. They are well suited to a natural-look border, as food for bees or a flowering hedge plant. They will tolerate just about any soil, except a waterlogged one, and have no problems thriving in semi-sunny locations.

The species rose may have a reputation of being a fussy and capricious garden diva, but as long as some basic conditions are met it will certainly show its more robust side. The most important conditions for healthy growth and profusion of flowers are sun, air, and shelter.

▶ *Rosa* 'Heritage' ('Ausblush')

English rose, shrub rose

This is another popular English rose. The densely-packed, round flowers hardly open; they appear in clusters and decorate this pretty shrub almost to ground level.

Up to 1.2 m | Summer to late autumn

◀ *Rosa* 'Kathryn Morley' ('Ausvariety')

English rose, shrub rose

During the season, 'Kathryn Morley' will bloom every three to four weeks, with flowers that really are worth seeing. In warm, dry regions, it will soon reach heights of over 2 metres. Good repeat bloomer, intense fragrance.

Up to 1 m | Summer to autumn

▶ *Rosa* 'Leander' ('Auslea') English rose, shrub rose, climbing rose

Individual plants of beautiful, vigorous 'Leander' can be persuaded to flower more than once. The sturdy apricot flowers with their fruity scent grow in long-stemmed clusters. They will later change colour through salmon pink to white. In a warm climate, treat this rose as a low-growing climber.

Up to 2 m | Summer

Rosa 'Mary Rose' ('Ausmary')

English rose, shrub rose

Beautiful 'Mary Rose' is one of the first and last roses in the season to flower. The slightly-curled, deep pink petals give the densely packed flowers a frilled effect. A good repeat bloomer.

Up to 1.2 m | Summer to autumn

▶ *Rosa* 'The Pilgrim' ('Auswalker') syn. *R.* 'Gartenarchitekt Günther Schulze'

English rose, shrub rose

An extremely profuse bloomer, 'The Pilgrim' forms an unmissable fragrant yellow sea of lavish flower clusters in the season. The contrast between the pale outer and brilliant inner petals is very beautiful. A good repeat bloomer.

Up to 1.5 m		Summer to autumn			

Rosa Rose

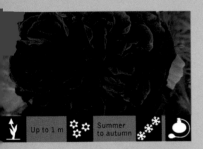

◀ *Rosa* 'Tradescant' ('Ausdir')

English rose, shrub rose

These dark red to violet flowers are among the darkest of David Austin's English roses. 'Tradescant' has earned a special place in any garden that can give this sweetly scented rose the right setting.

Up to 1 m		Summer to autumn			

◀ *Rosa* 'Wife of Bath' ('Ausbath') syn. *R.* 'Glücksburg', *R.* 'The Wife of Bath'

A robust, reliable bloomer, deep pink in the centre with paler outer petals. A good repeat bloomer, this rose will tolerate full sunshine.

Up to 1 m		Summer to autumn			

Up to 80 cm		Summer to autumn			

◀ *Rosa* 'Yellow Button'

English rose, shrub rose

The deep golden-yellow flowers, fading towards white on the outer petals, look their best in a cooler climate, as the flowers lose the intensity of their colours too quickly in the heat. Fruity scent.

Roses love a light location with good air circulation, allowing the leaves to dry quickly after a shower of rain. Roses are sun-worshipers and will certainly tolerate several hours of direct sunshine a day, but do not like heat. East- or west-facing sites are therefore preferable to south-facing ones, which are likely to be too hot. Some varieties will tolerate a position out of direct sunlight or in semi-shade; dark corners, dripping water, or pressure on the roots will, however, simply not be accepted.

Roses have deep roots, and therefore need plenty of space in the ground. The soil should be deep, humus, moist but well-drained. Soils that have had roses growing in them recently are unsuitable for new plantings. The best times to plant are frost-free periods in the winter or early spring.

Rosa 'Blanchefleur' Centifolia rose

The tightly-filled, double, pale pink to creamy-white, fragrant flowers grow in dense clusters on slightly overhanging stems. This rose flowers once early in the season, but the flowers are long-lasting.

| Up to 1.5 m | | Early summer | |

Rosa 'Boule de Neige' Bourbon rose

'Boule de Neige', with its large clusters of white, sweetly-scented roses, is almost a perpetual bloomer. The flowers are rather fragile and should be protected from rain.

| Up to 1.5 m | | Summer to autumn | |

Rosa 'Camaieux' Gallica rose

This small, compact Gallica rose has a striking colouring. Crimson and white streaks glow against a pink background; the flowers fade within a few days to delicate shades of lilac and grey. This rose flowers once in a season, with a sweet fragrance.

| Up to 80 cm | | Summer | |

Rosa 'Cardinal de Richelieu'
Gallica rose

The petals of this beautiful crimson Gallica rose are closely packed and give the flower a lush appearance. The bright contrast given by the inward curve of the petals is a pretty feature. Flowers once in a season.

| Up to 1 m | | Summer | |

◀ *Rosa* 'Charles de Mills' syn.
R. 'Bizarre Triomphant' Gallica rose

The almost thorn-free stems of 'Charles de Mills' bow down elegantly under the magnificent weight of their flowers. Its crimson to violet colouring, its vigorous growth, and its undemanding nature make this sweet-scented variety a highly esteemed rose. Flowers once in a season.

Up to 1.5 m | Summer

Rosa Rose

◀ *Rosa* 'Commandant Beaurepaire' Bourbon rose

In some years, 'Commandant Beaurepaire' will flower a second time in the autumn, but as a rule its pretty, irregularly-streaked flowers appear only once. It has a sweet citrus fragrance.

Up to 1.75 m | Summer

Up to 2.5 m | Summer

▲ *Rosa* 'Complicata' Gallica rose

'Complicata' turns up trumps with its easy-going simplicity. The single flowers, shallow but large, have a light sweet fragrance and close overnight. This vigorous plant bears flowers in little clusters on its overhanging stems.

◀ *Rosa* 'Comte de Chambord' Portland rose

This bushy Portland rose with dense foliage bears almost perfectly-formed pink flowers throughout the whole season, and has a sweet fragrance.

Up to 1.75 m | Summer to autumn

▶ *Rosa* 'Duc de Cambridge' Damask rose

Once every season, 'Duc de Cambridge' shows off its splendour. The flowers are a beautiful pink, growing paler toward the edges, and have a powerful, stimulating fragrance.

| ⬆ Up to 2.5 m | ✿✿ | Summer | ✳✳✳ | 🏺 |

◀ *Rosa* 'Félicité Parmentier' Alba rose

A robust character and vigorous growth make this bushy, erect Alba rose with its rough, blue-green foliage the jewel of the garden. The pale pink flowers grow in dense clusters and turn white as they fade.

| ⬆ Up to 1.5 m | ✿✿ | High summer | ✳✳✳ | 🏺 |

▶ *Rosa* 'Ferdinand Pichard' Hybrid Perpetual rose

The semi-double pink flowers with their irregular crimson streaks and flecks have a scent of raspberries. 'Ferdinand Pichard', erect and repeat blooming, is sturdy and robust, one of the most beautiful of the streaked roses.

| ⬆ Up to 2.5 m | ✿✿ | Summer to autumn | ✳✳✳ | 🏺 |

Rosa 'Général Jaqueminot'
Hybrid Perpetual rose

Its origins date back to 1846. Its profuse flowering made it the most frequently cultivated rose in the world for many years. It has a strong, sweet scent and is a good repeat bloomer.

| ⬆ Up to 1.5 m | ✿✿ | Summer to autumn | ✳✳✳ | 🏺 |

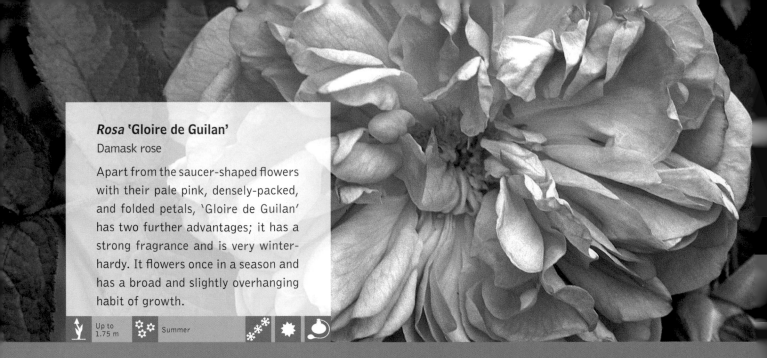

Rosa 'Gloire de Guilan'
Damask rose

Apart from the saucer-shaped flowers with their pale pink, densely-packed, and folded petals, 'Gloire de Guilan' has two further advantages; it has a strong fragrance and is very winter-hardy. It flowers once in a season and has a broad and slightly overhanging habit of growth.

Up to 1.75 m | Summer

Rosa Rose

Up to 2.5 m | Summer

Up to 80 cm | Summer to autumn

◀ **Rosa 'Goethe'** Moss rose

The mossy flower stems and buds make 'Goethe' look very attractive even after flowering is over. It is popular as a hedge plant due to the densely-placed long thorns.

Up to 1.5 m | Summer

▲ **Rosa 'Henri Martin'** Moss rose

It is not only the magnificent red flowers of 'Henri Martin' that offer an unforgettable experience of fragrance. The green mossy growth also has an intense resinous scent. In winter, the rose bears furry orange-coloured rosehips.

◀ **Rosa 'Hermosa'** China rose or hybrid China

'Hermosa' will display its nodding flowerheads right up into the early winter if it is in a sheltered spot. It has a scent of tea.

▶ *Rosa* 'Jacques Cartier' syn. *R.* 'Marchesa Boccela' Portland rose

The deep pink, quartered blooms seem to have an endless number of petals. It flowers like a dream, and is very robust.

Up to 1.5 m | Summer to autumn

◀ *Rosa* 'La Reine' syn. *R.* 'Rose de la Reine'* Hybrid Perpetual rose

The thin petals stick together in the wet, making the large-flowered 'La Reine' better suited to warm, dry regions. This compact hybrid Perpetual dates from 1842.

Up to 1.75 m | Summer to autumn

▶ *Rosa* 'Maxima' Alba rose

Modesty coupled with extravagance; a good summary of the essential qualities of 'Maxima'. This tall, broad Alba rose with the grey-green foliage is not just extremely sturdy and very winter-hardy, it is also suited to poor soils, as long as there is enough sun. In return for such treatment, it will gratefully produce masses of double white flowers and sweet fragrance.

Up to 2 m | Summer

Up to 1.5 m | Summer to autumn

◀ *Rosa* 'Mme. Louis Lévêque' Moss rose

The large, round buds are lightly covered with green moss. They open to form large, pink, densely-packed double flowers, which have a sweet fragrance. This rose is most effective in dry climates and is very winter-hardy.

▶ *Rosa* 'Mme. Pierre Oger'
Bourbon rose

The especially translucent, porcelain-like creamy-pink petals make 'Mme. Pierre Oger' one of the most popular of garden roses. After the first profuse flowering, delicately-scented, dense double blooms will appear until the first frost.

Up to 2 m | Summer to autumn

Rosa Rose

Up to 80 cm | Summer to autumn

Up to 2 m | Summer

◀ *Rosa* 'Portland Rose' syn. *R.* 'Duchesse of Portland', *R.* 'Paestana' Portland rose

This profuse flowering Portland rose forms a dense thicket of slender stems and glowing dark pink, semi-double flowers that have a wonderful fragrance. Repeat bloomer.

Up to 1 m | Summer to autumn

▲ *Rosa* 'Roger Lambelin'
Hybrid Perpetual rose

The dark carmine-red, loosely-packed double flowers have noticeably variegated petals. This rose tends toward a shrubby growth.

◀ *Rosa* 'Tour de Malakoff' Centifolia rose

The splendid play of colours of these incomparably fragrant, large flowers is somewhere between magenta, crimson, and a pale lilac grey.

▶ *Rosa* **'Tricoloure de Flandres'** Gallica rose

'Tricolour de Flandres' is small and delicate in growth. The well-arranged, densely-packed, double, streaked blooms have a green eye in the centre. This rose has a slight fragrance.

 Up to 1 m · Summer

◀ *Rosa* × *odorata* **'Viridiflora'** syn. *R. chinensis* **'Viridiflora', *R.* 'Lü E',** *R.* **'Viridiflora'** Tea rose

The green rose 'Viridiflora' is a rather curious example of the species. The flowers are green to start with but gradually turn an attractive shade of copper.

Up to 75 cm · Summer to autumn

▶ *Rosa canina* Dog rose

For many people, *R. canina* is *the* wild rose. Its short-lived flowers, white to deep pink in colour, are delicate and have a fresh scent, and they open once during the summer. After blooming, they develop coral-red rosehips, which can be used to make a tasty jam.

Up to 4 m · Summer

Rosa glauca
Red-leafed rose

The reddish-blue shimmer on its leaves, the many brilliant red rosehips and in winter the brownish-red stems with their blue bloom give *R. glauca* its inestimable value in the garden.

Up to 2 m · Summer

▶ **Rosa moyesii** Mandarin rose

From late summer onward the elongated, bottle-shaped rosehips appear on the slightly overhanging branches. They are an intense, brilliant, autumnal cinnabar orange. *R. moyesii* flowers in every shade of pink through blood-red to dark crimson.

Up to 4 m · Early summer

Rosa Rose

Up to 1.75 m · Early summer

◀ **Rosa pendulina** var. **pendulina** Alpine rose

The delicate alpine rose has single flowers in a strong pink, and almost thornless stems. In the autumn, bottle-shaped orange rosehips appear. This rose is very winter-hardy.

Up to 2 m · Early summer

◀ **Rosa pimpinellifolia** var. **altaica** Pimpinel rose

After the creamy flowers with their light fruity scent, the round, black rosehips take their turn to attract the eye in the autumn.

▶ *Rosa villosa* syn. *R. pomifera* Apple rose

The dark red hips, which usually have bristly hairs, are very noticeable. In the autumn, large numbers of them appear, large and round, on *R. villosa*. The flowers are pale pink with a light fragrance.

Up to 2 m   Summer

Rosa xanthina f. *hugonis*
Yellow rose

This is often the first rose of the season to bloom. It has primrose-yellow flowers, which appear in profusion along the arching stems. It has particularly attractive fern-like leaves.

Up to 2 m   Late spring

CLIMATE ZONE MAPS

Average annual minimum temperature
Table and maps follow USDA (US Department of Agriculture) climate zone divisions

°F (°C)	Zone
Under –58 (Under –50)	1
–58 to –40 (–50 to –40)	2
–40 to –31 (–40 to –35)	3
–31 to –20 (–35 to –29)	4
–20 to –9 (–29 to –23)	5
–9 to 0 (–23 to –18)	6
0 to 10 (–18 to –12)	7
10 to 19 (–12 to –7)	8
19 to 30 (–7 to –1)	9
30 to 41 (–1 to 5)	10
41 to 59 (5 to 15)	11

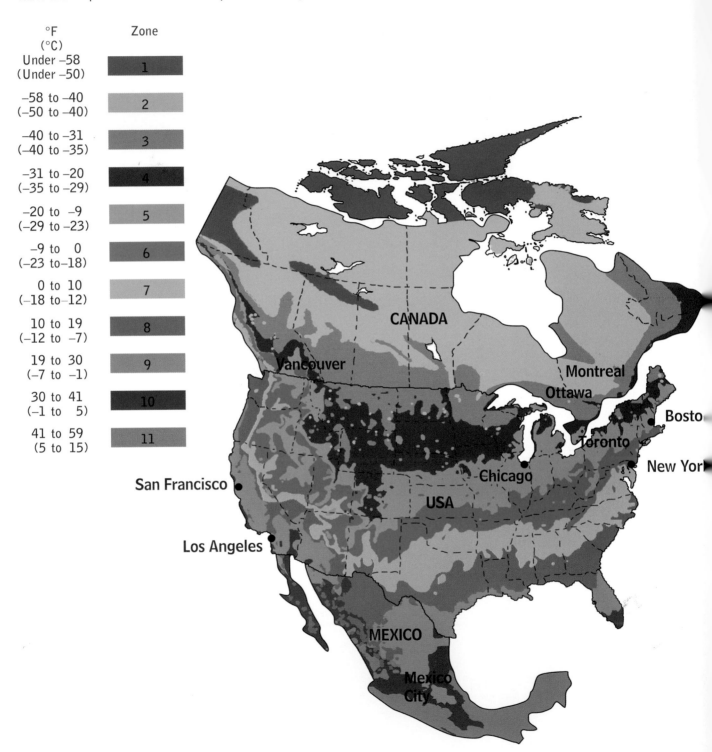

Each plant in this book is given a mark for frost-hardiness. However, the microclimate within the yard is the factor that decides whether a plant survives and thrives. The frost-hardiness of plants is favourably influenced by factors such as a warm site, along a wall for instance, sufficient shelter from cold and dehydrating winds, a constant covering of snow, and also a well-drained soil.

Many plants can survive low temperatures, given favourable conditions, for a brief period of time. As cultivated varieties of plants within a species can also differ widely, frost-hardiness can only be considered a general guideline.

KEY TO PICTOGRAMS

General information

 Height of growth

 Width of growth

Flowering period

Cut flower

Container/pot plant

! Take care

Fruits

Fragrance

Site

Sun

Semi-shade

Shade

Water requirements

Low

Medium

High

Frost-hardiness

 Limited frost-hardiness, to 32°F (0°C)

 Frost-hardy, to 23°F (−5°C)

 Fully frost-hardy, to 5°F (−15°C)

The colours of the pictogram vary according to the plant.

The plants marked by an exclamation mark are partly or entirely poisonous and are not suitable for consumption or can cause skin reactions. In some families of plants, the risk of poisoning, although marked only for the first plant of that family, apply to all the plants.

Do not plant poisonous plants in a garden where children play. Though the active principles of herbs taken in moderate amounts can be good for your health, their effect may become negative if consumed in excessive quantities. Not all berries and fruits can be eaten without unfortunate consequences. If you have the slightest doubt, do not consume them and get further information from a specialised garden centre. All the information given reflects the best of our knowledge.

INDEX

twinspur 132
tworow stonecrop 193

U
umbrella bamboo 216
Ursinia anethoides 89
Uvularia grandiflora 199

V
Valeriana officinalis 331
variegated cotoneaster 246
variegated giant reed 208
variegated manna grass 218
variegated palm sedge 213
Verbascum thapsus subsp.
   thapsus 101
Verbena bonariensis syn.
   V. patagonica 200
Veronica teucrium 'Shirley Blue'
   200
Veronicastrum virginicum syn.
   Veronica virginica 200
Viburnum × *bodnantense* 288
Viburnum × *burkwoodii*
   'Anne Russell' 288
Viburnum davidii 288
Viburnum opulus 288
Viburnum opulus 'Roseum' 289
Viburnum plicatum 'Mariesii'
   289
Viburnum tinus 288
Viburnum tinus 'Eve Price' 289
Viola 40, 101, 199, 201–3
Viola 'Etain' 201
Viola 'Jackanapes' 202
Viola 'Rebecca' 202
Viola 'Roscastle Black' 202
Viola tricolour 203
Viola × *wittrockiana* Imperial series
   102
Viola cornuta hybrid 202
Viola odorata 203
Viola riviniana 203
Virginia creeper 312

viridiflora tulip 62, 63
Vitis coignetiae 318
Vitis vinifera 'Purpurea' 318

W
Waldsteinia geoides 204
wallflower 98
walnut 260
watercress 327
waterlily dahlias 23, 25
wax begonia 120
weeping brown sedge 212
weeping butterfly bush 236
Weigela florida 'Variegata'
   290
western spirea 285
white baneberry 106
white cedar 287
white fir 231
white foxglove 97
white sagebrush 324
white spruce 271
white stonecrop 193
white trillium 57
white wood aster 114
whorled tickseed 127
wide-leaf grape hyacinth
   48
wig tree 246
wild garlic 322
wild potato 316
wild sweetwilliam 178
wild tulip 68, 69
willow 283
winter aconite 30
winter creeper 302
winter currant 282
winter daffodil 56
winter jasmine 307
wintergreen barberry 234
Wisteria floribunda 'Alba' 319
Wisteria sinensis 319
Wisteria sinensis 'Alba' 319
witch hazel 254

witch's moneybags 193
wood anemone 15
wood sorrel 54
wood violet 203
woodbine 310, 311
woodland cranesbill 145
woodland crocus 21
woodland forget-me-not 99
wooly hedgenettle 196
wormwood 324

X
Xeranthemum annuum 90

Y
yarrow 104
yellow archangel 162
yellow foxglove 97
yellow granadilla 313
yellow lady's slipper 22
yellow loosestrife 167
yellow marsh marigold 121
yellow meadow rue 198
yellow monkey-flower 169
yellow mountain saxifrage 190
yellow onion 11
yellow star of Bethlehem 34
yellow trumpet vine 296
yellow-eyed grass 195
yew 287
Yoshino cherry 276
Yucca filamentosa 'Bright Edge'
   290

Z
Zantedeschia aethiopica 70
Zantedeschia aethiopica
   'Green Goddess' 70
Zinnia elegans 'Envy' 90
Zinnia elegans 'Orange King' 91

Picture credits

Modeste Herwig all photos, except:

Jürgen Becker Vakat, page 12 top, 19 bottom right, 32 all, 33 top right, 58 top and middle right, 61 bottom, 62 middle left, 64 bottom left, 65 top right, middle right and bottom, 66 top and bottom left, 67 top left, right and middle right, 68 top, 69 middle right, 83 bottom right, 217 both right, 326 bottom, 328 top, 332–333, 334 top, 2nd from top and bottom, 335 all 3 top, 336 2nd from bottom, 337 top left, 2nd from top right and bottom, 339 all, 340 all 3 bottom, 341 all, 342 all, 343 top right, 344 top and bottom, 345 top left and 2nd from top right, 346 top left, 350 all 3 bottom, 351 both top right, 353 top left, 354 all, 355 all, 356 top, 257 all, 358 all, 359 all, 360 all, 361 top left, 2nd from top right and bottom, 362 all, and 363 bottom.

blinkwickel page 11 top right, 16 both, 22 bottom, 34 top, 43 top left, 46 middle left, 48 top left, 76 top, 78 top, 81 left, 82 middle, 92–93, 94 both, 96 top and middle, 99 both right, 100 top, 101 left, 113 both right, 120 bottom, 134 top, 158 top, 160 middle, 161 top right, 164 top, 165 top right, 172 bottom, 175 bottom, 182 middle right and bottom, 185 bottom, 189 right, 190 top, 192 bottom, 193 top left, right and middle, 199 bottom right, 202 bottom, 203 top right and bottom, 232 top, 233 top right, 235 right, 237 top, 241 bottom right, 250 top left, 254 middle, 256 bottom, 268 bottom, 269, 322 bottom left, 325 top right, 329 left.

International Bulb Center page 11 bottom right, 14 top, 25 both top right, 30 middle, 31 top, 36 bottom left, 37 top left, top right and bottom, 43 top right, 45 bottom, 46 middle right and top, 46 middle.

Special thanks

In recognition of their indefatigable efforts in the exceptional quality of this work, we thank Phoebe Päth, Justyna Krzyzanowska, Claudia Wester, and the whole Makro Chroma team.